◇◇◇◇◇◇◇◇◇◇◇◇◇◇

# New Structures
# of Campus Power

## SUCCESS AND FAILURES OF
## EMERGING FORMS OF
## INSTITUTIONAL
## GOVERNANCE

◇◇◇◇◇◇◇◇◇◇◇◇◇◇◇◇◇◇◇◇◇◇◇◇◇◇◇◇◇◇◇◇◇◇◇◇◇

◇◇◇◇◇◇◇◇◇◇◇

# John D. Millett

◇◇◇◇◇◇◇◇◇◇◇◇◇◇◇◇◇◇◇◇◇◇◇◇◇◇◇◇◇◇◇◇◇◇

◇◇◇◇◇◇◇◇◇◇◇◇◇

# New Structures
# of Campus Power

◇◇◇◇◇◇◇◇◇◇◇◇◇◇◇◇◇◇◇◇◇◇◇◇◇◇◇◇◇◇

Jossey-Bass Publishers
San Francisco • Washington • London • 1979

NEW STRUCTURES OF CAMPUS POWER
*Success and Failures of Emerging Forms of Institutional Governance*
by John D. Millett

Copyright © 1978 by: Jossey-Bass, Inc., Publishers
433 California Street
San Francisco, California 94104
&
Jossey-Bass Limited
28 Banner Street
London EC1Y 8QE

Library of Congress Catalogue Card Number LC 77-82911

International Standard Book Number ISBN 0-87589-350-3

Manufactured in the United States of America


JACKET DESIGN BY WILLI BAUM

378.101
M653n

FIRST EDITION
*First printing: January 1978*
*Second printing: August 1979*

*Code 7750*

LW 198087

◇◇◇◇◇◇◇◇◇◇◇◇◇

# The Jossey-Bass Series
# in Higher Education

◇◇◇◇◇◇◇◇◇◇◇◇◇◇◇◇◇◇◇◇◇◇◇◇◇◇◇◇◇◇◇

◇◇◇◇◇◇◇◇◇◇◇◇◇

# Preface

◇◇◇◇◇◇◇◇◇◇◇◇◇◇◇◇◇◇◇◇◇◇◇◇◇◇◇◇◇◇◇◇◇

When I left active administrative life in higher education in the summer of 1972, I received an invitation to join the Academy for Educational Development and to direct a management improvement program of the academy made possible by a grant primarily from the W. K. Kellogg Foundation. The original objective of the program was to explore transferring the management experience of business enterprise to academic enterprise. It became evident, however, that such a transfer of management experience from one institutional context to another was scarcely feasible.

Although there are similarities among business enterprises and higher education enterprises in matters concerning their management, there exist fundamental differences in social purpose and in method of operation (Millett, 1975). The similarities include definitions of purposes and objectives, selection of the work force, selection of managers, and use of problem-solving techniques. The differences are substantial: differences in production processes appropriate to an output of business goods and services as opposed to an output of learning, and differences in the economic method for financing the two kinds of operations. Business executives find it difficult to comprehend the peculiar organizational structure of colleges and universities, with their emphasis on the individual professional role of faculty members, the autonomy of instructional departments, and faculty and student participation in campus governance. My experience from 1972 through 1974 reinforced the conclusion I had reached as a university president: Managers of business enterprises and managers of academic enterprises inhabit very different worlds.

As the management improvement programs of the academy proceeded, college and university presidents were heard to assert more and more frequently that their management efforts were being substantially impeded by new agencies of campus governance. It became increasingly evident that there were conflicting concepts of governance and of management on various college and university campuses. It also became evident that these conflicting concepts could pose a major obstacle to higher education planning and decision making in attempts to adjust to the changing social circumstances and expectations of the 1970s. Because I have had a strong interest in academic governance ever since I was first a university president in 1953, I was deeply troubled by reports of a gathering storm over campus governance and management.

In the autumn of 1974 I proposed to the Lilly Endowment that recent experience in campuswide governance be carefully analyzed and reported. Because of the particular interest of James B. Holderman, then vice-president for education of the Lilly Endowment, a grant was made to the academy from the endowment for 1975 and 1976. The grant made it possible for me to give major attention to the subject, and this book reports on the results.

In this study, *campuswide governance* is defined as a formal arrangement for involving various groups or constituencies of the campus in a decision-making structure and process. The constituencies involved might be two or more of the following: the faculty (full-time and part-time), the students (full-time and part-time, undergraduate and graduate), the professional nonfaculty staff, the operating staff, and the administrative staff.

A *campus* is defined as a particular geographical location in which an academic enterprise might operate. In the public sector of higher education in particular in recent years, the multicampus system operating under the governance of a single governing board has become increasingly familiar. In this study, our interest is not directed toward systems but toward individual campuses.

In legal prescription, the authority for governance of a campus is generally vested in a governing board. Even in legal expectation, however, there is often an implied—if not specified—provision for faculty participation in governance, often in terms of establishing degree requirements and of prescribing student conduct regulations. In practice, a board of trustees and its academic agent, the president, have recognized the authority and responsibility of faculties to decide many issues of so-called academic affairs. In American higher education, faculties have long been involved in campus governance.

A new development in American higher education during the 1960s was the growth of formalized structures and procedures whereby campuswide governance extended participation to students. And, at the same time, faculty and students became involved in the decision-making process about issues usually considered institutional affairs. The 1960s were a period of innovation in campus governance.

Obviously the impetus for innovation arose from the fact that the 1960s were a time of trouble for American higher education. Much has been written about the "student revolution," about student unrest and disruption. There is still much we do not know about the motivation, the organization, the objectives, and the process of student activism in the decade now behind us. The objective of this study is not to analyze the student revolution but to analyze experience with campuswide governance.

In practice, it appeared that the student revolution was an excuse for, rather than the cause of, new forms of campuswide governance. Throughout the 1950s and into the 1960s, faculty members had sought to translate the "academic revolution" into some new machinery of academic governance. The interest of faculty members expressed a point of view rather than a program. Faculty members generally tended to perceive presidents, administrative officers, and boards of trustees as somehow not fully cognizant of or properly deferential to the new faculty power of the post-war era. Influential and decisive in scholarship, faculty members felt they were also entitled to be influential and decisive in college and university affairs. Student unrest and student disruption provided faculty members with the opportunity to push their claim.

It seems likely that both the structure and the practice of campus governance changed substantially in American higher education, beginning about 1966. Hodgkinson (1974) in his study of campus senates found 85 percent to have been in existence seven or fewer years. Boards of trustees and college and university presidents found it expedient, perhaps desirable, to extend the institutional decision-making process to include some form of participation by faculty and students.

As of 1974, I found that very little evaluation of the experience with campuswide governance had taken place. In 1971 the National Association of State Universities and Land-Grant Colleges had published four case studies on university governance prepared by David D. Dill. These studies were more concerned with structure and representation than with evaluation of performance.

On the basis of my own exposure to the problem of campuswide governance, I wrote *Strengthening Community in Higher Education* (1974). This commentary was directed to a discussion of issues involved in both *governance* and *government* of colleges and universities. The book expressed my view that a structure and process of decision making could not and should not be separated from an equal concern with a structure and process of leadership and a structure and process of management. At the same time I indicated my own continuing commitment to the concept of the campus as a community of different but interrelated groups, a concept I had propounded as early as 1962 in *The Academic Community*.

In 1974 it seemed to me that sufficient time had elapsed to evaluate actual experiences in campuswide governance for the decade 1966 through 1975. It was time to determine, if possible, the accomplishments of campuswide governance. What had happened in decision making, in leadership, and in management as a result of senates or councils established to bring together representatives from various constituent groups of the campus community?

I was not interested in structure and representation as much as I was in process and consequences.

It seemed best to base this study on actual experience rather than on questionnaires and statistical analyses. For this reason, the study plan was developed in terms of thirty case studies of specific colleges and universities.

In selecting thirty institutions for careful analysis, I was guided by obvious criteria: diversity of type and enrollment size, of sponsorship, and of geographical location. I was also interested in exploring particular situations about which I had some general knowledge. In addition, in selecting institutions for case studies, I was influenced by the availability of competent individuals to prepare the evaluative analyses.

In designing the study, apart from the selection of the thirty institutions and case authors, two procedures were employed. One procedure was to establish a set of evaluative criteria by which experience in campuswide governance could be judged. A second procedure, resulting from the first, was to determine which of four models seemed best to describe the performance of campuswide governance.

In the effort to evaluate experience, eight questions were formulated:

1. What has campuswide governance accomplished in the clarification of institutional purposes?
2. What has campuswide governance accomplished in the specification of program objectives, both for primary or output programs and for support programs?
3. What has campuswide governance accomplished in the reallocation of income resources among various programs?
4. What has campuswide governance accomplished in the development of new or expanded sources of income for the institution?
5. To what extent has campuswide governance become involved with issues for improvement in the management or the technology of program operation?
6. To what extent has campuswide governance become involved with issues of degree requirements or with the issue of instructional program outcomes?

7. To what extent has campuswide governance become involved with issues of academic behavior (academic standards, academic freedom, academic responsibility, academic interests of students), and with issues of student behavior (social conduct, housing regulations, recognition and support of student organizations, student political activity)?
8. To what extent has campuswide governance become involved with issues of program evaluation, utilizing such criteria as personal benefit, social utility, economy, cost effectiveness, and public accountability?

The authors of case studies were asked to examine the actual experience with campuswide governance on their respective campuses and to evaluate the performance in terms of the eight questions posed above. It was thought that answers to these questions would provide some reasonable conclusions about the contribution and the effectiveness of campuswide governance to the process of institutional decision making.

In addition to the eight questions, the study design set forth four different models of campus governance. The case authors, in light of their evaluations of experience with campuswide governance, were asked to determine which model most nearly represented the reality of their respective campuses. The four models set forth as hypotheses of campuswide governance were:

1. *The Dual-Organization Model.* A structure involving one set of arrangements and participants for deciding issues of academic affairs and a different set of arrangements and participants for deciding issues of institutional (or administrative) affairs.
2. *The Academic Community Model.* A structure and process bringing together three or more constituent groups of a campus to decide issues of campus governance on the basis of common interest.
3. *The Political Model.* A structure and process bringing together three or more constituent groups of a campus to decide issues of campus governance on the basis of divergent political interests and of necessary compromise.
4. *The Organized Anarchy Model.* A structure and process of cam-

pus governance characterized by problematical goals, an unclear technology, and fluid participation resulting in a high degree of individual rather than organizational decision making.

These models of campus decision making were obviously drawn from the literature about college and university governance, a literature that will be reviewed in Chapter One. Other models could have been included, but these four seemed to be the most useful analytically and so were incorporated into the study design.

A conference of the thirty case authors was held in March of 1975. During a two-day period, the study design was reviewed and the objectives of the inquiry delineated. Subsequently, my associate, Winifred Thompson, or I visited twenty-nine campuses and one nearby city to review the progress of the case studies and to obtain first-hand impressions of each campus environment. In March 1976 a second conference was devoted to reviewing the campus studies. (All but three of the case studies had been completed by that time; the other three were finished by June.) This discussion was very useful in underlining both similarities and particularities of institutional experience with campus governance.

From time to time during 1975 and 1976, the Lilly Endowment convened a panel of advisers to discuss issues of college and university governance, a major thrust of the endowment's interest during these years. I found the discussions most helpful during the course of this study and in preparing the final report.

I am truly indebted to the authors of the case studies. Chapters Three through Five are summaries of the studies prepared by the collaborators, and I endeavored to retain as much as I could of the content and actual wording contributed by each case author. I wish to express my deep appreciation to those who assisted me so substantially by preparing these separate studies. While I accept responsibility for the final version, this book would not exist without their excellent participation.

I especially thank Ken Metzler, professor of journalism at the University of Oregon. I had been much impressed by his book, *Confrontation* (1973). Perhaps I was especially attracted by the subtitle of the volume, *The Destruction of a College President*. Because of the careful investigative reporting that characterized this book about the University of Oregon, I was eager to persuade Metzler to turn his attention to the broader interest of campus governance, a subject of only peripheral concern in his account of one year in the life of the acting president of the university that ended so tragically in death in June 1969. I was successful in recruiting Metzler's expertise, and the results fulfilled my expectations.

I am also indebted to Winifred Thompson, who assisted me in visiting various campuses, in preparing summaries of the case studies, and in performing various editorial chores. I extend a grateful thank you to the Lilly Endowment for the support that permitted me to give part of my time over a two-year period to this study, and I am appreciative of the continuing encouragement and help I have had from my colleagues in the Academy for Educational Development, especially from the academy's president, Alvin C. Eurich.

For some readers the summaries in Chapters Three through Five may seem unduly long and the accounts overly detailed or even repetitious. But since these accounts form the basis for the generalizations about governance in Chapters Six and Seven, I believe that such detailed information is essential to the present report. The reader who prefers the generalizations to the particulars is free to skim the case study summaries and to examine more carefully my conclusions drawn from them.

*Washington, D.C.*                                          JOHN D. MILLETT
*August 1977*

◇◇◇◇◇◇◇◇◇◇◇◇

# Contents

◇◇◇◇◇◇◇◇◇◇◇◇◇◇◇◇◇◇◇◇◇◇◇◇◇◇◇◇◇◇◇◇◇◇

◇◇◇◇◇◇◇◇◇◇◇◇◇

# The Author

◇◇◇◇◇◇◇◇◇◇◇◇◇◇◇◇◇◇◇◇◇◇◇◇◇◇◇◇◇◇◇◇◇◇◇

JOHN D. MILLETT since 1972 has been senior vice-president of the Academy for Educational Development, a private nonprofit agency for educational planning. Millett received his bachelor's degree from DePauw University in 1933, his master's degree from Columbia University in 1935, and his doctor's degree in government from Columbia in 1938. While working for his doctorate, he was a teaching assistant at Columbia (1935–1937) and a full-time instructor (1937–1938). From 1935 to 1938 he was also a part-time instructor in political science at Rutgers University.

During 1938–1939 John Millett was a postdoctoral fellow of the Social Science Research Council, studying at the London School of Economics and Political Science. From 1939 to 1941 he served on the staff of the Committee on Public Administration, Social Science Research Council. In 1941 he joined the staff of the National Resources Planning Board in Washington, and in 1942 entered the U.S. Army as a major. Millett was released from active duty in 1946 with the rank of colonel and the award of the Legion of Merit. Appointed an associate professor of Public Administration at Columbia University in July 1945, Millett began his faculty duties in February 1946. Promoted to the rank of professor in 1948, Millett served on the staff of the first Hoover Commission in 1948–1949.

From 1949–1952, on partial leave from Columbia, Millett served as executive director of the Commission on Financing Higher Education, sponsored by the Association of American Universities with grants from the Rockefeller Foundation and Carnegie Corporation of New York. In 1953 he became president of Miami University in Oxford, Ohio. He became the first chancellor of the Ohio Board of Regents, a state government planning and coordinating agency for public higher education in 1964. He retired from the position in 1972 at sixty years of age.

John Millett is the author of fifteen books on public administration and higher education, co-author of six other volumes, and has written more than one hundred fifty articles. He has been president of the American Society for Public Administration, of the State Universities Association, and of his college fraternity, Phi Delta Theta. He has also served as chairman of the National Academy of Public Administration, secretary-treasurer of the National Association of State Universities, a trustee and chairman of the Board of Educational Testing Service, a trustee of the College Entrance Examination Board, a consultant to the Ford Foundation, a consultant to the Office of Education, and a trustee of the Institute of American Universities. In 1975 *Change Magazine* listed him as one of forty-four leaders of American higher education. He has received twenty-four honorary degrees and various other awards.

John Millett and his wife, a fellow student from DePauw, were married in 1934. They have three sons, two who have received the Ph.D. degree and one the M.D. degree, and five grandchildren.

*To future college students,*
*including my grandchildren*

## Authors of Case Studies

MARK BARLOW, JR., vice-provost, Cornell University

JAMES A. BAYTON, professor of psychology, Howard University

JOSEPH R. DUNN, JR., director of research, Central Connecticut State College

STEPHEN L. FINK, associate dean, Whittemore School of Business and Economics, University of New Hampshire at Durham

ROBERT L. GALVIN, former director, Institutional Research and Testing, West Virginia Wesleyan College

THOMAS R. GIDDENS, associate dean, Rockford College

NELSON P. GUILD, president, Frostburg State College

WILLIAM H. HARVEY, vice-president for student affairs, Tuskegee Institute

FERREL HEADY, former president, University of New Mexico

JOHN C. HONEY, professor of political science and higher education, Syracuse University (with Robert H. Davidson, Jr.)

SISTER MARIE LOUISE HUBERT, director of institutional research, Albertus Magnus College

FREDERICK S. HUMPHRIES, president, Tennessee State University (with Sterlin N. Adams)

M. GLEN JOHNSON, professor of political science, Vassar College

JOSEPH F. KAUFFMAN, professor of higher education, University of Wisconsin

EDWARD J. KORMONDY, vice-president and provost, The Evergreen State College

WILLIAM S. LIVINGSTON, professor of political science, University of
Texas at Austin

ELEANOR C. MAIN, associate professor of political science, Emory
University

HARVEY C. MANSFIELD, professor emeritus, Columbia University

LEWIS B. MAYHEW, professor of higher education, Stanford University

T. R. McCONNELL, former director, Center for Research and Development in Higher Education, University of California at
Berkeley (with Steward Edelstein)

KEN METZLER, professor of journalism, University of Oregon

WILLIAM R. OLIVER, professor of chemistry, Northern Kentucky
State College (now University)

DANIEL H. PERLMAN, dean of administrative services, Roosevelt
University

H. DEAN PROPST, dean, Armstrong State College

RODGER A. REMINGTON, assistant dean of community education,
Aquinas College

ROBERT M. RODNEY, dean, School of Liberal Arts, Eastern Montana College

BARDWELL L. SMITH, professor of religion, and former dean, Carleton College

HERBERT WALTZER, professor of political science, Miami University

CHESTER B. WHITNEY, director of institutional research, Augustana
College

PHILIP S. WILDER, JR., academic vice-president, California State
College at Bakersfield

◇◇◇◇◇◇◇◇◇◇◇◇◇

# New Structures
# of Campus Power

## SUCCESS AND FAILURES OF
## EMERGING FORMS OF
## INSTITUTIONAL
## GOVERNANCE

◇◇◇◇◇◇◇◇◇◇◇◇◇◇◇◇◇◇◇◇◇◇◇◇◇◇◇◇◇◇◇◇◇◇◇

# CHAPTER ONE

◇◇◇◇◇◇◇◇◇◇◇

# Academic
# Governance
# and Government

◇◇◇◇◇◇◇◇◇◇◇◇◇◇◇◇◇◇◇◇◇◇◇◇◇◇◇◇◇◇◇◇◇◇◇◇◇

Since the publication in 1960 of a little study by John J. Corson on the governance of colleges and universities, a substantial volume of literature has appeared on the subject of how institutions of higher education operate as organized enterprises. Governance attracted interest in the 1960s partly because these were the years in which the American public's expectations of colleges and universities had reached their zenith in terms of anticipated social benefits. Partly interest was aroused because the 1960s were a time of extensive conflict on higher-education campuses, expressed in student protest and riots and even student deaths. Among all solutions to campus conflict that were within the control of the campus leaders themselves, some reconstruction of the agencies of campus governance was the one most frequently offered.

1

Corson defined *governance* in a relatively restricted sense: Governance was the authority to make rules governing the conduct of, and relations among, those persons banded together as a college or university. In essence, Corson was interested in the authority and the responsibility to make decisions and largely ignored other aspects of the academic enterprise—its structure and process as a productive activity providing society with certain definite outputs and its structure and process of leadership. Governance became synonymous with decision making, and the Corson definition tended to dominate both discussion and action throughout the 1960s and into the 1970s. But some attention to the various kinds of ideas and concepts discussed in the literature on governance is important as a backdrop to the present study.

In some respects the story of college and university governance begins with Riesman (1958). In his commentary about constraint and variety in American higher education, the author anticipated his later work with Jencks (1968) about the academic revolution in America. The nature of scholarship during World War II and in the years thereafter produced not just an academic profession but also academic power. In the late 1950s, the American Association of University Professors (AAUP) established Committee T on College and University Government, which in 1960 set forth a statement of principles for faculty participation in university governance. This statement declared that the basic functions of a college or university in fostering knowledge and creativity were performed by a community of scholars who must be free to exercise their independent judgment in planning and in performing their educational activity. The AAUP statement recognized three groups as having important roles in the government of a college or university: the faculty, the administration, and the governing board. The statement called for a careful delineation of the role of each group in university government and declared that no one group had any "exclusive claim" to represent society in the conduct of higher education. It was asserted that the "actual practices" of academic operation did recognize this joint authority. The statement went on to set forth six so-called principles involving faculty participation in institutional governance.

As already noted, the Corson study of actual practices in

various institutions also appeared in 1960, and it will be considered in more detail below. In 1962 I responded to the Corson volume with an essay of my own entitled *The Academic Community* (Millett, 1962). As far as I know, this title was the first contemporary usage of the phrase *academic community*. Thereafter followed a good many commentaries and studies about governance. I shall mention only some: Perkins (1966); Demerath, Stephens, and Taylor (1967); Gross and Grambsch (1968); Goheen (1969); Howard and Franklin (1969); Hodgkinson and Meeth (1971); and McConnell (1971). For the most part these studies and commentaries accepted the definition of governance as decision making.

In 1966 the AAUP joined the American Council on Education (ACE) and the Association of Governing Boards of Colleges and Universities (AGB) in issuing a joint statement (*Statement on Government of Colleges and Universities*, 1966). This joint statement began with a call for "mutual understanding" about college and university government. It endorsed the need for participation of faculty members, administrative officers, and governing boards in determining "general educational policy." It proposed "joint endeavor" in long-range planning, in preparing plans for physical facilities, in budgeting, in selecting a president, in appointing other academic officers, and in conducting external relations. The joint statement set forth certain general duties of a governing board, emphasized the role of the president as institutional leader, and declared that the faculty had primary responsibility for the curriculum, methods of instruction, research, faculty status, degree requirements, and "those aspects of student life which relate to the educational process." The joint statement advocated faculty participation at each level of decision making in a college or university where a faculty responsibility was present.

The 1966 joint statement incorporated one element that had been missing in 1960, a recognition of possible student interest in institutional governance. The joint statement urged that when students desired "to participate responsibly" in government their interest should be recognized as an opportunity for student education and involvement in the affairs of a college or university. The statement said: "Ways should be found to permit significant student participation within the limits of attainable effectiveness" (p. 14).

It mentioned limitations to such effectiveness: inexperience, time demands, transitory status, and student subjection to faculty evaluation. The joint statement recommended that, at a minimum, students should have the right to discuss institutional policy and operation without fear of any reprisal, the right to due process when charged with violation of any regulation, and the freedom to hear speakers of their own choice. Thus, the possible role of students in institutional governance began to take shape in an important higher education document.

In 1967 another statement appeared—the report of the Task Force on Faculty Representation and Academic Negotiation of the American Association for Higher Education (AAHE). This task force reported that faculty discontent had become evident in many institutions, especially in public junior colleges and in the emerging four-year teachers colleges and certain state universities. The report identified the principal source of this discontent as the nonrecognition or nonaccommodation of a faculty desire to participate in policies affecting the professional status and performance of faculties. A further cause of faculty discontent was concern about the establishment of state boards of higher education and their threat to the autonomy of campus decision making. The task force advocated "shared authority" between faculty and administrative officers, to be exercised preferably through an academic senate in which faculty members would constitute a clear majority. The academic senate should resolve most issues of concern to a college or university, although the task force did not specify how these issues should be defined. Some issues, such as grading standards, were acknowledged to be primarily matters for faculty determination, while other issues, such as business management, were held to be "primarily under the control of the administrators." The task force report recommended that the academic senate create a budget committee "to deal with the general allocation of resources" among component programs of the college or university. The academic senate was expected to rely upon information sharing and appeals to reason as the "preferred approach" in resolving any conflicts about particular issues. But the report spoke of political, economic, and educational sanctions as possible faculty responses to situations of serious dispute with administrative officers and governing boards.

The 1967 report of the AAHE task force brought up two matters not appearing in earlier documents mentioned here. First, the report recognized the emergence of faculty collective bargaining upon the American academic scene. Although little was said about the bargaining process as such, the report stated that "formal bargaining relationships between the faculty and the administration are most likely to develop if the administration has failed to establish or support effective internal organizations for faculty representation." In addition, the report urged academic senates to create a formal appeals procedure to resolve disputes between individual faculty members and the administration. It pointed out that such a grievance procedure might provide for neutral third-party intervention, including arbitration. In a far-seeing observation, the report noted that "the relationships between the bargaining agency and the senate will probably be highly unstable."

Yet another extensive document about campus governance appeared in 1971—a report from the Assembly on University Goals and Governance sponsored by the American Academy of Arts and Sciences. The assembly brought together a number of leading faculty members and administrative officers, who with staff assistance undertook to set forth in its first report a number of "theses" about campus governance. The report began with an acknowledgment that a college or university was an "intricate organization," involving trustees, administrators, students, professors, staff, alumni, legislators, and public officials. The report asserted: "Good governance depends on a reasonable allocation of responsibilities that makes the structure of authority credible for all these groups" (p. 24). The assembly did not propose any particular organizational pattern for campus governance. Rather, the report declared that the educational mission of a university was most likely to be accomplished if there was a division of authority among various groups, a sharing of information, and a well-defined system of accountability. It asserted that "too few" colleges and universities had developed these characteristics in their structure of governance.

The "theses" about governance put forth by the assembly were generally consistent with the kinds of discussions then taking place within colleges and universities. The legal authority of the lay governing board was accepted, but the report urged that membership on such boards should be more representative of women and blacks and other minority groups. The report did not advocate faculty and student representation on governing boards, arguing that such membership might encourage board intervention in "day-to-day academic decisions." It did suggest that faculty members from other universities and young alumni might be elected or appointed to governing boards. The report recognized the unique importance of the college or university presidency and urged that the office be strengthened in order to represent the "general interest" of the university as a whole and in order to provide faculty leadership.

The assembly's report recommended that the faculty and administrative systems of university decision making should be combined into a "system of delegated, responsive governance." It advocated a limited term of not more than a "dozen years" for service by academic administrators, with one review of performance within this period of time. Faculty members were urged to give greater attention to the work of faculty senates and faculty committees. It was suggested that when faculty members and students were joined together in a universitywide senate the separate faculty senates and student senates should not be abolished but should continue to function. Student government was declared a "misnomer." The primary opportunity for student influence upon educational policy of a university would occur on a "decentralized basis." The report proposed that colleges and universities publish an official journal of the actions of their various governing bodies. And it suggested that alumni be regularly informed about the concerns of their college or university affiliations.

One other document requires mention in this review—the report of the Carnegie Commission on Higher Education in 1973 on *Governance of Higher Education*. The Carnegie Commission identified six "priority problems": (1) adequate provision for institutional independence, (2) the role of the board of trustees and of the president, (3) collective bargaining by faculty members, (4) rules and practices governing tenure, (5) student influence on campus, and (6) the handling of emergencies. The report made clear that it was defining governance as "the structures and processes of decision making." And it acknowledged that it was distinguishing governance from administration or management. But the attention

of the commission was directed in part to an off-campus problem—
the governance of multicampus systems—and in part to two issues
of substance rather than of structure and process—the rules concerning tenure and the desirability of contingency planning to cope with
campus disruption and violence. Only three of the six Carnegie
Commission problems were strictly issues of campus governance.

The commission opposed the membership of faculty members and of students on governing boards but advocated faculty and
student membership on appropriate board committees, or at least
an arrangement for joint consultation. The commission urged that
board membership should reflect the different age, sex, and racial
groups served by an institution and, like the Assembly on University Goals and Governance, asked that faculty members from other
institutions and young alumni be considered for governing board
membership. Insofar as the role of presidents was concerned, the
commission recommended that governing boards seek "active presidents" and provide them with the authority and staff needed to
provide leadership in a "period of change and conflict." The commission then added that boards might wish to consider the establishment of stated review periods for evaluating the performance of
presidents; it proposed that faculty members and students be associated in an advisory capacity in both the initial presidential
appointment and in the review process.

On the subject of faculty power and of collective bargaining,
the Carnegie Commission recommended that faculties be granted,
wherever it had not already been done, the "general level of authority" proposed by the American Association of University Professors;
but the commission did not make clear which proposal it was en-
dorsing, the AAUP statement of 1960 or the joint statement of
1966. The commission seemed to accept the current and prospective
practice of faculty collective bargaining; it recommended the en-
actment of state laws to permit faculty members in public institutions to engage in collective bargaining if they desired to do so. It
then went on to urge faculties to carefully analyze the implications
of collective bargaining as compared to other forms of governance,
advocating that collective bargaining agreements should cover only
economic benefits and should leave academic affairs in the hands
of a faculty senate.

In relation to student influence, the commission found little evidence that students wanted to take control of academic life. The commission proposed "adequate academic options" from which students might choose their preference and advocated the right of students to be heard on important campus issues. Students should serve on joint faculty-student committees in such areas of special interest as educational policy and student affairs. Students should be given the opportunity to evaluate faculty teaching performance. Formal grievance machinery should be available to students, and "impartial judicial tribunals" should decide charges of violation of conduct regulations.

These various documents issued between 1960 and 1973 are important because they clearly indicate the considerable attention being given to the whole subject of campus governance. Obviously, campus governance had become a major preoccupation of academic communities throughout the United States. These documents further identified the issues involved, even if they tended to be short in practical recommendations about actual structures and processes.

## Governance Versus Government

As suggested earlier, the discussions of governance dealt extensively with the subject of decision making but much less so with the subjects of leadership and management. The discussions of the 1960s generally tended to accept a set of common assumptions. One assumption was that there were certain identifiable and different group interests concerned with the operation of a college or university. The groups most commonly identified were faculty members, students, administrators, and members of governing boards. A second assumption was that there were such differences in interests among these constituent groups that conflict about purposes, policies, programs, and procedures was inevitable. A third assumption was that some machinery of participation in decision making would somehow resolve these conflicts or at least make the resolution of conflict more acceptable to the concerned parties. And a fourth assumption was that the critical process in conflict resolution was decision making rather than leadership or management.

In this book we shall accept the definition of governance that has generally prevailed in the literature on the subject: that governance refers to a structure and process of decision making, within a college or university, about purposes, policies, programs, and procedures. All organizations need structure and process for decision making, and a college or university is no exception. Within the academic community, however, this kind of decision making is especially cumbersome, for a variety of reasons. Purposes are often confused and even inconsistent. Policies in turn reflect the confusion of purposes. Programs and program objectives tend to be general rather than specific. And procedures, including work technology, are varied and often uncertain in output accomplishment. Most important of all, the academic community is not financially self-supporting but must rely upon extensive external subsidy. Because of these circumstances, some conflict between faculty members, students, and administrators may indeed be inevitable. A structure and process of governance must somehow unite these conflicts so that academic service is in fact produced.

If we accept that the concept of governance is limited in scope to a structure and process of decision making, then we need a broader concept that also encompasses a structure and process of leadership and a structure and process of management. In this discussion, I use the word *government* in this broader, more inclusive sense. I recognize that any attempted distinction between governance and government must, at best, be an arbitrary one. In many ways, I prefer the terms *decision making, leadership,* and *management* to *governance* and *government.* Unfortunately, much of what has been written about academic governance has used *decision making* in its restricted sense; thus, a broader concept is necessary—that of government, which includes leadership and management, as well as decision making.

In essence, decision making means the formal act of adopting ordinances, rules, regulations, and resolutions of purpose having the effect of law within an academic community. Legally, this authority to make rules and to establish purposes within a college or university is vested in a governing board. In fact, by specific delegation, or by custom and tradition, a good deal of rule-making authority may be exercised by faculty bodies (such as a faculty council or senate), by student bodies (such as a student senate), or by an ad-

ministrative council. In addition, these various bodies may adopt
resolutions that are, in effect, recommendations or petitions to the
governing board to adopt or approve particular rules of policies.
Whatever the structure and process, decision making or governance
is the authority to establish the law that governs the operation of an
academic community.

Leadership is different from decision making. To be sure, a
college or university president may be delegated authority to carry
out details of certain broad policy decisions and regulations as enacted by a governing board. Such an implementation of rule making
or action is essentially a part of the business of management. Leadership is the exercise of the authority to recommend decisions, and
it is having the status and prestige to ensure the probability that
these recommendations will become law. Decision making is a deliberative process in which several or many individuals participate.
Without leadership, deliberation may simply result in no decision at
all. Leadership proposes action, and it exercises authority to persuade or encourage that the recommended action becomes the decided action.

Management is the structure and process of implementation,
of executing decisions. Management involves the act of work planning, including the preparation of proposed lines of action to be
recommended by leadership and to be considered by the decision-
making body. Management is also work performance, the actual
enforcement of standards of behavior determined by the decision-making authority. Management means getting specific tasks
accomplished.

An academic community is, above all else, a productive
enterprise. A college or university does not exist just to cultivate a
sense of brotherly interest among all the individuals who compose
the whole. If we use the formulation of the 1973 Carnegie Commission report on the purposes and performance of higher education, a
college or university exists to produce instruction, research and
creative activity, public service, educational justice, and constructive criticism of society. As a producing enterprise, a college or university engages in decision making to ensure the accomplishment of
its intended outputs. Government, and not just governance alone, is
essential for a college or university.

In many discussions about governance, there has been a tendency to overlook the importance of government in higher education: that is, the importance of leadership and management in addition to decision making. There has also been a tendency to overlook the complexities of purpose. The 1971 report of the Assembly on University Goals and Governance did have the virtue of linkage. That report discussed such general problems as access to higher education, alternatives to higher education for American youth, the interrelationship of learning and experience, the importance of teaching, the reforming of general education, the relationship between higher education and professional practice, and the conduct of research. But the 1971 report was by no means specific about the actual conflicts raging in every college or university about these issues or how the conflicts confused or compounded the complexities of governance.

The basic conflict in higher education centers on the appropriate relationship to be formulated between higher education and society. Internally, colleges and universities usually agree that society should provide an ever-increasing subsidy to their operation. But when the question turns to higher education's obligations to society in return for this nurture, the agreement disappears. Some assert that the obligation of higher education is to be neutral with regard to the social conflicts that exist beyond the academic community: Colleges and universities should continue to perform their own missions of instruction, research and creative activity, educational justice, and responsible social criticism; what various social groupings and political parties do with these products is not for colleges and universities to determine. Others argue that the posture of social and political neutrality is in fact an alliance of higher education with the wealthy, the powerful, and the influential in society. These persons are inclined to argue that higher education should be active in providing assistance to the socially disadvantaged, to those individuals and groups who suffer from ignorance, poverty, racial discrimination, and lack of power and influence.

The Carnegie Commission, in its 1973 report on purposes, argued that a major goal of colleges and universities was to protect the right of individual faculty members to engage in the critical evaluation of social performance "for the sake of society's self-renewal." The commission acknowledged that there was conflict about the purposes of higher education and endeavored to state purposes so as to command the greatest possible degree of social acceptance. An important part of this effort was defending the academic function of producing social criticism in the context of institutional neutrality, on issues of social conflict.

The problems of governance for colleges and universities need to be approached, I believe, in a larger context. This context is that of conflict about the purposes, policies, programs, and procedures of colleges and universities as they relate to the internal interests of faculty members and students and as they relate to the external interest of social expectation and social support. Moreover, it is a context of government, not just of governance, and embraces the functions of guidance and performance as well as the structures and processes of decision making. Governance within a college or university is not enough; government is also essential.

## Models of Governance

The literature of governance has provided a number of models or generalizations about the reality of the decision-making process within colleges and universities. From study and research, from experience and observation, various individuals have sought to provide an understanding of decision making in terms of some overarching concept that explains the incidents and episodes of particular experience. In the years since 1960, several of these models have attracted a good deal of attention.

*The Dual-Organization Model.* In his 1960 landmark study, Corson declared that the decision-making process within institutions of higher education presented a "unique dualism of organizational structure." In effect, Corson identified a faculty hierarchy and an administrative hierarchy. Although he did not assert his generalization in quite these precise terms, Corson found governance in higher education divided into two different and separate spheres: academic affairs and administrative affairs. Decisions about academic affairs were made by the faculty, while presidents and governing boards made the administrative decisions. The problem of coherence and of overlap between these two spheres of governance did not appear to be important in this model.

To summarize Corson's observations in a few words and in a precise generalization is to do an injustice to the wealth of his comments and observations about higher education in the 1950s. It seemed to me, however, that essentially Corson was calling attention to an important distinction between the process of learning and the environment of learning. The process of learning is an interaction between faculty members and students, of course reinforced by their experiences outside the classroom and the laboratory. It was this process of learning that had become the special province of decision making by faculty members. But a college or university as an organized enterprise is also an environment of learning, requiring support services and income. It was this environment of learning that had become the special province of decision making by administrators and governing boards.

The dualism of governance found by Corson to prevail on various campuses was borne out in the testimony of the autobiographical accounts of university presidents themselves, such as those of Stoke (1959), Wriston (1960), and Dodds (1962).

The dual-organization model of college and university governance failed in practice when subjected to the stress of student disorder and disruption during the 1960s. The issue was then sharply posed: Was the maintenance of campus law and order an administrative matter or a faculty matter? Because campus law and order became a critical subject demanding the attention of both faculty members and presidents, an earlier practice of dual decision making could no longer be sustained. New arrangements became necessary.

Some fifteen years after his original study, Corson (1975) returned to the subject of governance in a revision of his earlier work. In his commentary about higher education in a turbulent decade, Corson abandoned the concept of organizational dualism that had constituted the innovative, unique contribution of his 1960 volume. Instead, Corson spoke of a "bifurcation" problem in college and university governance, and identified this separation as academic organization and operational organization. Corson appeared to endorse the idea of university councils, senates, or assemblies. He proposed that the functions of a college or university be narrowed and clarified, that the autonomy of individual institutions be reaffirmed, and that mechanisms for reestablishing a sense of academic community be developed. Corson then proposed a new concept of primary and communal authority for decision making. The primary authority of the faculty to make some decisions should be recognized, as should the primary authority of students to make other decisions. But there was a need, Corson maintained, for a communal authority as well. Unfortunately, the nature and extent of this communal authority were not specified.

The dual-organization model of governance was probably a realistic generalization about campus decision making in the 1950s. The arrangement proved to be inadequate to cope with the problems of the 1960s.

*The Academic Community Model.* As a response to Corson's concept of organizational dualism, I argued (1962) that colleges and universities were producing organizations different from other familiar types of organizational entities, such as a business enterprise, a government department, a church, or a voluntary association. I further argued that a unique characteristic of this organized entity was its bringing together of several quite different groups with quite different roles to fulfill. I identified four constituent groups of a college or university: faculty, students, alumni, and administrators (including president and colleagues as well as the governing board). I contended that the power relationship among these groups was not a relationship of hierarchical authority but of community and common interest. I did not present, however, any prescription of a structure for this relationship. I assumed that existing structures of faculty senates, student governments, and administrative councils could by a process of interaction arrive at a consensus about desirable decisions.

My objective in 1962 was to broaden the discussion of the academic community's constituents to include students and alumni. I was also intent upon presenting the proposition that, while these groups might have different points of view about many issues, they also had a very important common interest, which was the wellbeing and viability of the college or university enterprise itself. I closed my essay with a plea for the constituent groups to recognize that a struggle for power was inconsistent with encouraging the learning process and that a community of interest was essential to their endeavor.

It was noteworthy that after 1964 efforts at reconstruction of the structure and process of governance at many colleges and universities were directed to achieving community governance. I had obviously not foreseen either the student revolution that stimulated these efforts or the particular structures that they would produce. Community governance was attempted by many colleges and universities as they devised new arrangements for faculty members, students, and others to participate in decision making.

*The Political Model.* Drawing upon a study of New York University and its difficulties in matching income with expenditures, Baldridge (1971) presented a different model of university governance. He rejected the idea of community consensus in favor of the concept of political process. Baldridge perceived faculty members, students, and administrators as interest groups, each with a distinct point of view about what the university should do and each seeking to impose that point of view upon all other groups. He also recognized that within the broad categories of faculty members, students, and administrators there were many subdivisions of interest that were not always consistent with those of others with similar status in the organization. Baldridge saw the conflicts of interest as a struggle for power, and the outcome of this power confrontation was a necessary set of compromises and adjustments that would permit all groups to continue to function with some degree of effectiveness. This struggle for power and this set of compromises could best be described, he decided, as a political process. Hence the reality of governance within a university was the reality of a political model of behavior.

Baldridge gave very little attention to a structure and process of leadership within the university that could help achieve political compromise, and he said even less about the university as a producing organization concerned with providing certain particular outputs. He did not present any clearly defined structure or process by which political compromises could be effected. He did not resolve the dilemma of internal political process versus external subsidy. Baldridge was impressed by the existence of conflict within the university and by the fact that somehow the university continued to function. What enabled the university to continue in existence was identified as a process of political compromise.

Certainly the idea of a struggle for power within colleges and universities was a popular explanation for the very evident conflicts and disruptions occurring on college and university campuses during the 1960s. Becker (1970) pointed to the issues that had given rise to dispute: free speech, student political activism, racism, faculty involvement in war research, the campus relationship to a surrounding urban community, drug use, and restrictions on student conduct. The common theme in these conflicts was that students had deeply held positions on all these issues but were denied the power to compel colleges and universities to bring about the kind of institutional behavior they sought.

No doubt conflict had been building up within many colleges and universities as the decade of the 1960s began. Many undergraduate students were unhappy about the attention given by faculty members to graduate instruction, research, and public service. Many faculty members were unhappy because their status and their compensation did not advance as rapidly as they thought desirable. Administrators were harassed by substantial enrollment increases, lagging building programs, conflicting social pressures, and the increased complexity of institutional financing. These various attitudes tended to erode past patterns of accommodation and of trust within academic communities. Civility in social discourse and etiquette in personal relationships gave way to impolite language, strident demands, and disruption or violence. The campus of the 1960s did indeed present the picture of a struggle for power and a conflict about power relationships, both within the campus community and externally.

*The Organized Anarchy Model.* In their study of the role of forty-two college and university presidents for the Carnegie Commission, Cohen and March (1974) propounded the thesis that the American college and university belonged to a class of organization that they labeled "organized anarchy." The authors declared that the principal properties of an organized anarchy were problematic goals, unclear technology, and fluid participation. Cohen and March declared that institutions of higher education were uncertain about their purposes, practiced a technology that they did not understand and that might or might not produce intended outputs, and brought together participants who devoted varying amounts of time to the enterprise. Because the organization was thus characterized by a substantial degree of anarchy, Cohen and March found the leadership role of the president to be ambiguous.

The authors did not explore other models of governance that had been put forward in the literature about colleges and universities. Obviously they rejected all models except the one they considered applicable to a college or university. Apart from a considerable discussion about the special circumstances of the president in this organizational setting, Cohen and March said very little about the organizational concept itself. The authors were concerned about presidential leadership more than about organizational theory.

Yet the concept of organized anarchy is an intriguing one as a model of governance for the American college or university. The properties set forth by Cohen and March had to do with purposes, performance, and participation. There was almost no discussion of structure and still less about processes of governance. The different interests of faculty members and of students were recognized, but leadership rather than governance was the expected procedure of reconciliation. The concept of organized anarchy was put forward as an idea rather than as a fully developed construct. The concept was essentially a basis for discussion of leadership rather than of governance.

*The Bureaucratic Model.* On the basis of Max Weber's discussion of the characteristics of bureaucracy, some American sociologists have held that the attributes of bureaucracy are evident in the organization and governance of the college or university. Andes (1970) utilized this point of view in his discussion of a systems approach to higher education. The bureaucratic position, however, is most clearly presented by Blau (1973) in his discussion of the organization of academic work. This point of view argues that the academic enterprise, no less than any other enterprise, has explicit procedures for organizing and coordinating its productive output.

Blau finds characteristics of bureaucracy within the university in the formal division of labor among departments, in the existence of an administrative hierarchy, and in the presence of a clerical apparatus. At the same time, Blau notes that bureaucratic "rigidity and discipline" are incompatible with academic scholarship. He acknowledges that colleges and universities tend to be different from other bureaucracies since the work performed by faculty members is not directly supervised and since "detailed operating rules" governing the performance of academic work are lacking.

In spite of these differences, Blau insisted that he found "striking parallels" in organization between government bureaus and academic institutions. He did draw a distinction between the professional authority of faculty members and the bureaucratic authority of administration. Blau postulated that the distribution of decision-making influence among faculty members and administrative officers determined the extent to which professional authority or bureaucratic authority dominated the college or university work. Blau went further and correlated larger size, recognized quality in faculty performance, and an emphasis upon research activity with professional authority (as distinguished from bureaucratic authority).

Blau drew several conclusions. He suggested that the allocation of economic resources was a major source of power for presidents and governing boards. Because larger universities tended to devote proportionately less of their resources to administrative apparatus than did smaller institutions, he argued that the larger academic institution was in most respects less bureaucratic. He concluded that bureaucracy did come into conflict with scholarship, observing that the bureaucratic features of an academic institution had no negative effect upon research performance but did have "deleterious consequences" for educational performance. Blau argued that the "threat of bureaucratization" in higher education should be resisted and that faculty members were the persons to resist it.

Blau's study is important here for two reasons. Without saying so specifically, Blau in effect emphasized the production role of a college or university. Much of the literature about governance presents colleges and universities as debating societies or legislative assemblies. Blau pointed to colleges and universities as organizations producing an output that was presumably important and socially useful. In addition, although he did not make the distinction explicit, he observed an important organizational characteristic, the difference between operations and housekeeping, between output programs and support programs. Moreover, the high degree of "anarchy" noted by Cohen and March was really applicable to the performance of the output programs of instruction, research, and public service. The bureaucratization observed by Blau was to be found in the administration of support programs. In a sense, Blau was noting an aspect of organizational dualism, even though this concept was not mentioned in his study.

## Academic Constituents: Partners or Adversaries

A considerable part of the literature about governance has attempted to articulate faculty, student, and administration points of view or interests in the academic enterprise. In their study of university goals and academic power, Gross and Grambsch (1968) found that the goals expressed by faculty members were quite similar to those expressed by department chairmen and academic deans. These goals tended to be elitist, scholarly, and professionally oriented rather than practical and institutionally oriented. Faculty members professed to want participation in campus governance, rewards based upon professional accomplishment, academic freedom, and a maximum opportunity to pursue their individual professional careers. Similar points of view have been expressed by others, such as Milton and Shoben (1968), Clark (1970), Nichols (1970). They also appear in the collection of essays edited by Harcleroad (1970) and those presented in *Daedalus* (1970, 1974, 1975).

In commenting about the idea of community, Lewis (1975) wrote: "If academic administrators were as concerned about the needs of the faculty as they are about those of politicians, the press, the clergy, the rich, the poor, and the like, the development of such a community would be immeasurably enhanced" (p. 200)'. Such a comment may well express the viewpoint of many faculty members. Two other faculty members, both economists, have a somewhat different perspective. Buchanan and Devletoglou (1970) have observed: "University education, when examined through economists' eyes, assumes characteristics of a unique industry. This is because:

(1) those who consume its product do not purchase it; (2) those who produce it do not sell it; and (3) those who finance it do not control it" (p. 8).

Acknowledging faculty preoccupation with "participatory democracy," Zyskind and Sternfeld (1971) argued that the problem within a university was not how to equitably distribute power but how to minimize it. They insisted that the essential processes of a university were nonpolitical and that decision making must give greater concern to reasoned argument than to numerical voting strength. In his study of faculty participation in governance, Dykes (1968) found a "pervasive ambivalence" in faculty attitudes about participation in institutional decision making. On the one hand, he observed an attitude in favor of a strong, active, and influential faculty role in decision making, especially in relation to the educational affairs of a college or university. On the other hand, Dykes encountered nostalgia for a simpler, smaller academic community and a tendency to believe that faculties of an earlier era possessed more influence than may have actually been the case. He also reported an inclination among faculty to make a distinction in their own thinking between educational and "noneducational" affairs and a belief that faculty members ought not become involved in decisions about the latter. Other inquiries, such as those of Dressel and Faricy (1972) and Wilson (1972), suggest an inability of faculty to articulate a definite set of objectives to be achieved through their participation in the structure and process of institutional decision making.

To some extent it may be argued that students have had a more definite objective of what they have wanted to achieve through participation in campus governance than have faculty members. That objective has been repeal, or at least substantial modification, of student-conduct regulations by colleges and universities. In his study of student participation in campus governance, McGrath (1970) found that student membership on committees and councils dealing with student affairs was widespread. In his report about student concerns at Cornell University, Morrison (1970) stated that a great deal of student discontent centered in their sense of conflict between the structure of the university and their own "spontaneity," their own freedom of behavior. Students seemed to believe that the university was structured as a hierarchy of power from which they were barred. Student interests centered on the quality of their life in the university community, on the quality of their educational experience, and on the relationship of the university to external society.

Extensive student discontent, disruption, and violence in the 1960s was evident. This fact in turn resulted in various studies and inquiries: Williamson and Cowan (1966), Magrath and Sindler (1968), Becker (1970), Rossman (1971), the National Commission on the Causes and Prevention of Violence report (1969), and the President's Commission on Campus Unrest report (1970). In every instance the alternative to disruption and disorder on campus was seen as student participation in campus governance. Kellems (1975) has summarized the scope and extent of student influence upon college and universities operations, and Astin and others (1975) have analyzed the power of student protest.

In reviewing the attention given to student interests and concerns in the various reports of the Carnegie Commission on Higher Education, Wren (1975) referred to the survey of student attitudes undertaken by the commission that reached 70,000 undergraduate students and 30,000 graduate students. These students ranked their interests in participation in decision making in this order: (1) student discipline, (2) provision and content of courses, (3) degree requirements, (4) admissions policies, and (5) faculty appointments and promotion. In his own analysis of student concerns, Wren listed these interests: breaking the barriers to college opportunity, the costs of attending college, the need for more student options in pursuing instructional programs, student participation in decision making, and alternatives to a college education.

When we turn to discussions about the role of governing boards, the array of literature is extensive indeed. We shall mention here only Burns (1966), Henderson (1967), Rauh (1969), Zwingle (1970), Heilbron (1973), and Nason (1974). By common consent, boards of trustees constitute the link between the academic community and the external community. Among others, Epstein (1974) makes this situation clear; the external community of active alumni, influential business and professional groups, public officials, legislators, the media of mass communication, and others are all viewed as a solid phalanx hostile to the academic freedom of faculty members and to the behavioral inclinations of students.

Because of the financial dependence of the academic community upon external sources of support and because of their concern with the attitudes of this external community, presidents and governing boards are viewed by faculty members and students as the possessors of the "real" power within the academic community. Thus are sowed the seeds of conflict.

## Community Governance

Whatever the differences in attitudes and interests among campus constituencies, we do know that the 1960s were a period of experimentation in the development of structures and processes designed to achieve community governance within colleges and universities. Dill (1971) presented case studies of changes at Florida Agriculture and Mechanical University, the University of Minnesota, Columbia University, and the University of New Hampshire. Dill concluded that much of the current experimentation in university governance had been motivated by a desire to include students in the decision-making process. From the early experiences of these four institutions, Dill noted several problems: the demand for new institutional activities without the necessary income; the tendency to politicize academic issues; the expense in time for faculty members and students active in campus governance; and confusion about the relationship of campus governance to the governing board.

Hodgkinson (1974) presented the results of his own study of campus senates, which he described as experiments in democracy. Upon the basis of replies from 1,863 institutions, Hodgkinson identified 688 as having a "broadly based campus senate." One third of these respondents were two-year institutions, about one fourth were general baccalaureate colleges, and some 44 percent were comprehensive and research universities. About one third of the institutions had enrollments of 1,000 students or less, about 38 percent had enrollments from 1,000 to 5,000 students, and 28 percent had enrollments over 5,000. Of 364 institutions responding in detail to a questionnaire, Hodgkinson found that the campus senate had been in existence less than seven years at 80 percent of these colleges and universities. Hodgkinson presented eleven conclusions from his survey, as well as details of experience drawn from four case studies.

In 1974 I attempted to call attention to various deficiencies in the experience to date in campus governance and to suggest how the concept of community governance might be strengthened (Millett, 1974). Cleveland (1974) raised a pertinent question of criticism: "How do you get everybody in on the act and still get some action?" Against the openness and wide participation of a campuswide senate, he presented a number of flaws: apathy, nonparticipation, procedures tending to polarize various representatives, an excess of voting and parliamentary procedures, a tendency to restrictive legalisms, the encouragement of mediocrity, and the discouragement of innovation.

Some commentators, such as Johnson (1971) and Helsabeck (1973), have called for greater organizational effectiveness on campuses. Still others, such as Jellema (1972) and Balderston (1974), have stressed the management performance of colleges and universities as even more vital than governance.

A well-known and highly respected university dean provides us with an appropriate conclusion. Brown (1973, p. 1) wrote: "Science and technology have provided new knowledge and devices for human organizations to use. . . . Science and technology have not altered the persistent and controlling attribute of human organization—namely, whatever the organization's size or form, it continues to be subject to the complex and unpredictable initiatives and responses of the individual human beings who make it up."

# CHAPTER TWO

◇◇◇◇◇◇◇◇◇◇◇

# Studying
# Campus Governance

◇◇◇◇◇◇◇◇◇◇◇◇◇◇◇◇◇◇◇◇◇◇◇◇◇◇◇◇◇◇◇◇◇◇

The thirty colleges and universities chosen for case studies of experience in campuswide governance are shown in Table 1. These institutions were selected on the basis of an equal distribution between colleges and universities having public (state government) sponsorship and those having independent sponsorship. Apart from specialized professional schools and two-year institutions, categories which were purposefully omitted from this study, the number of higher education institutions under independent sponsorship exceeds the number of institutions under public sponsorship. In terms of enrollment, however, about two thirds of all students are to be found in the public colleges and universities. Since this study focused upon institutional experience, the fairest procedure seemed to be to divide the sample equally between public and independent sponsorship.

*Table 1.* Colleges and Universities Chosen for Case Studies.

| Public | Private |
|---|---|
| *Leading Research Universities* | |
| University of California at Berkeley | Columbia University |
| University of Wisconsin at Madison | Cornell University |
| University of Texas at Austin | Stanford University |
| *Other Universities* | |
| Miami University, Ohio | Emory University |
| University of New Hampshire | Howard University |
| University of New Mexico | Roosevelt University |
| University of Oregon | Syracuse University |
| Tennessee State University | |
| *General Baccalaureate Colleges* | |
| Armstrong State College | Albertus Magnus College |
| California State College at Bakersfield | Aquinas College |
| Central Connecticut State College | Augustana College |
| Eastern Montana State College | Carleton College |
| Evergreen State College | Rockford College |
| Frostburg State College | Tuskegee Institute |
| Northern Kentucky State College | Vassar College |
| | West Virginia Wesleyan College |

The sample was divided into three categories by type of institution: leading research universities, other universities, and general baccalaureate colleges. I devised these categories in 1973 as modifications of the institutional classification scheme developed by the Carnegie Commission on Higher Education and published that year. A leading research university was classified as one granting more than fifty Ph.D. degrees a year and receiving over $10 million a year in federal government support of academic science. In our sample the six universities in this category were all classified by the Carnegie Commission as Research Universities I.

The designation *other university* was utilized for other institutions with one of two kinds of characteristics. In general, these institutions all had enrollments of more than 3,500 students, offered an array of professional programs in addition to the arts and sciences, and were involved in graduate education. In the Carnegie Commission classification, three of these universities (Emory, Oregon, and Syracuse) were classified as Research Universities II; three (Howard, New Mexico, and New Hampshire at Durham) were classified as Doctoral-Granting Universities I; one (Miami)' was classified as a Doctoral-Granting University II; and two (Roosevelt and Tennessee State) were classified as Comprehensive Universities I.

The label *general baccalaureate college* seemed more appropriate to me than the Carnegie Commission designation, *liberal arts colleges*. Of the fifteen institutions in our sample shown as general baccalaureate colleges, the Carnegie Commission had classified four as Comprehensive Colleges I, four as Comprehensive Colleges II, five as Liberal Arts Colleges I, and two as Liberal Arts Colleges II. It seemed preferable to me to consider all of these particular institutions as general baccaluareate colleges in terms of the data available about them as of 1973. (We should note, however, that as of 1976–77 two or three public colleges in this category could more properly be considered universities.)

Some diversity by type of institution, in terms of program thrust and enrollment size, was obtained in the sample. Although the numbers of institutions in each of the three categories by type were not closely proportionate to the total in each category, some balance was achieved. The number of leading research universities in the sample was disproportionate to the total of such institutions in a universe of some 1,300 colleges and universities, and the number of public general baccalaureate colleges was also disproportionate to the total of such institutions.

The geographical distribution of the sample is shown in Table 2. Institutions were selected from all six designated geographical areas of the United States. The thirty institutions were located in twenty-three different states. This geographical spread appeared to provide a reasonable variety of experience as far as the various parts of the United States were concerned.

## Case Authors

The individuals recruited to serve as authors of the thirty case studies are listed in the front of this book. Thirteen were administrative officers of the college or university about which they wrote; another four were directors of institutional research, and a fifth was the former director of a research center on higher education. Twelve were faculty members; six of these were professors of

*Table 2.* Geographical Distribution of the Thirty Colleges
and Universities.

*New England*—three (two public and one private)
   Central Connecticut State College, University of New Hampshire;
   Albertus Magnus College
*Middle Atlantic*—six (one public and five private)
   Frostburg State College; Columbia University, Cornell University,
   Howard University, Syracuse University, Vassar College
*Southern*—six (three public and three private)
   Armstrong State College, Northern Kentucky State College, Tennessee
   State College; Emory University, Tuskegee Institute, West Virginia
   Wesleyan College.
*Middle West*—six (two public and four private)
   Miami University, University of Wisconsin at Madison; Aquinas Col-
   lege, Carleton College, Rockford College, Roosevelt University
*Southwest*—two (two public)
   University of New Mexico, University of Texas at Austin
*West*—seven (five public and two private)
   California State College at Bakersfield, Eastern Montana State Col-
   lege, Evergreen State College, University of California at Berkeley,
   University of Oregon; Augustana College, Stanford University

political science, two were professors of higher education, and four
taught in the varied disciplines of psychology, chemistry, philosophy
and religion, and journalism.

In recruiting case authors, a balance between administrative
officers and faculty members seemed desirable. The study was not
intended as an attack upon presidential leadership or upon administrative behavior nor was it intended either as a defense or advocacy
of any particular faculty role in making decisions about the operation of a college or university. As far as possible, the study was intended to be an objective and empirical analysis of the behavior of
various persons in the organizational setting of a higher education
campus.

With three exceptions, all of the faculty members participating in this study had previous administrative experience in the institution or had played a prominent role in faculty leadership. Such
persons tend to have greater personal interest in institutional affairs
than faculty members who concentrate their professional attention
on a given discipline.

I found that professors of higher education and directors of
institutional research tended to have both the most balanced and

the most sympathetic concern with all individuals and groups involved in campus governance. These individuals were well aware of institutional objectives and constraints and were also inclined to support faculty aspirations and student interests. The two graduate students who participated as co-authors of case studies contributed to the balance in the evaluation of governance activities.

## The Faculty and Governance

Before we look more particularly at the various kinds of governance experience within the thirty colleges and universities of this study, some general issues deserve discussion. In the preface I have set forth the eight criteria chosen for evaluating governance experience. But there are other, and larger, matters requiring attention. It is unfortunate that in the extensive literature about governance I find very little consideration of them.

The first question that should be asked in a discussion of campuswide governance is fundamental: What is the role of the faculty in a college or university, and what is there in this role that justifies faculty participation in the governance of the institution? If we accept the basic proposition that the governance of a college or university is legally vested in a governing board of lay trustees, we must ask the further question: Why should the authority of this board of trustees be shared with the faculty?

Without endeavoring to bring together historical and other evidence that might illuminate the proposition, I suggest that boards of trustees, early in their experience in the United States, begin to share their authority with faculties. I believe that the concept of a board of lay trustees as an agency of governance was never intended to mean that such boards would make decisions about "academic" affairs. The determination of what constitutes a degree program, the establishment of degree requirements, the development of a set of courses or of a curriculum satisfying those requirements, the development of course objectives and course content, the handling of instructional procedure (the work technology), the evaluation of the learning achievement of students—all of these decisions were entrusted to the faculty of a college virtually since the first college was founded in colonial America.

In the due course of events, the scope of affairs or decisions labeled *academic* expanded: the determination of desired competencies needed in a faculty, the recruitment and selection of faculty personnel, the decision about faculty members worthy of tenure and promotion. Nominally and officially these actions might still be endorsed by a board of trustees, but the initiative for action became a province of faculty determination. The faculty role might be called advisory, but, except in unusual circumstances engendering public attention outside the academic community itself, faculty advice was translated into board decision as a matter of routine.

There were several reasons why the faculty role in a college, or later in a university, was quite different from the role of a laborer in a factory or of a clerk in a store. The faculty role was a professional role, involving individual expertise based upon educational preparation and experience. The faculty member was not told what to do by a supervisor or a manager; the faculty member was expected to know how to encourage learning on the part of students. Moreover, boards of trustees did not pretend to be managers of learning. The board's role was not that of a manager; the board's role was that of liaison between the world of learning and the world of social interest in learning, including interest in providing needed economic resources.

In order to complete this organizational sketch we must acknowledge the peculiar position of the college or university president. The president was both executive officer for the governing board and presiding officer of the faculty. The president was expected to share both the world of learning and the world of social expectation about higher education performance. The president represented the faculty to the governing board and the governing board to the faculty.

There can be no doubt that faculty power within the academic community was strengthened by the so-called academic revolution: by the expansion of knowledge, the specialization of knowledge, the need to acquire new knowledge through research, and the growing social utility of knowledge. These factors combined to give faculty members a new status in society, especially in the middle years of the twentieth century. And these factors encouraged faculty members to join together to further their influence, institutionally and socially. Faculty identification of a group interest helped to promote faculty power within the academic community.

For a considerable period of time, faculty power was satisfied with its authority to decide all major matters involving academic affairs. If John Corson's concept of organizational dualism in 1960 did represent the reality of college and university governance, then there was a category of decision making to be identified as institutional affairs, somehow different and distinct from academic affairs. The new issue of the 1960s was the competency and legitimacy of the faculty role in institutional affairs; the faculty role in academic affairs was no longer subject to question. The current issue was that of the faculty role in decision making about institutional affairs, and it was this role that the present study was intended to explore.

Rationalization for this faculty claim, insofar as one can be said to exist, arose from the student revolution of the 1960s. The essence of the faculty case seemed to be that a distinction between academic and institutional affairs had broken down when students disrupted the operation of the institution. Faculty members then asserted their appropriate concern with decision making that would restore campus order and prevent the necessity for police action to overcome student violence and student interference with the learning process to which the institution was committed.

The claim to a faculty role in institutional affairs could be made good only if an effective structure and process could be devised to fulfill this role. The claim quickly became an issue in organization, as well as a question of role legitimacy. There appeared a disposition to debate organization rather than role, structure rather than performance. This conclusion was my perception of the situation. Would empirical evidence confirm, reject, or modify this perception?

## Students and Governance

A second set of issues in governance necessarily concerns the role of students in the academic community. Are students to be considered as customers or clients for the professional services of the faculty? What is the relationship of students to the institution they are attending? What role could and should students have in the decision making about institutional policies and programs?

As one reviews the student activism, or indeed the student revolution, of the 1960s, one quickly becomes aware of at least three quite different thrusts. First, there was an attack upon the social conduct or behavioral standards that faculty or board regulations imposed upon students. Second, there was an attack upon the basic concept of higher education purpose in relation to the power structrue and the other institutions of society. And, third, there was an attack upon the educational priorities of the day that appeared to favor research, public service, and graduate instruction over undergraduate instruction.

There has been a long and discordant history of debate about the appropriate standards of student social and personal conduct within the academic community. The American college of the eighteenth and nineteenth centuries was essentially an austere learning environment in which the student was expected to concentrate on his or her intellectual endeavors and to avoid student social activity and any contact with a corrupting external world. The standards of personal behavior expected of students were unrealistic, and revolts and rebellions periodically occurred, as the histories of many American colleges make abundantly clear.

Slowly colleges and then universities changed their expectations to accord a place within the community for various kinds of student social organizations and activities. The college or university continued to supervise these organizations and activities to an extent, to require faculty advisors, and to set certain standards of acceptable social behavior.

The 1960s were different from preceding decades in that students tended to insist that no standards should be imposed by colleges and universities upon personal and social behavior, at least none different from those applying to all individuals in American society. Presumably a permissive family experience and a changing set of personal values in society at large suddenly engulfed higher education. Rules that affected residence-hall life, the possession of alcoholic beverages, the organization of like-minded individuals to discuss any subject of current interest, and other matters of personal choice were questioned. Students demanded that they be considered adults, not children.

A different kind of student concern raised a profound issue of higher education purpose. A fundamental understanding had developed between higher education and society in America: The price of academic freedom was academic restraint in social and political conflict outside the campus itself. The college and the university took a neutral stance with regard to the social, economic, and political struggles of the day. The student activists of the 1960s rejected this fundamental understanding.

The Vietnam War was ostensibly the reason for repudiation of the traditional social and political neutrality of American higher education. Some students argued that higher education was not in fact neutral; that, in terms of research activities and of placement of college graduates, higher education was allied with a gigantic governmental-military-industrial complex dominating the political process of American society. Some student activists, by disruption of research activity, of military and industrial recruitment, and of military education on campus, sought to express their disapproval of the Vietnam War.

At the same time that the conduct of war was a target of student activism, other aspects of American social life came under critical scrutiny—racial discrimination, poverty, environmental pollution, urban congestion, traditional attitudes about the role of women. Students demanded that colleges and universities be neutral in fact rather than in theory or align their commitment with those groups that students identified as progressive and liberal.

A third student attack was directed at the very heart of the educational enterprise: the priorities of educational endeavor. A university is engaged in producing not one but several outputs: research, creative activity, and various kinds of public service, in addition to student instruction. Moreover, student instruction is divided into undergraduate and graduate categories and general and professional, or specialized, areas as well. The years after 1945 in America were a period in which research became a major endeavor of American universities, graduate education took precedence over undergraduate education, and professional and specialized education took precedence over general education. It may not be an exaggeration to assert that as undergraduate and graduate student enrollments expanded in the 1950s and 1960s, graduate students occupied the place in faculty interest that was extended so often to undergraduate students in the years before 1940.

My perception was that the student revolution tended to express itself in action rather than in discussion, in disruption rather than efforts to achieve a legitimacy in the power process. Much of the attention of faculties, presidents, and governing boards was necessarily addressed to the issue of how to interest students in the orderly exercise of power in an atmosphere of civility and reasoned discourse. Would empirical evidence confirm, reject, or modify this perception?

## Presidents and Governance

Although only occasionally asserted as such by either faculty or student spokesmen, much of the power struggle of the 1960s was aimed at reducing or curtailing the perceived power of presidents on a college or university campus. Criticism of the composition and actions of boards of trustees merely reflected a belief that presidents dominated board decision making and that boards were rubber stamps for presidential recommendations. Faculty members in particular seemed to believe that, since governing boards merely echoed faculty academic recommendations, these boards must be equally subject to the president's authority in institutional matters.

As early as 1962, Harold W. Dodds, who was president of Princeton University from 1933 to 1957, asked the question in *The Academic President—Educator or Caretaker?* (1962). The question was important, even if the answer was somewhat less than convincing. Dodds accurately observed that presidents had become decreasingly influential as educational leaders and were increasingly perceived as institutional managers. But any expectation that presidents could regain a major voice in academic affairs was probably misplaced.

Presidents began to lose their influence as educational leaders because of two or three forces over which they were powerless to assert control. One force was, of course, the increasingly specialized nature of research and of instruction. Presidents could not provide an intellectual leadership encompassing the range of knowledge professed in a college or university. A second force was the increasing burden of institutional finance confronted with the depression of the 1930s, the war years from 1939 to 1945 and the loss of male students after 1941, the tremendous influx of veterans after 1945, and the uncertainties of the 1950s as higher education faced the prospects of further enrollment growth in the 1960s. As my own experience verified in a study I directed from 1949 to 1952, the financing of higher education necessarily became the preoccupation of college and university presidents, with such assistance as they could garner from individual members of their boards of trustees. And the third force affecting presidential behavior was the growth of support services within colleges and universities after 1945, especially in the area of student services. Presidents did become managers-in-chief of these support services. If concern for financing and for support services made presidents into institutional caretakers, there was little they could do to avoid this situation. Someone had to worry about the institution as an economic and organized enterprise.

Specialization of scholarship within the faculty brought about two organizational developments that have been little discussed in the writing about higher education. One of these developments was a high degree of decentralization in the decision-making process concerning academic and faculty affairs within a college or university. Academic departments became the key organizational unit to decide questions of instructional objectives and courses and of faculty qualifications. The second and corresponding development was a decline in important decisions about academic and faculty matters made at the college or university level. To be sure, colleges and universities continued to exercise authority to approve departmental recommendations, but increasingly this authority was exercised as a matter of routine rather than as a matter of substance. If one department objected to the program and personnel actions of another department, it invited similar objection on some future occasion when it presented actions for approval. To live and to let live became the process of faculty decision making about academic and faculty affairs. There were occasional exceptions to these two organizational practices, but the exceptions were sufficiently unusual to confirm the general arrangement.

The president's role as educational leader diminished because the role of the faculty as a whole in academic decision making had diminished. Just as faculty members of highly specialized competence in a particular area of knowledge were cautious in offering advice and counsel to other faculty members, presidents were also cautious in offering leadership in academic affairs. The president's role remained one of leadership in resolving those academic matters that were subject to central decision making. The real issue was: What kinds of academic matters could properly be handled on a centralized basis while preserving intellectual integrity in the various specialized fields of knowledge cultivated by the institution?

In his or her relationship to the governing board, the president became the professional (or full-time) adviser in two vital areas of interrelated concern: institutional financing and institutional viability or integrity. On the one hand, the president had to find an appropriate admixture of sources of financial support: pricing, governmental subsidy and grants, and philanthropic. On the other hand, the president had to recommend the allocation of these available resources among various primary programs (instruction, research, public service, student aid, and special operations), among various support programs (academic support, student services, plant operation, institutional support, and mandated or desirable transfers), and among various auxiliary enterprises. Moreover, this financial planning pertained to both current operating and capital improvement budgets. In addition, budget planning was necessarily closely related to institutional planning, to the question of policies and programs appropriate to the mission of the institution as a whole.

As chief executive officer for the board of trustees, the president was expected to be the institution's principal planner and its budget officer as well. And in both areas the president's task was to determine the viability of the enterprise—its reasonable expectation of accomplishing its stated mission. If there was no reasonable prospect for such accomplishment, liquidation or merger might have to be considered as alternatives. The president could not avoid a concern for survival—and survival at some appropriate level of per-

36 New Structures of Campus Power

formance. Moreover, in the search for survival, the president could not afford to be indifferent to threats or actions leading to disruption of operation.

The president also became manager-in-chief of support services. As universities expanded in enrollment and budgets, they did not decentralize support programs, which also demanded enlarged resources. Libraries grew and became a broader instructional resource; academic support was enlarged to include computers, broadcasting, and audiovisual materials; institutions provided museums and art galleries. Student services expanded to embrace personal counseling, health care, recreation, cultural affairs, and other activities. Plant facilities grew and became more expensive to operate. Logistical, administrative, fiscal, legal, informational, and other services likewise became more extensive. The president was expected to ensure that support services facilitated the production of the primary outputs of the college or university and remained subordinate to the mission and primary programs of the institution.

When presidential leadership of institutional survival was criticized by both faculty and students in the 1960s, a new constituency in the academic community suddenly made itself evident. This constituency was the professional and technical staffs of a college or university operating the various support services, including auxiliary enterprises. For a long time these staffs had been vaguely identified as part of the administration of the institution. When *administration* became a suspect word, both professional and technical support personnel sought acknowledgment of their particular identity within the academic community. Indeed, on many campuses, craft technicians and custodial, food service, and even clerical personnel had resorted to unionization and collective bargaining as a device for improving salaries, wages, and working conditions. This technical staff was not satisfied to be considered just a part of "administration." Moreover, when faculty members began to challenge faculty designation for librarians, student personnel officers, doctors, nurses, architects, lawyers, accountants, and others, then this professional staff insisted upon some other appropriate recognition. Presidents had to assist in ensuring that professional and technical staffs operating support services were accorded a status in governance.

The role of presidents underwent substantial change on college and university campuses in the years after 1920. But that role did not thereby become unimportant; it simply became different. In their concentration upon institutional performance and institutional financing, presidents could not be indifferent to or ignorant of academic affairs. But presidents became supporters rather than instigators of faculty endeavor. The relationship of faculty management of academic affairs and presidential management of institutional affairs was destined for readjustment.

My perception was that the student revolution of the 1960s precipitated that readjustment. Would empirical evidence confirm, reject, or modify this perception?

### Governing Boards and Governance

Beginning in the 1930s and gaining momentum in the 1950s, governing boards, or boards of trustees, of colleges and universities, were criticized on two major issues. One criticism was that board members were largely Protestant, male, experienced in professions and business, and wealthy. As colleges and universities enrolled more women, blacks and other minority students, as well as students from less affluent economic circumstances and from diverse religious affiliations, it was argued that boards of trustees should be more representative of the composition of society. Second, boards of trustees were criticized as knowing little or nothing about the educational process—about educational inputs, about educational technology, and about educational outputs. As a consequence, how could a group of individuals so ignorant about education presume to "govern" an educational enterprise?

Without endeavoring to assess the merits and the deficiencies in either criticism, we can observe one very important omission in the discussion about governing boards. If the income of higher education was largely derived from government and philanthropy and not from charges to students, how was the governance of a college or university to be structured in order to reflect social expectation and social accountability? And a further omission, as far as state universities were concerned, was the failure to perceive that the alternative to governance by a board of trustees was governance by the chief executive and the legislature of the state.

It is not necessary here to sketch various concerns and various responses involving the governance role of governing boards. The current study assumed that the importance of governing boards was self-evident. The issue of campuswide governance was essentially an issue of who advises and influences the governing board rather than that of abolition or even of modification of the authority vested in it. Here again, this was my perception of the situation. Would empirical evidence confirm, reject, or modify this perception?

### The Academic Community

The academic community is, in my view, a unique kind of organizational arrangement. I have argued for many years that a college or university as an enterprise cannot be compared with, or evaluated by, experience in other kinds of enterprises. The academic community is subject to the authority of a governing board that does not in fact govern; the board has delegated substantial authority to faculties and to students. The academic community is led by a president who exercises management authority over support services, an institutional budget, and an institutional plan but who lacks management authority over the essential output programs of instruction, research, and public service. Moreover, the tenure of a president may well be determined by faculty and student confidence in his or her leadership. The essential or productive outputs of the academic community are determined on a highly decentralized basis, as are management planning and management performance of these outputs. And the student "customers" of higher education constitute a clientele who insist upon a role in the operation of the academic community, even if that role is one of disruption.

The academic community is a productive organization. The essence of the enterprise is the accumulation of resource inputs, the operation of a productive procedure or technology, and the output of certain particular but often somewhat indefinite outputs: degree recipients, educated talent for the labor market, new knowledge and even new technology for use by society, various creative or cultural activities, and knowledge services to society. The academic community is neither the legislature nor the chief executive nor the judiciary of any governmental jurisdiction. The academic community does not exercise control over any other kind of enterprise. The academic community produces certain essential services for society but does not control that society.

The academic community does not "sell" its services to society and does not offer its services at a price designed to recover all costs of production. Some auxiliary services, such as student housing and student feeding, may be priced at cost, but the primary services tend to be priced below the cost of production—the difference expected to come from governmental subsidy and philanthropic giving. The academic community requires public or social support.

The academic community does consist of identifiable constituent groups: faculty, students, professional support staff, technical support staff, and a leadership group. Many of these persons as individuals or the institution as an enterprise belong to numerous associations designed to promote a common interest across institutional boundary lines. External to these groups are an even larger number of persons and groups: a governing board, alumni, governments, professions, voluntary associations, business and corporations, general purpose foundations, the media of mass communication, interested citizens. All of these persons and groups have an interest in the performance of colleges and universities and express that interest in various ways, including the granting or withholding of economic resources.

The constituent groups of an academic community tend to seek self-government, that is, self-determination of mission, policies, and programs. Just which constituent groups should dominate this decision making is one of the issues of campuswide governance. The other major issue is how constituent groups can be self-governing and still obtain external support and externally provided economic resources.

Governance in higher education, as a subject of study, is an account of how particular colleges and universities have sought to resolve this dilemma of internal self-government versus external economic support.

# CHAPTER THREE

◇◇◇◇◇◇◇◇◇◇◇◇

# Governance in
# Leading Research
# Universities

◇◇◇◇◇◇◇◇◇◇◇◇◇◇◇◇◇◇◇◇◇◇◇◇◇◇◇◇◇◇◇◇

The six leading research universities reviewed in this study on campuswide governance are, in order of their founding dates, Columbia (1754), Wisconsin at Madison (1848), Cornell (1865), California at Berkeley (1868), Texas at Austin (1881), and Stanford (1891). They are among the luminaries of the American higher education firmament. Two of them operate under private sponsorship, three under public sponsorship, and one under a unique private and public sponsorship; all six have achieved the status of institutions to whom the federal government looks for extensive research in the sciences and engineering and to whom society in general looks for educated talent of the highest order and for public service of exemplary quality.

The two privately sponsored universities have student enrollments of from 13,000 to 15,000 students; two thirds of Columbia's
and over one half of Stanford's are enrolled as graduate and graduate professional students. On the other hand, about two thirds of
Cornell's some 16,000 students, about two thirds of Berkeley's
28,000 students, about three fourths of Austin's 40,000 students, and
nearly 70 percent of Madison's 35,000 students are undergraduates.
The annual budgets of these universities range from $110 to $190
million, and the number of their faculty members (full-time and
part-time) ranges from 1,300 to 3,800. By various kinds of measure-
ments, these six universities tend to be sizable as well as of substantial quality in student and faculty inputs.

Each university can be considered unique in its history, in
its traditions, in its record of outstanding faculty members and administrators, in its location (only Columbia is in the middle of a
large city, although Berkeley and Stanford are located in large
metropolitan areas), and in its structure of governance prior to
1960. Five of the six universities experienced severe student disorders during the 1960s, and Austin experienced some student dis-
affection, although by no means on the scale of the other five. The
"student revolution" of the 1960s began at Berkeley in 1964. Critical events occurred at Columbia in 1968, Cornell in 1969, Stanford
in 1969 and 1970, and Madison in 1967 and in 1970. Troubles
brought change in these leading research universities. But again the
changes varied one from another.

## Columbia University

A university senate was established by the board of trustees
of Columbia University in May 1969. This action followed months
of argument, turbulence, and discussion in the aftermath of the student revolt and police action in April 1968. By 1975 it appeared
that the senate was a smoothly operating but somewhat inconspicu-
ous element in the governance structure of Columbia. As an organizational arrangement it had found some previously unfulfilled,
relatively modest functions to perform. By 1975 new issues confronted the university, and the competence of the senate to assist in
resolving them appeared uncertain.

Prior to 1968, Columbia had a long history of first strong and then of ineffectual leadership (1933 to 1953), coupled with a high degree of departmental and college autonomy in performing educational programs. The university consisted of sixteen colleges and schools with seventy departments and more than a dozen research institutes. It occupied sixty buildings crowded into just under thirty acres of land at Morningside Heights on the island of Manhattan. The College of Physicians and Surgeons was located fifty city blocks to the north, and some research institutes occupied areas farther removed from the main campus. By affiliation agreements, Barnard College and Teachers College were related to the university but remained separate educational corporations. The Union Theological Seminary also had a cooperative arrangement with the university.

The official and formal governance of the university was vested in a twenty-four-member board of trustees, which was self-perpetuating. Six of the trustees were nominated for staggered six-year terms through an alumni nominating committee, and in 1969, when the university senate was created, the board agreed that six more of the trustees should serve six-year terms and be nominated by the board's executive committee meeting in joint session with the executive committee of the new senate. As other trustees reached the mandatory age limit of seventy-two, elections for life were being replaced by elections to six-year terms.

Prior to 1968, the only campuswide agency of governance had been a university council. The president presided over this council and controlled its agenda. The membership consisted of fifteen deans and directors, along with two elected faculty representatives from fifteen colleges and schools. Another ten or twelve administrative officers and heads of professional support services (such as the director of libraries) served as members as designated by the president. The council met regularly once a semester, seldom for more than an hour. The council served primarily as an approving agency for matters previously negotiated between a faculty and the administration. If any item was objected to by a council member, the matter was not debated but referred to its originator for further negotiation.

The university council had been created in the 1890s, soon

after Columbia had expanded its educational mission and had established three graduate faculties that were in time to become the very center of the university. The board of trustees had in effect delegated to the council the authority to deal with academic and faculty affairs. Actions of the council were laid before the board, and council decisions became final if, in two subsequent meetings, the board neither amended nor disapproved the action. In effect, the council became the device whereby the president and representatives of the various faculties determined those academic and faculty affairs deemed to require university action. By objecting to some proposed council action, a dean or a faculty member could protect the perceived interests of any particular part of the university. Nevertheless, by practice and presidential inclination, the council was not a forum for discussion of any campuswide issues. The faculties of the university never met as a single body but only as the faculty of a particular college, school, or graduate division (political science, pure science, and philosophy). During the late 1950s, President Kirk agreed to the creation of a faculty advisory committee to the council, but the device had never been important. The president continued to name ad hoc inquiry committees to study vexing problems, and the faculty advisory committee was reluctant to spend the time required to become an effective voice of faculty interest in university operations. The faculty "style of life" at Columbia emphasized individual commitment to scholarship and public service but not commitment to the university as a community. Faculty members in general pursued their individual professional, cultural, and social life in the City of New York and its suburbs rather than on Morningside Heights as such.

When the university senate was established by the board of trustees in 1969, the board resolved the internal conflict about governance by making the senate the lineal successor to the university council. The powers of the council became the powers of the senate, with a few additional concessions. The differences between the council and the senate were not differences in authority but differences in organization, membership, and method of operation. The senate device was the product of a year's active discussion involving an executive committee of the faculty, student organizations, administrative officers, and board members. At one time a bicameral arrangement for a faculty senate and a student assembly had been contemplated. The final product was a university senate of ninety-five members. The composition of the senate was forty-two members of the tenured faculty, fifteen members of the nontenured faculty, twenty-one students, nine members of the administration (including the president), two alumni, two from the library staff, two from the research staff, and two from the operating staff. To these ninety-five places were added representatives of affiliated bodies. The numbers of faculty members and students were distributed among the sixteen academic units of the university roughly in proportion to size, with the guarantee of at least one faculty member and one student per unit. It was further provided that at least 40 percent of a constituency would have to vote in order to elect a senator; this requirement was later reduced to one third because of the low rate of student participation in senate elections. If the necessary participation was absent, the constituency went unrepresented. As of 1975, students in the graduate faculties of political science and of pure science had not elected a senator for five years.

The university senate, by terms of its bylaws, was required to meet monthly. Meetings were held on Friday afternoons at 2:15 p.m. and could continue beyond 5:00 p.m. only by majority vote. Attendance between 1969 and 1975 averaged about 80 percent of the membership. The president was the presiding officer. This arrangement was finally accepted as a means of ensuring presidential interest in and acceptance of the role of the senate. In practice, the president began senate meetings with a review of current university problems from his perspective and then invited questions and opinions. In general, the impression prevailed that the president listened carefully to senate discussions, responded to individual suggestions (if they didn't cost much money), and found senate meetings an important device for two-way communication within the academic community. Since the meetings were open to the public and the press, the president found it necessary on occasion to respond to inquiries by saying that some matter was under consideration and that it involved issues or personalities too sensitive for public release. The senate's executive committee might designate a particular meeting as a closed meeting. In the first two years of its existence, senate meetings were sometimes disrupted by heckling and unruly behavior on the part of visitors. By 1975 this kind of difficulty had disappeared.

The executive committee of the senate was a thirteen-member group consisting of six tenured faculty members, two nontenured faculty members, three students, and the president and one administrative colleague. The executive committee controlled the agenda of the senate, including submission of reports from other standing committees. The executive committee might at times be given authority by the senate to make decisions in its name. The executive committee participated in the selection of the president, the provost, university professors, and six trustees. The senate by 1975 had authorized twelve standing committees. Both the executive committee and the committee on budget review were made up exclusively of senators. The other committees might draw membership from throughout the academic community. The committee on faculty affairs was composed solely of faculty members; the committee on student affairs was made up exclusively of students. The senate as of 1975 had a four-person staff and special office space. The minutes of the senate were open to public inspection.

When one turns from structure to deliberation and action, the story of Columbia's university senate was largely one of reaction and changing social circumstances. The senate began to function in September 1969; during 1969–70 there continued to be campus disruptions. A meeting on February 27, 1970, was broken up by a demand from the "gallery" that the university provide funds for the legal defense of the Panther 21. The last such episode occurred on February 22, 1974, and was occasioned by a demonstration by a group calling itself the "Columbia Community Against Tuition Hikes and Financial Aid Cuts." A session in September 1975 produced a number of Hispanic students who sat glum but silent while the senate debated and approved the president's proposal to withdraw pledged support for a Latin studies program because of stringent financial constraints and because of the inability of rival factions to agree on a director acceptable to the university. In general, senate proceedings by 1975 were conducted in order, with civility, some interest, and occasional wit. On special occasions the senate meetings were used as a gathering to hear an outside speaker, as in April of 1974 when a dissident Russian physicist recently expelled from the USSR addressed the gathering.

On the whole, in the years after 1970 the president did not confront an angry or hostile senate. This circumstance resulted in part from the respect and attention given to the senate by the president and in part from complexities in arriving at any decisions affecting the "bread and butter" life of the university. The senate might, and did, agree on desirable restrictions affecting operation of a Navy ROTC program on campus and later insist that these restrictions be observed if an ROTC program were to be reinstated. But, on the larger issues of how to resolve the deepening financial crisis of the university, the senate could do no more than hope that, somehow, the president and the board of trustees could end the deficit without alienating deeply held faculty or student sentiments. The expectation was probably unrealistic and unreasonable.

Since the authority of the old university council did not extend to the university budget, the senate's charter provided only that a committee on budget review should serve as a kind of watchdog of budget formulation and execution. Apart from the reluctance of the board of trustees to diffuse the budget role beyond the authority of its agent, the president, faculty members realized, even in 1969, the inherent dangers in a parliamentary budget determined on the basis of political influence and logrolling. In practice, the budget review committee found its assignment confusing and frustrating. The committee was unable to resolve the question of just how far it should intervene in the budget process. The nature of so many accounts, involving an almost proprietary role of individual faculty members or groups of faculty members in special projects, defied scrutiny without arousing faculty hostility. Program budgets appeared to be nonexistent. The committee found itself turning from substantive to procedural improvements.

Between the two extremes of conditions for an ROTC program and the handling of a financial crisis, the senate did find problems to consider that were susceptible to amelioration. The senate acted to revise university statutes and voted to join the three graduate faculties into the Graduate School of Arts and Sciences. The senate concurred in the decision of the board of trustees to

discontinue the School of Pharmacy. The senate joined the president
and board in reviewing relationships with Barnard College and
eventually gave its formal approval to a new affiliation agreement
in 1973. As a part of a measure setting forth standards of academic
freedom and responsibility to be observed within the university, the
senate agreed to a mandatory retirement age of sixty-eight years.
Under pressure from faculty and student activists, the senate called
the board of trustees' attention to the desirability of considering the
social consequences of endowment investments.

From time to time, the university senate considered the
question of the university's role in its neighborhood and in its city.
On the one hand, there were those who argued that the concern
of the university was the life of the mind, not the life of an urban
population; on the other hand, there were those who argued that
the university was and should be part and parcel of its urban environment. The difficulty was one of resolving how a university confronted with current operating deficits could be a positive force in
a city confronted with current operating deficits. The senate discussed relations with tenants in university-owned buildings, relations
with the New York City police, the security of person and property.
Ironically enough, the chairman of the senate's committee on community relations was stabbed and killed by young muggers as he
walked from his office.

The senate insisted that university construction contracts involve minority hiring. The senate voted for a day care center for
children of staff and students. The senate debated conditions attached to grants from both the federal and the state governments, but
tended to express resistance to governmental interference by verbal
protest rather than by declining governmental support. The senate
did adopt a sweeping policy statement prohibiting the university
from accepting any governmental grant or contract calling for outside censorship of research results, the approval of research personnel, or the handling of classified information. When Columbia
University was picked as a target institution to be required to develop an affirmative action plan acceptable to the Office of Civil
Rights of the U.S. Department of Health, Education and Welfare,
the senate established a commission on the status of women to work
with the administration in developing such a plan. The senate's

48                                        New Structures of Campus Power

committee on faculty affairs performed notable service in mediating
faculty grievance cases. The committee devoted much effort to
developing a statement on professional ethics and academic responsibility that was finally adopted by the senate in 1972.

In the senate's early years, student activists sought to involve
it in discussing and resolving the ills of the world: the war in Vietnam, the Cambodia invasion, racial discrimination, poverty, and
like matters. Each such effort triggered debate about the nature of
the university. On a more mundane level, the committee on student
affairs sought to resolve issues involving rules of conduct on campus, the academic calendar, improved campus lighting, campus
housing, campus religious life, and commitments to student financial
aid. The financial crisis of the university prevented the realization
of student expectations.

By 1976 the Columbia University Senate was perceived as a
useful but not spectacular addition to governance of the academic
community. One difficulty was the tendency for well-known members of the Columbia faculty to avoid election to the senate. Several
faculty members whose reputations were of national dimension were
to be found in the senate at its beginning, but these individuals
dropped out because they considered attendance too great a drain
on their time and their energies.

### Wisconsin at Madison

The story of campuswide governance at the University of Wisconsin at Madison is different from the experience of other institutions in two or three particulars. The tradition of strong faculty
influence in campus management was firmly fixed. To the student
difficulties of the 1960s was added a political complexity in 1971 by
the governor's insistence that the university become a statewide
operation; suddenly Madison found itself no longer a state university but a campus in a state system of public higher education. And,
out of anxiety about their own future, faculty members began to
flirt with the idea of faculty collective bargaining as a means to
preserve and protect faculty status in the new political environment.

A faculty senate document prepared at Madison in 1974
pointed out that the faculty had more of a governing role than did

faculties at most other colleges and universities in the country, even if this role was difficult to define or to describe. The document acknowledged the "technical" authority of campus administrators, which the faculty did not expect, in fact, to be fully utilized or to stand against faculty opposition. The faculty at Madison was conscious of a substantial capacity to affect the destiny of the university. The emphasis of the "Wisconsin idea" as a link between education and service to the state and the insistence upon academic freedom, symbolized as early as 1894 in a plaque affixed to the principal campus building, were the twin underpinnings for faculty authority within the university. Composed of twelve colleges and schools and 125 academic departments, the university had achieved a national reputation for instruction, research, and public service.

There was also a history of student political activism. The troubled years from 1966 to 1970 left an indelible imprint upon the university. A massive sit-in demonstration protesting university cooperation with the Selective Service System was staged in 1966, to be followed by further demonstration against campus recruitment by Dow Chemical Company in 1967. A demand for a black studies program arose in 1969; in 1970 there was a strike by teaching assistants. Campus protests against the invasion of Cambodia and student deaths at Kent State and Jackson State were climaxed by a bombing of a building in August 1970 that caused the death of a young researcher, injury to several other persons, and property damage estimated at $6 million.

In 1971 a new threat to the ordered life of the Madison campus suddenly appeared. The disorders of five years had sadly damaged the political status of the university. The governor and legislature combined forces to enact legislation establishing a University of Wisconsin system on a statewide basis. No longer was the board of regents a governing board for a flagship campus with two or three satellite campuses. Now the board became the governing board for a statewide system embracing thirteen campuses. The Madison faculty, in a special meeting in March, 1971, strongly opposed the reorganization, fearing the budgetary and educational consequences of endeavoring to build thirteen state universities like Madison. The protest was ignored. (Perhaps it would be more accurate to say the protest was politically ineffective.) The budget

50                                    New Structures of Campus Power

law mandated the merger of the University of Wisconsin system
and the Wisconsin State University system, and a merger law was
enacted by a special session of the legislature in April 1974.

As at many other universities, the academic departments at
Madison have enjoyed substantial self-government in academic and
personnel matters. While department chairmen served for only one-
year terms, there was no limit to the number of terms they might
serve. In essence, department chairmen were elected by their colleagues, although they were formally designated by deans. Student
participation in departmental management was entirely in the discretion of each department, but participation on various departmental committees became quite common during the 1960s. In
addition to membership in the faculty of a school or college, each
faculty member was also a part of one of four academic divisions:
(1) the biological sciences; (2) the humanities; (3) the physical
sciences; and (4) the social sciences. Through divisional executive
committees, the faculty exercised the authority of approval on curriculum matters and on all faculty personnel decisions. The action
appeared in the form of a recommendation to particular deans;
such recommendations were almost never disregarded.

Until January 1970 the entire faculty of the University at
Madison met in town meeting on a periodic basis. In ordinary circumstances not more than 100 faculty members might attend, and
the agenda was largely one of ratifying division and college actions.
During the disturbances between 1966 and 1970, faculty meeetings
swelled to as many as 1,400 or 1,500 persons. As a consequence, the
faculty began to think in terms of a representative body. A special
committee was appointed to prepare a plan for a faculty senate.
The committee rejected the idea of an academic community council
or senate. The faculty senate was designed to replace the all-faculty
meeting and hence was intended to represent only the faculty. The
plan called for the senate to receive communications from other
constituent groups of the university, including the Wisconsin Student Association, but participation of any of these groups in senate
membership was specifically omitted. After a three-year trial period,
the faculty voted at a general meeting in May 1973 to make the
faculty senate a permanent arrangement.

The faculty senate of the University at Madison consisted of

226 persons representing 2,200 "legal" faculty members. The apportionment of representation among colleges and schools was based upon their respective faculty strength and was subject to readjustment every two years. The chancellor, or chief administrative officer of the campus, served as chairman but voted only in the case of a tie. An executive committee of six elected faculty members chose its own chairman and controlled the agenda. It consulted with the chancellor about agenda items. The committee also served as a grievance committee. There were some thirty standing committees, and students were invited to serve on many of them. In general, the authority of the senate was to decide educational matters of campuswide concern and to submit recommendations to the chancellor when administrative action or follow-up was necessary.

At the outset of each senate meeting, questions might be addressed to the chancellor. These questions were submitted to the faculty secretary in advance and appeared on the agenda distributed at the beginning of the meeting. Issues of special interest were thus aired, and in turn the chancellor had an opportunity to present his own remarks prior to consideration of the formal agenda. Issues discussed by the senate in 1974–75 illustrated the activity of the body: approval of revised guidelines for fixing the academic calendar; approval of five committee recommendations on the admission of undergraduate foreign students; approval with amendments of undergraduate enrollment ceilings for the campus; and approval of a resolution against the adoption of faculty collective bargaining. The senate had also discussed but not acted upon such subjects as the regulation of faculty off-campus activities, a code of ethics for faculty behavior, a public relations agency to represent the faculty, more or less routine actions involving approval of degree requirements for various programs, receipt of information about creation of two new departments by the chancellor, and approval of a new grading system in the School of Medicine.

Historically the faculty had also been the body to enact rules and regulations governing student conduct. In 1963 a special committee to study the extracurricular life of students was created, and the committee subsequently recommended that such rules be restricted to matters threatening the safety of members of the university community, threatening the property of the university, and threatening the integrity of the educational process. Subsequently, various student-related issues occupied faculty attention, such as university cooperation with selective service boards and student participation in governance. In the autumn of 1966 students were added to almost all faculty committees, but the more militant students resisted any action that suggested "cooptation" by the university.

In 1967 the Wisconsin Student Association (WSA) demanded that the faculty withdraw from imposing any rules or regulations affecting students and student organizations in areas of "solely student concern." Instead, the WSA would establish all policies, rules, and regulations governing student social and group activity. The WSA insisted that it alone should define the areas of sole student concern, that individual conduct cases should be handled by a student court, and that an appeals body of five students and five faculty members should make all final decisions in conduct matters. The faculty paid considerable attention in 1967–68 to student affairs by means of an ad hoc committee on the role of students in the government of the university.

In two special meetings during October 1967, the faculty voiced deep regret about the violence attending the disruption of the campus recruitment effort of Dow Chemical, expressed "grave concern" about the damage of such occurrences to the integrity of the university community, and affirmed a resolve to join with students and administration in seeking ways to ensure the orderly functioning of the university. The Wisconsin Student Association then insisted upon its own student representation on an ad hoc committee concerned with university response to obstruction, recruitment policies, and related matters. The faculty consented to this arrangement, although some faculty members protested the issuance of a student body ultimatum to the faculty.

A questionnaire distributed to students revealed that 65 percent of all students desired the placement office to continue to operate as at present, and that 74 percent of all students were opposed to the protest tactics used to disrupt the Dow recruitment visit. The ad hoc committee in March 1968 recommended that all employment and recruitment interviews be terminated and not be resumed until approved by the Wisconsin Student Association. This recommendation was submitted by a majority of five students and three faculty members. A minority report by four faculty members and two students called for continuation of placement interviews without interruption.

The faculty adopted the minority report but eliminated a provision calling for appointment of an emergency advisory committee of three faculty members and three students to consult with the chancellor when the university confronted a crisis situation. The faculty wanted the chancellor to name his own committee rather than having such a committee named for him by the faculty and by the student association.

In February 1968 the ad hoc committee on the student role in university government made its report to the faculty. In general the committee agreed that faculty interest in student affairs should be restricted as proposed back in 1963, that freshmen and sophomores be required to live in supervised housing unless married or unless provided written consent by a parent or guardian to live elsewhere, that the university impose no general restrictions on student hours in supervised housing, that student residents of each housing unit determine visitation rules, that students be added to most faculty committees, and that the faculty committee on student life be replaced by four new committees concerned with student organization, student housing, student conduct standards, and conduct appeals. These new committees would have joint faculty and student membership (one more faculty member than student members), except that the appeals committee would be composed entirely of faculty members. These recommendations were adopted by the faculty.

In October 1969 an ad hoc committee on the grading system recommended that the committee be given permission to authorize certain experiments in the grading system in specific courses, such as use of the pass-fail grading. The permission was granted, and in 1971 the committee made eight specific changes in the grading system. These changes, debated at length and finally adopted with amendments, were later rescinded in favor of four modifications in the existing grading system.

During 1969 some disruption occurred on the part of black students dissatisfied with the programs and opportunities available to them. The faculty expressed sympathy with their concerns but objected to making changes in the face of disruptive action. Later in the year the faculty authorized the Department of Afro-American Studies in the College of Letters and Science. At the same time the faculty insisted upon the maintenance of existing standards of student academic achievement.

These illustrations of faculty issues and actions on a campus-wide basis underlined two basic propositions. In spite of student and other pressures, faculty domination of the decision-making process on academic matters remained intact. Students were added to various faculty committees, but the faculty made it clear that student participation in final decision making was unacceptable. Secondly, it was demonstrated that an increasing number of academic issues were demanding campuswide attention, and this circumstance helped to convince the faculty that it should act through a faculty senate rather than a town meeting.

The faculty senate that came into existence on the Madison campus in 1970 had less trying circumstances on campus to contend with than did the faculty in the preceding years. But the reorganization of the statewide higher education system in 1971 produced a new set of problems: the erosion of campus autonomy and the possible diminution of the flagship status of the Madison campus in the new system. The faculty senate had to wrestle with these issues but had little to offer in resolution of campus anxieties apart from authorizing a public relations committee.

At the same time, the faculty senate had to confront the question of faculty collective bargaining. On the four-year campuses of the university system, faculty organization had proceeded and preparations had been made for collective bargaining whenever the state legislature authorized the practice. Madison's faculty senate insisted that legislation should not require systemwide negotiation and agreement but should preserve for the Madison campus independence to decide whether or not to engage in collective bargaining, and to exclude from this bargaining any matters of faculty governance. The board of regents in 1975 indicated general agreement with the position of the Madison faculty. The legislature appeared to be more inclined to adopt the approach to bargaining urged by the American Federation of Teachers (AFT) and the National Education Association (NEA). Thereafter the faculty senate voted to oppose legislation that did not provide for campus autonomy. The legislature in 1976 did not enact the bill desired by the AFT and NEA.

In the meantime, the appropriation law for 1975–1977 authorized an interim legislative study committee to examine the extent to which differences in cost per student and in faculty compensation existed within the University of Wisconsin System. The faculty senate interpreted this action as legislative pressure for comparability and uniformity within the system, a further threat to the status of the Madison campus.

The tradition of faculty governance remained strong at the University of Wisconsin at Madison as of 1976. But the tradition was threatened by forces outside the campus over which faculty influence was at best only meager. It remained to be seen if the newly created Public Representation Organization of the Faculty Senate, Inc. (PROFS) could become an effective agency for faculty representation beyond the campus itself.

### Cornell

Cornell University, after 110 years of existence, differed in respects other than its youth from the institutions collectively referred to as "the Ivy League." Cornell included four colleges that were supported by the State of New York and that received over $40 million a year in subsidy. Yet the university considered itself privately sponsored and its lay governing board exercised the authority of governance over all of the institution. The board of trustees did include state government officials ex officio, two persons appointed by the governor, four persons named by the faculty, three students, and other persons named by alumni and outside groups. But a majority of the sixty-one-member board were selected by the board itself.

Internally, Cornell University consisted of eleven colleges, each headed by a dean and each having its separate faculty organization dominated by a powerful educational policies committee. The administration of the university, with president, provost, vice-provost, and vice-presidents, had a prominent role in the affairs of the university as a whole. The academic organization was once described as a "series of fiefdoms held together by a heating plant." New students were not admitted to Cornell University; they were admitted to individual colleges. By university statute, the academic programs were determined by each college.

The university faculty included all persons of professorial rank from all the colleges. The faculty met periodically but less than 200 usually attended a meeting. The faculty committee on student conduct supervised the judicial structure, and the faculty committee on student affairs supervised student campus life. For the most part, the university in practice gave considerable discretion to various student organizations to control their own activities with little if any direct supervision. Campuswide student government was relatively powerless.

In the 1960s student groups pressed for representation on faculty committees, and students were then added to the committee on student conduct and the committee on student affairs. Faculty members continued in the majority of both committees. The issues that demanded faculty attention in the 1960s were familiar ones: closing hours in women's dormitories, male and female visitation rules, chaperones for social events, and restrictions upon student conduct. Facultywide governance of academic affairs was minimal.

Then, beginning in 1965–66, the campus atmosphere began to change. Student requests gave way to student demands. And the idea of any university supervision of student conduct was challenged. A major confrontation developed about the question whether or not the university should administer selective service deferment examinations. Then military recruitment on campus aroused student opposition and student disruption. Cornell's wholly owned research corporation was involved in classified research, some sponsored by the U.S. Department of Defense. This situation was also attacked by students and by faculty members.

It quickly became apparent that the university as a community lacked the structure to resolve the issues that had arisen. Faculty organization on a universitywide basis was inadequate and student organization was weak. The president resorted to a series of ad hoc commissions to study individual problems; the membership was drawn from the faculty, the student body, and the administration. The chairman was usually a well-known and respected member of the faculty. One such commission was established to study the interrelationship of campus law with federal and state law. The commission recommended a major retreat from the doctrine of the university *in loco parentis*. Another commission was charged with the study of university governance. The published report seemed to arouse little interest on campus.

The issue that precipitated a concern with campuswide governance at Cornell arose from the action of black students. As early as 1964 the university had begun a concerted effort to recruit black students. By 1968 these efforts had increased the number of black students enrolled at Cornell by ten times, and the presence of a black minority on campus became visible. But the colleges had done little to prepare for an influx of black students, who themselves complained that the university was essentially white in tradition, socially inhospitable, and irrelevant to black needs. Late in 1968 a group of about one hundred black students began to demonstrate their dissatisfaction. A march to the infirmary protested the lack of a black psychiatrist. A march to the library protested the lack of books about black culture. A march to the Administration Building protested the absence of instructional programs related to black interests.

Many Cornell students and faculty members viewed these demonstrations with fear and anger. Some small damage occurred in one building. An attempt to identify those who had caused the damage led to a demand by the black students that all be judged by the judicial system. An impasse resulted. Then, after some actual personal assaults, the black students seized possession of the student union building and, upon hearing that white students were arming themselves, obtained guns. The blacks were persuaded to leave the building, but the photograph of black students emerging with guns and bandoliers of ammunition received national and international attention. The result was a paroxysm of emotion on the Cornell campus.

A faculty meeting of 800 persons displayed confusion and an inability to cope with the disintegration of reason and order on the campus. A meeting of 6,000 to 7,000 persons was held at the Drill Hall, but the leadership to bring the university out of the crisis was not evident. It was agreed by many students and faculty members that campus governance had disintegrated and disappeared. There emerged a constituent assembly of some 350 faculty, students, alumni, administrators, and trustees, which undertook to draft a constitution for campuswide governance.

After a year of effort, a constitution for a university senate was presented in 1970 to the faculty, to the students, and to the board of trustees. This constitution was ratified by the constituent assembly, by the faculty, and by a referendum of the student body. The constitution was "recognized" by the board of trustees at a meeting on April 10, 1970, and thereupon became effective. The new senate began to operate in the autumn of 1970.

The constitution declared that the university senate was to be the principal legislative and policy-making body of the university "in matters which are of general concern to the University community." The authority vested in the senate included:

1. General responsibility for "nonacademic" matters of campus life.
2. Legislative power over campus codes of conduct, the campus judiciary system, and the academic calendar.
3. The power to require the faculty to reconsider any action taken by it.
4. The right to obtain written or oral reports "on matters within its area of concern" from academic and administrative officers.
5. The right to maintain an interest in educational quality and innovation at Cornell and to formulate recommendations on such matters.
6. The power to formulate a statement of the principles of academic freedom of students.
7. The power to recommend desirable legislation to the faculty and to the board of trustees.
8. The power to examine current policies on any activities of the university that have "important social or political implications" and to recommend changes deemed necessary.
9. The power to draft a bill of rights for the protection of the civil liberties of all members of the university community.

Governance in Leading Research Universities                59

10. The power to examine short and long-range plans of the university, "including the broad allocation of the university resources," and to make recommendations thereon.
11. The power to provide for the election of four tenured faculty members, one nontenured faculty member, one faculty member to be elected by the students, four students, and three persons from outside the university to serve two-year, four-year, and five-year terms on the board of trustees.
12. The power to participate through a fifteen-member committee in any presidential search by the board of trustees.

A special article of the senate constitution provided that there should be in the university a division of campus life administered by a vice-president for campus affairs "under the policy making jurisdiction of the Senate." The division was to manage housing, dining, and university unions; athletics and recreation; the university health service; the campus store; public lectures and performances; a general counseling service; and traffic regulation and parking. It was also to supervise registered campus organizations and activities, the recruitment of students by "outside organizations," and campus religious groups and organizations. In the case of the university health service, the senate was to exercise its authority through a board on student health, composed of ten members, four of whom were to be elected by the senate, two to be elected by the professional staff of the health service (but not members of the staff), one to be appointed by the president, two to be administrators of the health service, and one to be the vice-president for campus affairs (without vote). The board's authority excluded "strictly medical questions." The vice-president for campus affairs was to be elected by the board of trustees on the recommendation of the president "with the concurrence of the Senate." The budget for the division was to be approved by the senate.

The constitution provided for a senate of ninety-five voting members: forty students, forty faculty representatives, and fifteen other members. The fifteen included nine staff employees, one alumnus, one administrative officer, one librarian, one "nonprofessorial academic who does not have faculty status," one person

from the Department of Military Sciences, and one person from the
"middle management" of the university. There were also to be a
number of ex officio members without a vote, including the president, the provost, the deans of the colleges, the trustees whose election was provided through the senate, the director of African studies,
the dean of the faculty, and ten persons from the "central administration." The senate was to elect its own speaker to preside and to
elect such other officers as it deemed necessary. The university was
to provide financial and other support "for reasonable staff and
facilities of the Senate." The senate was to have an executive committee and six other standing committees, including a committee on
campus life, a planning review committee, and a committee on educational innovation.

The constitution in effect accomplished three major arrangements: a redistribution of power between the administration and
other constituent groups of the university community, a new and
unusual arrangement for administering activities labeled "campus
life," and a forum for the discussion of issues of campuswide interest. But in large part the senate was excluded from any real influence over the academic affairs of Cornell University. Although the
board of trustees never formally approved the senate constitution as
such but simply "recognized" it and incorporated some of its provisions in resolutions and other actions, the board made it clear that
it retained the authority to disapprove any senate action it deemed
ill-advised.

Soon after the university senate was organized, the university faculty took steps to clarify its own role and to strengthen its
structure. The faculty created a council of representatives of some
ninety members apportioned among the various colleges. This
council was empowered to consider questions of educational policy
that concerned more than one college, school, or academic department or questions that were general in nature. With the approval
of the appropriate college or school faculty, the council might
recommend to the board of trustees the creation, modification, or
discontinuance of degree programs.

In addition, the provost set up a council of deans as a deliberative body to meet biweekly and to assist in considering general
academic issues. This council became particularly useful in helping

the provost and president to decide academic priorities in the light of budget constraints.

As circumstances changed at the university after 1970, the university senate found it more and more difficult to determine exactly what its role was. A great deal of time was devoted to matters of campus life. Students became concerned about the rising tuition charges, and much committee discussion was devoted to the issue, but the senate was unwilling to act upon the subject. The vice-president for campus life met monthly with the executive committee of the senate, but often no consensus emerged about desirable policies to adopt.

The president was disposed to adopt most of the recommendations submitted by the university senate. But on the most pressing issue confronting the university after 1970—the university budget—the president obtained little help. Once again the president turned to the special device of a presidentially designated task force to advise about budget priorities within the university. The task force reports were laid before the university senate and the faculty council, but neither body was able to provide a considered response to the various recommendations dealing primarily with the support programs of the university.

The senate gave consideration to a proposal to abolish ROTC within the university, but enacted legislation instead speaking to the quality of instructor personnel and course content. The senate considered several pieces of legislation to abolish physical education as a degree requirement, but the faculty council of representatives rejected the one recommendation on this subject passed by the senate. The senate debated the matter of the academic calendar several times but found no agreement on the subject. In practice the university senate found most of its time devoted to issues of campus life.

The senate took action on such issues as equal access for men and women to physical education and recreational facilities and on an expanded career counseling service for women. A good deal of time was given to a criticism of the Protestant bias of the chapel service, and the decision was made that the university would not sponsor worship services but only convocations, with "speakers" rather than "preachers." Another debate arose about the use on campus of Christian symbols at Christmas time. A determined effort by the university to make the dining service self-supporting produced criticism that the service had deteriorated and brought demands that the senate should dismiss the director. The issue was declared inappropriate for action by the senate, and the senate retreated. The senate enacted legislation governing the assignment of housing space to students. And periodically there were extensive, even heated arguments about the inadequacy of parking space on campus. The senate did intervene in athletic affairs to insist that intercollegiate athletics must be self-supporting. This action led to the discontinuance of several sports, amid the considerable unhappiness of alumni and others. By January 1976 the board of trustees was seriously considering action to remove jurisdiction over intercollegiate athletics from the university senate.

For four years out of six, the committee on campus life was chaired by a faculty member. Students learned that the time demands of the chairmanship exceeded their capacity to handle this effort along with academic and social activities. In general, campus opinion seemed to be that the senate had handled issues of campus life with some success but at the price of substantial faculty and student time. Almost no action was taken with which the administration had any substantial disagreement.

The senate also found itself debating national political and social issues: the war in Vietnam, the impeachment of President Richard M. Nixon, and the pardon of draft evaders and military deserters. On such matters as the boycott of lettuce and investments in South Africa, the senate recommended action to the administration and the board of trustees. All these actions brought with them criticism from both within and without the university.

The senate did undertake at an early stage in its history to prepare a statement on the academic rights of students, but the legislation was not enacted until the spring of 1975. Approvals were given by vote of the students and of the university staff, but the faculty refused to consent because of provisions that appeared to invade faculty prerogatives. The senate was able to approve a campus code of conduct and to reform the judicial system.

By 1976, however, the continued existence of the university senate was uncertain. Student voting to select senators fell to 20 percent of the student body, whereas 40 percent was deemed desirable if student selections were to be representative. The accomplishments of the senate tended to be overlooked, while the extraneous issues were given disproportionate attention. By 1975–76 about half of all senate meetings were held without the presence of a quorum. A small group of faculty members and students who had devoted a good deal of time to the senate declared in an open letter that the senate no longer commanded the confidence of the university community, that it was not encouraged to undertake useful work, and that it had become a forum for a few persons with "swollen egos."

In January 1976 the senate adopted a resolution to have a charge for a study commission that would consider the future of self-governance at Cornell drafted. The committee named to prepare the charge was unable to reach agreement. In March 1976 the president established his own commission on self-governance and named nine persons to the commission, including three faculty members (one served as chairman), a research engineer, an officer from one of the state-sponsored schools, a trustee, the vice president for research, and two students. This commission submitted a preliminary report in August 1976 calling for replacement of the senate by a university assembly to consider matters of campuswide interest and a separate committee on campus affairs to consider matters relating to campus life. All structures would be made in effect advisory to the president. A major reason for the change was given as the need to make "substantially fewer demands on the time of faculty, students, and employees than has the senate." The president, it was proposed, should be the presiding officer of the new university assembly, which would have a total membership of approximately seventy-five persons.

In March 1977, upon recommendation of the president, the board of trustees abolished the university senate and replaced it with a campus council of twenty-one members, including seven faculty members and seven students.

## Berkeley

Berkeley has been the flagship campus of the nine campuses that compose the University of California. Its standards and values have infused the entire system. Berkeley has been preeminent among the campuses in research activity and has considered extensive research as essential to good teaching. As a campus, Berkeley has valued faculty members and students who are committed to an intrinsic interest in ideas, the tolerance of complexity, and freedom from traditional patterns of thought.

The multicampus system of the University of California has been governed by a board of regents of twenty-four members, eighteen appointed by the governor for twelve-year terms and six persons ex officio. By recent constitutional amendment, the board of trustees has been empowered in its discretion to add one faculty member and one student to its voting membership. The academic senate of the system declined representation on the board, lest its participation encourage greater board influence over academic and faculty affairs. However, the chairman of the academic council of the senate agreed to serve, at the board's invitation, for two years as a faculty representative at board meetings, with the privilege of participation in all discussions; the arrangement was regarded as an experiment. A student representative has served on the board as a voting member.

The universitywide or systemwide administration is headed by the president, who enjoys the assistance of a sizable staff numbering some 1,250 persons of all ranks. Although the state government has possessed various means of influencing or controlling the various campuses, for the most part state influence has been exercised through the universitywide office. Pressures have been brought to bear, for example, to determine minimum enrollments for courses and to control campus size and development. Faculty members at Berkeley have tended to be fearful of increased controls exercised by the president's office, encouraged to some extent by demands from state government.

The bylaws of the board of regents have defined the role of the chancellor on each campus as "chief campus officer thereof" and as "executive head of all activities" on a campus, with certain prescribed exceptions. There has been an accretion of administrative authority in the chancellor's office in recent years. Budgetary constraints have led to a strengthening of both central planning and central budgeting. The chancellor has reserved to himself the authority to make final decisions about the allocation of budgeted resources. Flexibility in budget management has been impaired by the central office practice of allocating appropriations in ten budget categories without any campus authority to effect transfers. In recent years the chancellor has provided, from his discretionary fund, additional faculty positions in various professional colleges and schools. This practice has aroused discontent among faculty members in the academic disciplines, who have regarded their scholarly achievements as the basis of Berkeley's preeminence in higher education. At the same time, it has reflected the changing enrollment patterns of the campus and the quality of the achievements being realized in such professional disciplines as engineering, business, education, law, optometry, and architecture.

The chancellor at Berkeley has organized and managed the central administration as changing circumstances, needs, and personalities seemed to require. Recently there has been a provost for professional schools and colleges and a second provost for the departments in letters and science; this provost is also dean of the faculty in letters and science. Considerable discretionary authority has been delegated to each provost. The two provosts as well as the dean of the graduate division nominally report to the vice-chancellor. The chancellor's cabinet has been composed of the vice-chancellor, a vice-chancellor for administration, an assistant chancellor for budget and planning, the two provosts, and the graduate dean.

The current vice-chancellor at Berkeley has had considerable informal influence upon campus operations. He has met frequently with the senate's committees on educational policy, academic planning, and budget and interdepartmental relations. He has chaired a council on educational development set up to foster innovative and experimental programs. He has attended the monthly meetings of the chancellor with the chairpersons of all senate committees. Because of his long association with the work of the academic senate and because of his personal administrative style, the vice-chancellor has been able to guide and influence campus decision making substantially.

Faculty participation in university affairs at the system level has been governed by the bylaws and by standing orders of the board of regents. The bylaws have created an academic senate on a systemwide basis, which has functioned through a representative assembly, an academic council, and a roster of committees. The universitywide senate has authority, subject to the approval of the board, to determine conditions for student admission and to fix the requirements for degrees in course. In addition, the academic senate has been expected to approve and supervise all courses and curricula except those in professional schools offering work at the graduate level only and one or two other programs. The bylaws of the university senate have provided for divisions of the senate on each campus.

The Berkeley division of the university senate has operated through a representative assembly and various committees and especially through a committee on budget and interdepartmental relations. The Berkeley faculty has had a long tradition of involvement and authority in campus decision making. The two provosts have worked closely with all committees and especially with the budget committee. In the mid-1960s the committee on budget and interdepartmental affairs found that it could not efficiently handle both budget matters and faculty personnel matters. The committee therefore established a subcommittee on budget policy to serve as a watchdog for the Berkeley faculty. In the early 1970s the Berkeley division abolished the subcommittee and established in its place an academic planning committee.

During the 1960s the income of the Berkeley campus increased sufficiently to permit most departments and colleges to add to their faculty positions and to enjoy larger faculty compensation. In recent years the increases have diminished and the allocation of available resources has become a major problem. Because of greater universitywide controls exercised through the campus chancellor, the Berkeley division of the university senate has moved more aggressively and in more detail to exercise its prerogative of advising the provosts and the chancellor on the redistribution of faculty positions. Within the constraints of campus budgets and with the assistance of computer models developed in the chancellor's office, the faculty, through its committee on budget and interdepartmental relations, has had a decisive influence upon the allocation of faculty positions, upon faculty appointments and promotions, and upon tenure.

The organization and operation of the Berkeley division of

the university senate have been designed to maintain faculty power in campus affairs. With a few exceptions, administrative officers have been excluded from division committees. One exception has been a dean with long service on the committee on committees; another has been the position of the vice-chancellor as chairman of the council on educational development. Deans, provosts, and vice-chancellors have been explicitly excluded from the committee on educational policy. A study in 1970 indicated that membership on the most powerful faculty committees came preponderantly from certain departments, the higher academic ranks, and the older age groups. The situation had not noticeably changed by 1976. There has appeared to be a faculty oligarchy at Berkeley of persons interested in faculty and institutional problems, having the time and skill needed for committee work, and evidencing experience in the processes of faculty governance. When it first established the educational policy committee, the Berkeley division of the university senate refused to empower the committee to represent the faculty in any consultation with the campus administration. This position was subsequently reversed, but faculty-administration relationships at Berkeley have demanded careful, continuous attention.

Although the "student revolution" began at Berkeley in 1964 and although student activism and disruption continued into the early 1970s, the years of upheaval had only a minimal impact upon faculty governance. Faculty committees and the representative assembly debated various issues of conflict but were little inclined to change accustomed patterns of faculty behavior. A faculty committee report urged increased attention to the instruction of undergraduate students, but the implementation was left largely to the discretion of each department. Students were admitted in small numbers to some but not to all faculty committees. The chancellor in office from 1965 to 1971 found his time almost completely occupied with problems of student agitation, including efforts to ward off or blunt threatened punitive action from outside the campus. The conduct of academic and faculty affairs continued largely uninterrupted throughout these years.

The 30,000 students of the Berkeley campus are represented in campus governance by an organization entitled the Associated Students of the University of California (ASUC). Unlike other student organizations in the University of California system, the Berkeley ASUC represents both undergraduate and graduate students; a graduate assembly advises the ASUC about graduate student concerns. The ASUC has enjoyed only limited student support; in the 1970s only between 15 percent and 20 percent of the student body voted in ASUC elections. Over the years the ASUC has developed a relatively complicated organization. It appoints an executive director to control the operation of service units owned by the ASUC, including the bookstore and the student union food service. It has elected three presidents, three vice presidents for academic affairs, a vice president for administration, and two executive vice presidents. A 30-member senate, which allocates funds from student activity fees to various student groups and activities, approves policy statements, and ratifies student appointments to administrative and faculty committees, is supported by an array of student committees.

Students have been appointed to almost all of the advisory committees to the chancellor, and in general the ASUC has had cordial relationships with the principal administrative officers. Paid student interns have worked on the budget review of funds for student services. The relationship of students to the Berkeley division of the academic senate have been somewhat strained. The division's committee on student affairs seated students with the right to vote as early as 1966, but did not add students to the committee on educational policy until 1973. Students have obtained voting representation on five other committees, out of a total of thirty-three, since then. Informal student representation has been arranged by other faculty committees, but an extension of formalized and voting representation has been defeated by vote of the representative assembly, much to the frustration of student leadership. The Berkeley faculty has felt that the academic senate should exclusively represent faculty interests and has argued that student representation on committees sometimes resulted in a politicization of issues and impaired serious deliberation. A move by the chancellor several years ago to establish a campus council of faculty-student-administration representation encountered faculty hostility and was dropped.

The Berkeley ASUC has continued to feel hampered by an inability to keep current on all the major issues of campus concern, although student participation in committees has increased student access to information. Berkeley student leaders seem to believe that they can gain more leverage by their own capacity for independent analysis. In 1971, the University of California Student Lobby was established, and it represented all nine campuses. Staffed by two full-time lobbyists and several student interns, the lobby has worked hard at developing good relationships with state officials and with legislators, has selected a few issues on which to have an impact, and has earned considerable respect. The lobby has been credited with some role in forcing withdrawal of a bill to authorize collective bargaining in state government. In addition, it has supported student aid legislation, an appropriation for the improvement of teaching, and stabilization of student fee charges.

An important characteristic of the authority structure at Berkeley is the predominance of faculty members in administrative positions. Membership in important senate committees has often led to administrative assignments as a dean, provost, or vice-chancellor. In turn, individuals who have held administrative positions move back to faculty status and then on to membership on important senate committees. There are noticeable advantages in this practice in extending faculty points of view to administrative operations and in providing an administrative point of view to the deliberations of faculty committees. At the same time, this interchange raises the issue of whether there are separate faculty and administrative jurisdictions at Berkeley or one shared faculty-administrative jurisdiction. Organizational arrangements have suggested that there may in fact be two jurisdictions requiring a high degree of interaction, and this interaction has been encouraged by faculty-administration rotation in roles.

The board of regents continues to be a factor to be reckoned with; even as the board has delegated authority, it can also withdraw authority. The difficulty has been a tendency of the board to intervene on a selective basis in particular cases attracting considerable public attention, as it did in the widely publicized Cleaver Case of 1968 and as it did in 1970 on the matter of academic credit for ROTC courses. In 1976 the academic senate of the university and the board of regents made some overtures for improved collaboration but with no certainty of success.

In general, there has been little disposition at Berkeley to change its structure and process of governance. External pressures to change, especially with regard to Berkeley's priorities as between research and public service and instruction, have been resisted. Internally, the departmental structure has tended to restrict efforts to launch interdisciplinary and innovative instructional programs. Interdisciplinary graduate programs have succeeded better than those at the undergraduate level, in part because they have had an administrative structure for their support. The competition for financial resources has further tended to discourage efforts at curriculum innovation. One of the most extensive experimental efforts on the Berkeley campus has been the program in health and medical sciences. Administrative sponsorship of change has sometimes been a source of faculty suspicion and opposition. Although it has been possible to bring about incremental change in various kinds of programs, few if any faculty members or administrators have a vision of a Berkeley essentially different from the present institution. It has been pointed out that Berkeley is known as a graduate and research university of the highest distinction, and presumably that status is to be preserved and protected.

A major concern has been whether or not Berkeley can devise a plan to achieve faculty renewal in a time of steady state. Some recent campus conflicts, such as that involving the future of the School of Criminology, were partly inspired by doubts about the prospects for faculty positions and new appointments on the Berkeley campus as a whole. The committee on educational policy has struggled with the development of a policy and process for establishing priorities among academic programs but has encountered substantial difficulty in obtaining general faculty acceptance of either policy or process.

Campus planning as of 1976 has reflected the primacy of faculty interests over the desires of students or the expressed needs of groups outside the university. Although flexibility and adaptability have been acknowledged as conditions of program quality, planning initiatives have been left to departments and have been little exercised by central faculty committees. At the college and school level, there have been efforts to obtain more information about current circumstances and future prospects, but the plans and values have been those of departments rather than of the institution as a whole.

Administrative initiative and decision making need not be arbitrary and can be exercised after extensive consultation. But on occasion a chancellor may need to take action in disregard of advice offered by various campus constituencies. At the same time, a faculty needs a means of escape from continuing arbitrary authority exercised by a chancellor. The mechanisms for such action and such escape remain to be developed at Berkeley. Budget difficulties tend to force more and more decision making to the center of the campus, either by faculty committees or by administrative officers. The particular roles of the faculty and administrative officers in long-range campus planning still need to be defined. It seems both inevitable and appropriate that, in a well-defined system of shared authority and shared responsibility, a strong administrative influence will need to emerge at Berkeley.

## Texas at Austin

The University of Texas was originally located by popular referendum of the Texas voters in 1881: a principal campus in Austin, the state capital, and a medical branch in Galveston. Eventually the university was to become a system of six "general" campuses and four health science centers, all under the governance authority of a single board of regents. The Austin campus was gradually transformed from the "main university" to the principal instructional and research component of a multicampus system. With the transformation emerged the familiar concerns of status and support of the Austin campus in the complexity of a university of diverse parts and aspirations. During the 1950s the Austin campus, through a series of specializations and islands of high competence, surged toward genuine academic excellence. The University of Texas at Austin became a national, research-oriented, developed university. It saw its mission and its self-image as comparable to those of the leading state universities in the Middle West and at Berkeley.

By provisions of state constitution and law, the governance

of the University of Texas was vested in its board of regents, composed of nine persons serving six-year terms and appointed by the governor with the consent of the state senate. The board met frequently, in public, and with an elaborate agenda. Much of the detailed work and negotiation was accomplished in standing committees. The real decision-making process largely occurred in informal conferences between board members, system administrators, and campus administrators. The board viewed itself essentially as an arm of state government, as an intermediary between campus and state officials, including state legislators. Charged with management of an endowment exceeding $750 million and with direction of an extensive and important university operation, the board commanded power and prestige. When conflict arose between campus and board, the board rarely lost the argument.

Relationships between the central system office and the Austin campus have varied considerably since the system office was first established in 1950. From 1950 to 1954 the system office was headed by a chancellor, but from 1954 to 1960 the position of chancellor was not filled. From 1961 to 1967 the chancellor also served as chief executive officer of the Austin campus. Since 1967 the position of the chancellor of the system and president of the Austin campus have been distinct and separate, but the relationship between the two offices has remained troublesome. Austin was so close to the system and the system was so obviously located in Austin that the two worlds overlapped in many different ways. Moreover, there remained the confusing question whether the president was an agent of the campus or an agent of the chancellor and the system.

On the Austin campus the administrative organization has undergone frequent and sometimes kaleidoscopic changes in nomenclature and structure. At various times in the past twenty-five years the chief administrative officer has been called the president, the chancellor, the vice-president and provost, and the vice-chancellor for academic affairs. Since 1941 the administrative associates of the chief administrative officer have continually expanded in number and designation. As of 1976 the president was assisted by six vice-presidents who meet regularly to discuss and resolve major issues of campus policy and program.

The academic operations of the Austin campus as of 1976 were conducted through eighteen colleges and schools and fifty to sixty departments. In recent years, the council of deans has acquired something of a collegial character, and it may become an important agency for academic decision making. The faculty of the Austin campus exercises influence primarily within the context of the individual colleges and schools. In the smaller schools, the faculty meets as a body. In the larger ones, the faculty is necessarily organized into various committees. One college, for example, maintains three standing committees: buildings and space, courses and curriculum, and promotion and tenure. Another college has two of these same committees but has a committee on undergraduate advising in place of the committee on space. In another college, in addition to the standing committees, there is an elected faculty council; this arrangement avoids the need for the entire faculty to meet to accept or modify committee actions.

By direction of the board of regents, each academic department was once required to have a budget council, consisting of all the full professors in the department and presided over by the department chairman, to initiate all actions affecting faculty appointments, promotions, and salaries. While this arrangement was fairly satisfactory until the early 1960s, it then came under increasing criticism as departments expanded and acquired a larger number of assistant and associate professors. Some departments sought board legislation, approved in 1968, to permit the election of an executive council by all persons of assistant professor rank and above. In some instances the executive council might be fixed as requiring certain representation from each faculty rank. A proposal for admission of students to council membership was rejected.

The Austin campus experienced muted but evident student disorder in the last half of the 1960s. Some departments responded by providing for student participation in a departmental forum. To some extent departments also permitted student membership on departmental committees, even if the students were excluded from the budget council or the executive council.

In spite of the extensive authority vested in the board of regents, a tradition of faculty determination of academic matters took root on the Austin campus. The board of regents was satisfied with the arrangement as long as faculty actions did not prompt internal controversy and external criticism. Conflicts were occasional rather than frequent and usually arose in a kind of twilight area between academic and institutional affairs. The delegation of authority by the board to the faculty included general academic policies, student life and activities, admission and degree requirements, scholastic performance, the approval of the award of degrees, and the determination of faculty rules of procedure. The delegation was made, however, "subject to the authority of the board of regents."

The Austin faculty originally met as a whole, usually in a routine fashion, to act on recommendations from various standing and special committees. These committees were appointed by administrative officers of the university and generally worked in close relationship with them. As the university faculty expanded in size, it became too cumbersome to function well. In 1936 the general faculty adopted a motion urging the president to name a committee to study the organization and future of the university. The president did so, appointing a young assistant professor of government as chairman of a committee made up exclusively of assistant and associate professors.

In 1937 the Committee on University Organization submitted its report. It recommended appointment of a vice-president, the faculty election of various committees, more rapid promotion of junior faculty members and adoption of an up-or-out rule, a strengthening of the role of departmental chairmen, and faculty consultation in the appointment of deans and of the president. These recommendations, except for part of a proposal relating to department chairmen, were approved by the faculty, the president, and the board of regents. The committee considered the question of a representative council to act in the name of the general faculty and urged faculty acceptance of the device but submitted no specific proposal, asking only that five elected faculty members be added to the administrative council of the university. As of 1944 this council consisted of ten administrative officers and five appointed faculty members.

In 1944 the discussion of general faculty organization was resumed. The administrative council was criticized as performing a dual function, advisory to the president and legislative for the faculty. A special committee was appointed to make a detailed study of alternative organization arrangements. This committee recommended that the administrative council become exclusively a group of administrative officers and that the faculty create a faculty council of elected representatives apportioned among the colleges and the faculty ranks of the university. The recommendations were debated at length, some faculty members being reluctant to abandon the general faculty meeting. In September 1944 the report of the special committee was approved and the creation of a faculty council was authorized. The board of regents gave its assent, and the new council began to operate in the academic year 1944–45. The council continued to operate with virtually no change of substance until the spring of 1969.

The faculty council as established included the president and deans. This inclusion was a matter of considerable debate. It was argued that the president and deans were themselves members of the faculty and were important spokesmen for faculty interests. The faculty council was deemed to represent not two but only one constituency, the faculty of the university. The faculty council was charged with authority to act in the name of the general faculty, subject to approval of the entire faculty if a minimum number of protests were voiced. The first council consisted of thirty-six voting members, fourteen persons ex officio and twenty-two elected by the faculty. Of the twenty-two elected representatives, eight were elected at large and fourteen by particular colleges and schools. The president served as the presiding officer, even as he was presiding officer of the general faculty.

For a quarter of a century the faculty council served its purpose, on the whole with success and satisfaction. The membership expanded so that by 1967 there were fifty-one members, sixteen ex officio and thirty-five elected by the faculty. Another five administrative officers were members ex officio but without a vote. The administrative officers and the faculty lived amicably together in the council until the student disorders gained momentum in the late 1960s. The council set out to create and codify a new set of regulations governing student conduct, and enforcement of the rules fell almost entirely upon the administrative staff. Furthermore, the president as of 1968–69 was seen as a dominant figure who in large part determined university policy. To many faculty members the faculty council was seen as a rubber stamp for the administration. To the board of regents the president tended to appear as unduly "soft" on student disruption and protest.

In the autumn of 1968 two faculty members submitted a proposal to the general faculty that would remove the president as chairman of the faculty council and would deprive all administrative officers (or ex officio members) of a vote. The proposal was debated in a series of well-attended faculty meetings in 1968 and early 1969, approved in principle in November 1968, and modified during further discussion. Many faculty members were not disposed to approve any action that might be interpreted off the campus as personal criticism of the president.

The final action in 1969 was to recast the faculty council as a university council that would bring together representatives of three constituencies: faculty, students, and administrators. At the same time, the elected faculty members of this university council would constitute a separate faculty senate concerned with addressing in advance the issues coming before the university council. The arrangement was seen as a device whereby faculty representatives could do their homework in preparation for council meetings, even as was expected of the administration representatives. The council of deans continued to meet with the president and to provide him or her with advice. In addition, the student body would continue to have its student senate. Only the university council, and not the faculty senate, however, was entitled to adopt legislation for submission to the president and the board of regents. The new system was approved by the president and the board of regents and was set in operation in 1969–70.

As of 1976 the university council consisted of twenty faculty members elected at large (ten of whom must be professors and associate professors, and ten of whom must be assistant professors and instructors), thirty-one faculty members elected from individual colleges and schools, twenty-four ex officio members (the president, five vice-presidents, the librarian, and seventeen deans), and six students. The student senate appears to be underrepresented in the council, but, unlike the faculty senate, can submit legislation directly to the president. Some question remains about whether or not the nonacademic staff is adequately represented.

In addition to the university council, mention should be made of the graduate assembly, which exercises general legislative authority over graduate education. For a time Austin endeavored to control graduate education throughout the university system with a graduate legislative council. In 1964 this arrangement was superseded by a graduate assembly solely concerned with the Austin campus. This assembly consisted of forty elected faculty members and twenty administrative officers. The assembly elected its own chairman. Although large and somewhat clumsy, this structure continued for nearly a decade. In 1972 a committee was named to study a restructuring of the assembly, and the recommended changes were adopted in 1973.

The new graduate assembly consists of twenty-seven elected faculty members and the graduate dean. Other administrative officers may participate in the discussions of the assembly but are not permitted to vote. The assembly elects its own chairman and secretary. In practice, the exclusion of administrators from voting seems to make little difference in the operation. Administrative officers continue to attend the meetings and to take an active part in the deliberations of the assembly. Decisions appear to embody a consensus reached in debate in which the deans have had a considerable voice.

The graduate assembly approves new graduate programs, recommends the abolition or modification of existing graduate programs, determines criteria for membership in the graduate faculty, determines standards for student admission to graduate programs, sets policies concerning graduate student support and welfare, and establishes the functions of various committees on graduate studies. The assembly also advises the president about university research policies. In 1975 a graduate student council was organized; since then the graduate assembly has provided that six graduate students selected by this council shall be admitted to membership with the power to vote.

As would be expected, the university council has operated extensively through committees. In response to student demands, the faculty has included students on many of these committees at all levels, from departmental and college committees to those of the council. But the response initially was haphazard, following no coherent pattern. In 1972–73 a study of student participation was undertaken by the faculty committee on policy. The committee recommended that all standing committees be classified into three categories: Type A, dealing with faculty affairs with no student members; Type B, dealing with student services and activities with substantial (but not majority) membership; and Type C, dealing with institutional policy and governance with at least two student members. This proposal was approved by the university council in the spring of 1973. Eventually nine committees were classified as Type A. Students were then included on all Type B and Type C committees. Since 1973 almost all ad hoc committees appointed by the president or by the university council have included student members.

Up to 1976 there was no evidence that student interest in Austin affairs was waning. If anything, the interest seemed to be on the increase. Students were among the most faithful participants in meetings of the university council and reliably attended various committee meetings. The student organization acted to perfect its procedure for recommending student members for various committees. The final selection was made by the president but only from names submitted by the student president.

The procedure for selection of a new president of the Austin campus in 1975 was a two-step arrangement involving an advisory committee, composed only of faculty members and students, and a selection committee of regents, system administrators, presidents of other institutions, an alumnus, one student, and one faculty member. The advisory committee submitted five names to the selection committee but did not include the name of the acting president, Lorene Rogers. A continuing exchange of views took place between the two committees, but the selection committee did not consider itself bound by the advice of the campus advisory committee. The selection committee then recommended the appointment of Rogers as president to the board of regents, and board action followed by a 5-to-3 vote. Vigorous protest by the faculty followed throughout the year 1975–76. Both the faculty and the board of regents took action during the year to cool the conflict. The faculty abstained from participation in university decision making. Finally, the faculty senate recommended an end to the faculty boycott and the general faculty concurred, effective in September 1976.

As the principle of shared governance and campuswide governance has gained acceptance at Austin, alumni representatives from the Ex-Students Association have been included on more and more committees. Previously the practice had been restricted to the fields of intercollegiate athletics and development activities. More recently alumni have been added to various study committees and other planning and policy groups. The faculty senate and the executive council of the Ex-Students Association have developed a meaningful working relationship in the past two or three years. And, for the past three or four years, students have indicated a willingness to express and seek the accomplishment of student objectives through university organizational channels.

The appeal of campuswide or multiconstituency governance structures has been that it has brought together competing points of view about the well-being of the Austin campus. In many instances the structures have provided a mechanism for achieving a compromise or consensus about desirable action. The adjustment of the university calendar represented such a compromise. Yet in other instances there has been a lack of congruence between interests and eventual action. The attempt to achieve a core curriculum for all undergraduate programs in the 1950s was one of these, a proposal debated at length by the general faculty itself and then defeated by a narrow margin. A controversy about how to finance the student newspaper was eventually decided by the board of regents acting on its own initiative; the paper was dropped from the allocation of funds from the activities fee. Only after a lengthy conflict was the board persuaded to restore the previous arrangement.

In the past few years, however, the major disputes have increasingly been ones on which various agencies of campus governance have been arrayed against the board of regents. As of 1975–76 this circumstance appeared to be the one most likely to disrupt and harm the Austin campus. Tentative and confidential discussions about avoidance of continued confrontation were employed in an effort to overcome a circumstance of potentially great damage. Campus governance may not be equal to the stresses of a multicampus system and to the strength of such a powerful body in state government as the University of Texas Board of Regents. It appears that the prosperity of the Austin campus and its community of constituent interests will be shaped by its success in representing itself as a vital part of the public enterprise of the state and of the nation.

## Stanford

Stanford University was unique in the circumstances of its founding, in its location on the 9,000 acres of property of the Leland Stanford family, and in the authority exercised by Mrs. Stanford as the surviving founder after the death of her husband in 1893. The first president, a distinguished educational administrator, appeared generally satisfied with the decisions of Mrs. Stanford; not until legal and other issues were settled around 1902 did she transfer her authority to a self-perpetuating board of trustees. This history helped to establish a tradition of active trustee and presidential governance. In 1904 the trustees provided for "articles of organization" for the faculty of Stanford and for an advisory board. Both arrangements were still in effect in 1976.

Until the 1950s, the orientation of Stanford University was largely toward California. Faculty residence on campus and careful campus planning had helped to achieve a certain interrelationship between faculty and students and between disciplines that may have been somewhat unusual in American higher education. Stanford began to gain academic recognition primarily because of its professional schools. This circumstance reflected the wishes of the founder, who desired that graduates should not only be cultured and socially responsible citizens but also employed and productive citizens. In the 1950s, under the leadership of a new president, Stanford embarked upon a calculated course to achieve national distinction in the arts and sciences as well as in professional fields of study.

This development was made possible in part by the authority vested in the president by the founding grant. The trustees were required to delegate to the president the power to hire and fire faculty members at will, to prescribe the duties of professors, to determine and enforce courses of study and modes of teaching, and to take such other action as might be necessary to ensure the "good conduct" of the university. Early faculty fears led to provision for an advisory board to the president that had to be consulted on matters of faculty appointment and tenure. The development of Stanford was further made possible by a scheme for leasing part of the acreage of the university for research and other facilities; this practice produced new income for the benefit of the university.

The governance of Stanford University was vested in a self-perpetuating board of twenty-four trustees. The president was selected by the board and was responsible to it for the operation of the university. In addition, there was an advisory board to the president consisting of seven full professors elected by the academic council. All personnel actions were to be submitted to this advisory board before being referred to the board of trustees, and the president was required to indicate to the trustees whether or not his recommendations had the approval of the advisory board. The academic council at the beginning of the 1950s included all faculty members of professorial rank plus certain designated administrative officers. The president was also expected to consult the advisory board in making appointments such as deans and as department heads. Student affairs were handled through a committee on student affairs of the academic council and a dean of students. The Associated Students of Stanford University exercised some authority over student organizations and activities. The "Fundamental Standard" asserted that students were expected within and without the campus to evidence respect for order, morality, personal honor, and the rights of others. Failure to abide by this standard was cause for dismissal.

During the developmental processes of the 1950s and early 1960s, the president found it essential to work closely with faculty leadership. His relations were quite close with the advisory board, and there was no evidence that he recommended any personnel actions not previously approved by this board. He enlarged the executive committee of the academic council by the addition of various administrative officers into a committee on university policy. Moreover, the president was ably assisted by a provost from the College of Engineering who proved to be an especially competent academic administrator. The academic council met regularly but with meager

attendance. Major curricular matters were resolved by the several
departments and schools. Personnel decisions and broad university
policy were determined by the president working closely with a small
group of faculty and administrative associates.

By the end of the 1950s the board of trustees was concerned
about a threefold increase in expenditures as a result of the university's quest for academic excellence. With the assistance of certain
faculty and administrative colleagues, the president undertook to
prepare a long-range financial plan for Stanford. The plan as presented to the board called for still further financial expansion during
the 1960s, aided by a $25-million grant from the Ford Foundation
with the understanding that the university would match this amount
at three dollars to one from sources other than the government.
With the new resources from this endeavor, the increases in sponsored research, and the increases in annual giving and in student
tuition, Stanford began a program to recruit one hundred new full
professors in a five-year period. The university became known as
"marauding" Stanford. The planning and the decisions implement-
ing the plan were made by a small group of individuals working
informally and on a restricted time schedule.

As early as 1954 the president informed the faculty that he
desired a careful study to be made of undergraduate education at
Stanford. He appointed a nine-member faculty committee to undertake the assignment, assisted by a twenty-member advisory group.
The president served as chairman of both committees, with the
provost as vice-chairman. The committee distributed a questionnaire to faculty members, but only twenty out of three hundred
bothered to respond. The president provided the two committees
with a statement of undergraduate instructional objectives as the
framework for their discussions. The committee found reason to be
somewhat critical of undergraduate instruction but rejected the idea
of separating departments into undergraduate and graduate components. The committee reported that the intellectual tone and
motivation of the undergraduate student body did leave something
to be desired. The principal recommendation of the committee,
approved by the academic council, was to abolish the distinction
between lower-division and upper-division courses. General education courses henceforth might be distributed throughout the four

years of undergraduate education. The procedure involved in this study and change was illustrative of the pattern of campus decision making as it existed in the 1950s and early 1960s.

Student issues were handled in much the same way. In 1954 the president had established the office of dean of students to direct and coordinate all student service activities that had, up to that time, reported directly to the president. The dean of students was pictured as paternalistic, just, fair, patient, and kind and willing to spend many hours in discussion with student leaders and student groups. The reconsideration of the question of the use of alcohol on campus was indicative of problem-solving procedure. Because of student pressure and a student referendum in favor of student use of alcohol on campus, the president appointed a student-faculty committee to examine the issue. The committee recommended that campus regulations be made consistent with state law on the consumption of alcoholic beverages. The committee on university policy rejected this recommendation. But in 1962 the president and board agreed to review the 1960 decision, and this action paved the way for subsequent university action accepting the original 1960 proposal.

By the mid 1960s the informal governance procedures of the past became unworkable. The number of faculty positions had increased from 450 in 1955 to over 600 in 1960, to 850 by 1967, and to 1,000 by 1969. Enrollments increased from 7,600 students in 1950 to about 11,500 students by 1970. The admission standards had become more and more selective, and the student of 1967 and thereafter rejected the paternalistic role of the university. Moreover, the new faculty tended to be composed of persons uninterested in the Stanford of the past, committed to their own scholarship in particular and to faculty influence in university affairs in general. Student dissension and eventual disruption and destruction of property forced Stanford to react more quickly and more decisively to changing circumstances.

The issues that aroused campus agitation and ire were familiar ones: participation in ROTC education, participation in research projects for the benefit of the U.S. Department of Defense, university ownership of the Stanford Research Institute, the privilege to invite campus speakers of extreme views on social and economic issues, the appropriateness of faculty engagement in classified research, continued university supervision of the personal lives of students, whether or not the university should terminate the tenure of a faculty member who advocated student violence, whether or not the university as a corporate entity should take an official stand on the subject of American involvement in Vietnam. Students and faculty were not content just to discuss these issues or to vote on them. Students and perhaps others expressed the emotion of their commitment to a particular point of view by disruption of campus activities, the occupation of buildings, and the destruction of property on campus and adjacent to the campus.

In an effort to provide increased student and faculty participation in decision making about Stanford as a means of avoiding campus violence and destruction, a number of changes were introduced in the structure of campus governance. The provost retired in 1965, leaving a kind of power vacuum in the university. The position remained unfilled for a critical year and a half. The president retired in 1968. The position of provost was eventually filled internally, but the appointment of a president from outside aroused considerable opposition, and after a year he resigned. Thus leadership within the university suffered during a period when important decisions had to be made about its operation.

In 1968 the academic council voted to establish a senate as a faculty representative body. There were to be fifty-three members elected by the faculty according to proportional representation, with twelve administrative officers serving ex officio and without vote. All decisions of the senate were to be reported to all members of the faculty comprising the academic council. A council meeting to review a senate decision could be summoned by petition of one third of the senate representatives, fifty members of the academic council, or two thirds of the council members in a school or college. The senate was to have its own chairman and two standing committees: a steering committee and a committee on committees. The authority and scope of the senate were imprecise; presumably the senate spoke for the faculty in making appropriate recommendations to the president. But the committee proposing the senate and the action of the academic council approving the new arrangement excluded any student participation.

It is not easy to determine the full importance of the new senate. Its membership generally has consisted of strong, respected faculty members, and its leadership has involved the outstanding members of the faculty. Attendance at meetings has been good, and the senate has considered various issues of major importance. Much of the preparatory work preceding the senate discussions is handled by special committees, which require a good deal of time to arrive at recommendations and thus make the decision-making process a relatively slow one. Faculty members are increasingly reluctant to serve on these committees because of the time thus consumed. The administration in general has been inclined to accept the recommendations of the senate. The senate did decide, ultimately, to involve students in the membership of all special, or study, committees, and this student role has helped to avoid disruption similar to that of the late 1960s.

Between 1970 and 1975, the senate was involved in several significant processes. The senate asked the board of trustees to sell the Stanford Research Institute at the best possible price. It recommended that faculty members in the future not engage in classified research. It adopted a policy statement on faculty self-discipline. It approved a policy requiring each school to maintain a program evaluating faculty instructional performance. It adopted actions improving the status of graduate students. A move to involve the senate in the university budget process was headed off by presidential leadership in establishing new budget procedures and in keeping the senate fully informed about the budget difficulties and actions of the university.

In 1967 the president had again raised the question of the scope and adequacy of the educational programs undertaken by the university. A study committee was appointed to examine these matters under the chairmanship of a professor of law who was also named a vice-provost. Over a two-year period, the committee published ten volumes of analysis and recommendations. The underlying premise of the study was a belief that universities were deficient in their continuing internal introspection, and the overarching recommendation was to propose a spirit of self-examination and self-renewal supported by two principal institutional devices: (1) a standing committee of the senate, with student membership, to concern itself with identifying institutional problems and ensuring that these were studied; and (2) the establishment of an academic planning office. The study committee also affirmed the role of the president as an educational leader and of the provost as the president's chief deputy. Other recommendations dealt with selective admissions (the committee proposed greater heterogeneity in the student body), continuance of Stanford as a residential campus, a faculty commitment to both undergraduate and graduate education, the need to improve instructional performance, and further effort to reconcile research and instruction.

The reports of the study of Stanford education provided the senate with a rich agenda for discussion and action. The senate has been somewhat cautious in making decisions, however, preferring to undertake further study on a subject-by-subject basis. In the meantime, the budget difficulties of Stanford, requiring a concerted budget adjustment program to find more income and to reduce the growth rate in expenditures, transferred attention from program effectiveness to program cost. The days when program improvements could be made without concern for program costs came to an end. The task of academic planning was now attached to academic budgeting, and the initiative for action was now clearly in the hands of the provost and the president. The senate or the academic council might react but it was less and less an innovative or dynamic force in Stanford governance.

One other important change was made by the board of trustees, which expanded its own membership from twenty-four to thirty-two, with a provision that the eight additional members must be alumni, half of them under thirty-six years of age at the time of election. Moreover, faculty and students were invited to participate in the work of board committees. As of 1976 fears were expressed that the board had become too large for effective operation.

The Franklin affair of 1971 demonstrated the authority of the advisory board and its capacity to assert discipline of a faculty member. An associate professor of English with tenure, H. Bruce Franklin, was allegedly involved in actions occasioning disruption of campus activities. The president notified Franklin of his intention to recommend to the board of trustees termination of his appointment for cause and advised Franklin of his right to appeal to the advisory board. Franklin exercised this right. For six weeks in the autumn of 1971 the board, working six hours a day, considered the case and then voted 5 to 2 in favor of termination of employment. A subsequent appeal to the courts sustained the authority of the board of trustees.

Much of the ongoing activity of the university remained within the jurisdiction of the individual schools, institutes, and departments. The faculty committees, with students added in most instances, exercised authority wherever it was not exercised by the separate departments and individual faculty members. The two most important school committees were usually the committee on curriculum and the committee on faculty personnel. The leadership in school affairs was normally exercised by the dean. The heads of departments were appointed, mostly for three-year terms, by the president, upon recommendation of a dean. In turn, the deans by varying devices—a straw vote, individual consultation, small group meetings—determined the consensus of department personnel about desired leadership.

By 1976 Stanford University had moved beyond the conflicts of the 1960s into a period of more widespread faculty and student participation in governance processes but with administration leadership largely unimpaired and the authority of the board of trustees still extensive and respected. The faculty exercised much greater authority in matters of curriculum and faculty personnel than in earlier years, but budgetary constraints were becoming increasingly evident in this decision making. The president and the provost tended to consult more extensively and more formally than in earlier years. The period of institutional paternalism over the lives of students was gone. The techniques of institutional planning and institutional budgeting had been substantially perfected and were administered by professional personnel. Institutional information was more widely shared than in other years. Paperwork, much of it generated by federal government requirements, had substantially expanded. In an important sense, however, the governance of Stanford was still a governance of conversation.

## Conclusion

In these summaries of governance experience from 1966 through 1975 at six leading research universities, three themes predominate. One theme is that of faculty domination of faculty affairs, with some generalized leadership from presidents and provosts. Another theme is that of the emergence of new issues in the 1970s demanding a planning and budget leadership by presidents under the compelling force of a decreased rate of growth in institutional income. And a third theme is that of increased formal and informal participation by faculty and students with administrative officers in the decision-making process involving the university as a university.

The so-called golden age of the research university in the 1960s was interrupted by an increasingly restive and challenging student body, beginning around 1965 and 1966. Fundamental issues about the purpose of the university and its relationship to society were raised by a confrontation between students, with their power to disrupt, and faculties and administrators, with their vested interests in university effectiveness. Almost as suddenly as they arose, the conflicts began to disappear in 1971 and 1972.

By 1976 the universities were different from what they had been in 1965. The power of research universities to change society had waned; the power of society to change research universities had begun to grow.

# CHAPTER FOUR

◇◇◇◇◇◇◇◇◇◇◇

# Governance in
# Other Universities

◇◇◇◇◇◇◇◇◇◇◇◇◇◇◇◇◇◇◇◇◇◇◇◇◇◇◇◇◇◇◇◇◇◇◇◇

In addition to six leading research universities, another nine universities were included in this study of campuswide governance to ensure variety of type and to determine any possible correlation of type with experience. Of these nine universities, five are state universities and three are privately sponsored; the ninth (Howard University) is a mixture of public and private sponsorship.

In the order of their founding dates, the five state universities are Miami University (1809), the University of New Hampshire (1866), the University of Oregon (1872), the University of New Mexico (1889), and Tennessee State University (1909). These universities are quite divergent in their mission and program characteristics. Enrollment as of 1975 varied from around 5,000 students at Tennessee State to 20,000 at New Mexico, with New Hampshire at 11,000, Miami at 15,000, and Oregon at 16,000. Expenditures varied in that year from $12 million at Tennessee

89

State to $60 million at Oregon, with budgets between $40 and $55 million at the other universities. All but Tennessee State offer degrees at the doctoral level, and both Oregon and New Mexico are developing notable research capabilities. Tennessee State in Nashville has a predominant black enrollment.

In order of their founding, the three privately sponsored universities are Emory (1836), Syracuse (1870), and Roosevelt (1945). Emory University, with an enrollment of around 7,000 students and a budget of $80 million, is on the road to becoming a major research university. Syracuse has an enrollment of 15,000 students and a budget of around $85 million. More closely involved in educational services to its urban constituency than Emory, Syracuse is, like Emory, involved in extensive separately supported research activity. Roosevelt University, with an enrollment of around 7,500 students and a budget of $12 million, represents the privately sponsored institution committed to instructional service of an urban population in a large, congested city.

Howard University, founded in the District of Columbia by an Act of Congress to provide educational service principally to black students nationwide, claims a self-perpetuating board of trustees, but the major part of its income is derived from federal government appropriations and federal government grants and contracts. It has an enrollment of some 10,000 students and an operating budget of some $75 million, according to 1976 figures.

These nine universities surely represent diversity. They also represent diversity in their experience with campuswide governance in the years from 1966 to 1976.

## Miami University

Founded by state law in 1809 with a public land grant as directed by the Northwest Ordinance of 1787, Miami University throughout the nineteenth century had been a public college of the liberal arts. In the twentieth century, it had added various professional programs for undergraduates and has, since World War II, expanded its graduate program to include the development of several selected doctoral degree programs. Located in a small com-

munity of southwestern Ohio, Miami is a residential institution with
a selected student body. Like state universities generally, it has
grown in enrollment since World War II (its enrollment was about
3,000 students in 1940) to the maximum of 15,000 students fixed
by state law. Some 1,300 of these students are graduate students.

As of 1975–76 Miami employed nearly 3,200 persons, not
including part-time student workers. The forty-seven academic departments were staffed with 663 full-time faculty members on the
Oxford campus. Some 400 of these faculty members were in the
disciplines of the arts and sciences; 87 were in business administration, some 130 in teacher education, 67 in fine arts, and 40 in
applied science. The university had a physical plant valued at $140
million and an operating budget of $55 million. It received over
one third of its income as instructional subsidy from the State of
Ohio, about 30 percent from tuition, about 27 percent from residence-hall charges, and about 9 percent from miscellaneous sources
(federal grants and about $1 million in private gifts).

In connection with a decennial accreditation visit, including
final approval of ten doctoral degree programs, in 1974–75, Miami
prepared an extensive self-study. The occasion was employed as an
opportunity to reassess and restate the mission of the university; a
campuswide committee formulated a statement that was subsequently subjected to formal hearings and official adoption by the
legislative bodies of the university and by the board of trustees. The
distinctive elements of Miami's mission were held to be a liberal
arts heritage and the functions of a public university with many
qualities of an independent institution, a modern university committed to graduate study and research, and a residential university
seeking total student development.

The corporation of the university as embodied by provision
of state law in 1809 was the president and trustees of the Miami
University. From the end of the Civil War until 1963 the board
consisted of twenty-seven members, all residents of Ohio appointed
by the governor and confirmed by the state senate for nine-year
terms. Beginning in 1963, as set forth in a new state statute, a
planned reduction took place, so that by 1975 there were nine
trustees, one appointed each year for a nine-year term. The law

prohibited reappointment. The lengthy service of some earlier members of the board was no longer possible. The authority of government of the university was vested by law in the board of trustees.

The president, as chief executive officer of the university, is selected by the board. On the past two occasions, in 1953 and in 1964, the board voluntarily associated faculty members, students, and alumni with it in the selection process. The president is assisted by four vice-presidents; the college and five schools (including the graduate school) are headed by deans. From the beginning of formal instruction at the collegiate level in 1824, the faculty, as a group under the presiding influence of the president, has been a major element in the operation of the university, including detailed prescription of expected student conduct.

In 1856 a formal university senate was organized, with the president as presiding officer, to include all full-time faculty members and all administrative officers with faculty rank. In the early 1950s the senate was organized into four standing committees. For the committees on academic affairs and student affairs, the president appointed half the membership and designated the chairman; the senate elected the other half of the membership. For the faculty affairs committee and the committee on committees, the senate elected the entire membership and the committees selected their own chairman. The most active committees were the committee on academic affairs, which was concerned with degree requirements, the approval of new courses, and academic standards, and the committee on student affairs, which was concerned with student-conduct regulations and the judicial system. The committee on faculty affairs was concerned with faculty welfare; its preoccupation in the 1950s was with matters of fringe benefits. The president in the 1950s named a special committee to develop a universitywide requirement for general education and another special committee, later, to examine the academic calendar. The committees reported to the senate, which met regularly four times a year; almost always the committee recommendations were approved by the senate. The president was aided by a council of deans (including his closest administrative associates) and a committee on external relations. The board of trustees generally approved the actions of the senate. There were no conflicts between the two bodies in the 1950s or early 1960s.

Miami University experienced steady but modest enrollment growth from 1953 to 1965 (5,300 to 8,000 students) but almost doubled in enrollment between 1965 and 1975. As the size of the faculty grew in the late 1950s, faculty leaders became dissatisfied with the meetings of the senate, holding that the body was becoming too large to be a deliberative group and that committee recommendations ought to be subject to additional consideration. In 1965 a faculty council was established as a kind of executive committee of the university senate, with sixteen elected faculty representatives and eight appointees of the president. The president presided and served as one of the eight administration representatives. The actions of the faculty council were subject to an arrangement for senate review.

Miami experienced only slight student disruption in the period from 1968 to 1970. The Navy ROTC building was occupied by a group of students who were compelled to leave under threat of police action. There were several student demonstrations and some further threats of disruption but little violence or general disorder. In 1970 the board of trustees added eighteen student representatives to the university senate and approved redesignation of the faculty council as the university council, with twelve student representatives. Later the board approved a proposal to increase the eighteen student memberships in the senate to twenty-nine. The president withdrew from active participation in the university council and the provost became the presiding officer.

Another basic change took place in the 1970s. The university council and the senate found their agendas crowded with matters related to student affairs. A council on student affairs was then established to become the legislative body on matters involving student conduct and social activities. The senate and the university council divested themselves of further concern with student residential affairs. The council on student affairs consisted of nine faculty members elected by the senate, four administrators appointed by the president, and thirteen students selected by the student senate. The council had a considerable number of committees with generally equal student and faculty-administration membership. The council presented recommendations to the president, who might or might not transmit these recommendations to the board of trustees. In recent years the president and board found themselves largely preoccupied with student issues. The students wanted the university out of their lives, and the faculty has been inclined to agree. The president and board were unwilling to accede to the full range of student demands.

As of 1975–76 the university senate consisted of 906 voting members: 752 full-time faculty members, 29 students, and 125 administrative and professional staff officers. A quorum of the senate is 25 percent of its membership. The senate meets three times a year, but it has become more and more difficult to obtain a quorum. A special meeting may be called upon petition of fifty members. Senate rules reflect a kind of faculty apathy about the role of the body. The consequence of the general indifference is that the senate is given a diluted role in university governance. The president presides at senate meetings, and an agenda committee composed of the chairmen of standing committees of the university council controls the agenda. Almost no issue comes to the senate that has not previously been considered by the university council. Thus the university senate serves as a review agency of the university council but seldom finds it necessary or desirable to exercise its powers.

The university council by 1975–76 had become the campus-wide legislative body. Its thirty-six voting members include sixteen elected faculty members, twelve elected students, and eight persons appointed by the president. Faculty representatives are elected from a universitywide slate of nominees by the method of the single transferable vote. Nominees are chosen by academic divisions of the university in a number twice the proportionate share of each division to total faculty. Voting participation in recent years has been only about 50 percent of the faculty. At one time a "leftist" group of faculty members calling for a dramatic relaxing of academic requirements and student regulations and a "rightist" group advocating stricter standards gained some representation on the council, but the "centrist" majority has continued to dominate educational policy making.

The university council meets twice monthly, with a two-hour time limit that can be extended by majority vote. Meetings are open, the agenda and supporting materials are distributed in advance, and nonmembers may be heard upon request to the presiding officer. Actions taken by a two thirds vote are reported to the senate for information. Actions by a less than two thirds vote are placed automatically on the senate agenda. The council works through a series of committees. The council has been concerned in recent years with admission standards, the improvement of instruction, the general education requirement, academic regulations, the student aid program, and library operations. Faculty interest has been devoted particularly to the question of how to ensure faculty domination of academic decision making.

Some special mention should be made of the Committee on Faculty Rights and Responsibilities, which was created in 1967 by the university senate and which is an all-faculty committee elected by the senate. Administrative officers, including department chairmen, are not eligible for membership. This committee has reported directly to the senate on various recommended clarifications in university regulations concerning the duties and obligations of faculty members. Upon approval by the university senate, the committee negotiates directly with the board of trustees about the need for legislative action by the board. In addition, the committee has served as a grievance committee in instances where faculty members have believed that their academic freedom was threatened or impaired by actions of the administration or the board. In several instances the committee has been able to negotiate at least partial adjustment of such grievances.

Both the president and the provost have made use of advisory committees outside the structure of the university council and the council on student affairs. After a heated senate debate in 1969 about the allocation of resources in the university budget, the president named a budget advisory council presided over by the vice-president for finance and consisting of two students and five faculty members. By 1975 this council had ceased to function. The president has also made use of so-called blue-ribbon committees and task forces to study special problems. The reports of these special groups are usually submitted to the university council for action. Such special committees have dealt with academic priorities, establishment of a law school, the academic program for Western College (a new campus taken over in 1975), the general education program, the status of women, and relations with a university in Brazil. The most serious or controversial university issues have thus been assigned to special committees appointed by the president rather than to standing committees of the university council.

A student life research service was begun in 1971 to assist the work of the council on student affairs by conducting surveys of student attitudes and opinions about university issues. The university also publishes its own weekly bulletin to convey information to faculty members and other persons. Throughout the university in recent years extensive efforts have been made to improve and extend various devices for communication. Some faculty members have declared their inability to cope with this augmented flow of information, in which their interest is often peripheral.

During the past ten years Miami University has become constituency-conscious. Faculty, students, professional staff, operating staff, administrators, alumni, and board members have been identified as special groups, and their various interests increasingly have been articulated. There has been no pattern in determining the relative weight in decision making to be given to these constituent groups. The board of trustees remains the court of last resort. And in various ways Miami has had to accommodate its interests to the existence of two campus centers located in nearby Hamilton and Middletown and to a state government little disposed to invest generously in public higher education.

## New Hampshire

Founded in 1866 as the Morrill Act Land-Grant College of New Hampshire and originally attached to Dartmouth College for administrative purposes, the University of New Hampshire came into existence in 1893 at its Durham location. Only after World War II did the university experience any substantial enrollment growth, reaching 6,000 in 1960 and over 10,000 by 1970. In 1963 the general court added Keene State College and Plymouth State College to the University of New Hampshire, thus creating the University of New Hampshire system under a single governing board, a board of trustees. Until July 1975 the three campuses were administered more or less separately, however, and the University of

New Hampshire that is our concern here is the campus at Durham, which consists of five colleges.

The board of trustees of the university as of 1975 consisted of twenty-four members, the governor ex officio, twelve persons appointed by the governor, six alumni elected by the alumni associations of the three campuses, two state officials ex officio (the commissioner of education and the commissioner of agriculture), and the presidents of the three campuses. The board exercised the customary authority of a governing board. The political situation in New Hampshire has been such in recent years that the board has had to take a very active part in the governance of the Durham campus.

Although the board of trustees submits budget requests to the governor for needed appropriations for each of the three campuses, the governor's office presents its own recommendations to the general court. The final appropriation represents the result of considerable negotiation between the chief executive and the legislature. Capital improvements are financed by the issuance of bonds, for projects specifically authorized by the legislature. The board then determines the instructional charges to be paid by students. In the fiscal year 1974–75, 41 percent of the educational and general expenditures were financed by the State of New Hampshire, 48 percent by charges to students, and 11 percent by grants and other sources of income.

Prior to 1969 the university senate consisted of all faculty members presided over by the president. In addition, there was a student senate, elected by the student body, that worked closely with the administrative staff on matters of student organization and activities. The president who came to the university in 1944 had a concept of the university as a complex of faculty-student-administration relationships, along with relationship to various external groups. He wished both senates to be more active than they had been in the past, and he involved the university senate in basic policy issues to a greater degree than his predecessors. This innovation was not entirely agreeable to the board of trustees, which saw the development as somehow impairing its own governance role. When the president resigned from the university in 1949, the university senate became somewhat less active in the 1950s.

In 1952 the university senate disapproved doctoral programs in four fields, on the grounds that the financial resources of the university were not adequate to support them. The senate went on to pass various resolutions deploring the financial condition of the university and the low level of faculty salaries. In 1958 the student senate made a formal request for membership in the university senate but was rejected. The faculty did agree that two students should be added to the committee on student organizations and that students might be invited to meetings of committees and of the university senate when matters affecting students were under consideration. In 1960 the senate authorized the use of the Scholastic Aptitude Test as a condition for admission but set no minimum test score for entry into an instructional program. In 1961 the senate voted an expression of appreciation to the board of trustees for resisting an especially vigorous attack upon the university by the governor. The major work of the university senate in those years was approval of recommendations from its committee on educational policies regarding general education requirements for all students. Later, in 1969, the university senate approved a detailed and elaborate reorganization of all undergraduate instructional programs.

The university experienced a good deal of student agitation and disorder in the years from 1965 to 1969. Although no major confrontation occurred between students and the administration, the conflict was sufficient to induce the president in 1968 to appoint a committee to prepare a new organizational arrangement. The committee recommendations were adopted and made effective in 1969. As a result, the composition of the university senate was drastically changed.

The university senate in 1969 became a representative body embracing various campus constituencies. Originally the new senate consisted of thirty faculty representatives and thirty student representatives, along with the president and nine administrative officers. Later the membership was increased from seventy to eighty persons by adding five graduate students and five representatives of the professional-technical staff of the university. Faculty senators were elected for a two-year term, while other representatives served one-year terms. Expected to meet monthly during the regular academic year, the senate elected its own presiding officer and operated primarily through committees. An executive council including the chairman of the senate and the president of the university controlled the agenda, recommended committee membership, and generally served to guide the work of the senate. The executive council was also used by the president as an advisory agency.

A unique aspect of the governance structure devised in 1969 was the creation of caucuses and forums as participating bodies. The faculty representatives in the university senate became the faculty caucus, and all full-time faculty members constituted the faculty forum. The undergraduate student caucus was made up of all undergraduate student senators and the graduate student caucus was made up of all graduate student senators; the undergraduate forum consisted of all full-time undergraduate students and the graduate student forum consisted of all full-time graduate students. This arrangement was intended to facilitate communication and to permit general participation beyond the act of voting. The forums were expected to meet prior to each university senate meeting to discuss issues and to arrive, if possible, at a faculty consensus, an undergraduate student consensus, or a graduate student consensus. The caucuses, after consultation with their respective forums, might decide by a two thirds vote that an item on the senate agenda constituted a matter of "gravity" and should be acted upon only by a two thirds vote of the senate.

It is generally agreed that the university senate was most active and most innovative in the years immediately after its creation in 1969. The innovation included inauguration of a life studies program, a series of issue-oriented workshops that might be substituted for general education requirements in the first two years; the establishment of a student-designed major; and the elimination of a physical education requirement in favor of a voluntary program of physical education and intramural sports. The senate also voted to let each residence hall set its own hours by a two thirds vote. Moreover, the senate served as a vehicle for discussions and protests about the war in Vietnam and other public policies. The university did not have to close its doors in May 1970 at the time of the Kent State and Jackson State tragedies.

As the 1970s proceeded, however, campus interest in the university senate seemed to wane. The percentage of student participation in student elections declined to 20 percent. Faculty interest turned from the university senate to action controlled exclusively by faculty members. The university continued to be subject to political attack, and the senate felt helpless to respond to this external hostility. In 1973 both the executive council and the university senate endorsed the creation of a commission on university governance to be appointed by the president. A commission of eight faculty members and eight students was named, and a report was completed in April 1974.

The commission report reviewed various sources of dissatisfaction with the university senate: vagueness of jurisdiction, cumbersome procedures, exorbitant consumption of members' time, lack of confidence in the body, concerns about its representative character, and faculty feelings of disenfranchisement. The two major concerns of the commission were frankly acknowledged: the perception that "real" power rested with departments, colleges, and the administration, and the perception that the senate was dealing with issues peripheral to the real problems of the university, which were being resolved elsewhere.

The commission on governance in 1974 recommended a new structure, to consist of a steering committee, a faculty senate, a staff senate, a student senate, an academic senate, and three boards concerned with faculty, staff, and student welfare. A steering committee of nine members was to decide whether or not an issue of universitywide interest was a policy or nonpolicy matter. Only policy issues would be considered by an appropriate decision-making agency. The steering committee was to consist of a designate of the president as chairman, three faculty members, three students (one being a graduate student), one member of the professional staff, and one member of the support staff. The faculty senate would be the deliberative body on universitywide issues of concern to the faculty. The staff senate would be the deliberative body on universitywide issues of concern to the professional and support staff. The student senate would have the same jurisdiction on student affairs. The academic senate of sixty-eight members (thirty-one faculty, thirty-one students, and six academic deans) would deal primarily with academic (as distinct from faculty and student) affairs. The vice-provost for academic affairs was included ex officio as one of the faculty members. The commission report designated various matters to be handled as "operating" matters by the administration and then urged consultation with appropriate bodies. These administration issues included: university planning, administrative organization, budget preparation, plant use, development, tuition charges, student services, parking and traffic, athletic and recreation programs, and cultural events.

In reviewing the work of the university senate between 1969 and 1975, it was observed that most of the discussions centered on three areas of concern: improvements in instructional programs, degree requirements, and regulations about student life. Faculty criticism tended to be directed at the amount of time devoted to issues of student life. Academic issues before the senate included a pass/fail grading option; a directive to departments to evaluate the quality of all courses in relation to the credit hours awarded; the award of an associate of arts degree; the establishment of a teaching-learning council to encourage instructional innovation and to carry out an evaluation of instructional effectiveness; and the requirement that selection of a department chairman be ratified by a majority vote of all faculty members in the department.

Faculty opinion within the University of New Hampshire was generally favorable toward the 1974 recommendations of the commission on university governance. Student attitudes tended to be hostile, as were staff reactions. Interestingly enough, the members of the university senate opposed the recommendations; criticism seemed to give the university senate a new cohesiveness and sense of purpose. There was some question about who should act on the commission's proposals, the president or the university senate. Moreover, a change of presidents was under way in 1974, and a new president was not selected until the beginning of the 1975–76 academic year. The new president in 1975 recommended that the existing university senate be retained, with some modifications in jurisdiction in the direction of augmenting the authority of the faculty caucus. He also proposed that a faculty council be elected by the faculty to serve directly as an advisory body to him. The president's proposals were greeted with some sense of relief and were implemented during the year. In the meantime, the possibility of faculty collective bargaining arose as an issue that might come to a head in 1976–77.

It appeared as of 1976 that the governance structures of the university were not well suited to a time of deep uncertainty and rapid change. Yet the direction of appropriate and acceptable alteration in these structures was by no means clear.

## Oregon

Established in 1872 as the University of Oregon, separate and distinct from the Morrill Act Land-Grant College (now Oregon State University), the university began collegiate level instruction in 1876 in Eugene. Initially, the authority of government of the university was vested in a board of regents for the Eugene campus; in 1932 the state legislature abolished the board of regents and replaced it with a state board of higher education with the power of government over eight campuses comprising the state system. But a statute of 1876 was not repealed in 1932; this law specified that the president and professors constituted the faculty of the university and were to exercise the "immediate government and discipline" of it. The faculty was, subject to the "supervision" of the board of regents, to prescribe the course of study in the university. The president was designated the "executive and governing officer of the school" and, subject to board supervision, was vested with authority to "control and give general direction to the practical affairs of the school." The legislation of 1876 continued, one hundred years later, to provide the legal foundation for governance at the University of Oregon.

The University of Oregon became and has remained a town-meeting system of faculty governance. Originally the university had three professors, one of them the president; by 1976 there were 922 professors, including the president and many administrative officers. The curriculum was a simple one one hundred years ago; in 1976 there were nine colleges and schools, plus a graduate school, and the budget of the university was around $60 million. But few persons are disposed to criticize or abandon the faculty town meeting. One hundred years of legislative accretion encrust the operation of the university. The regulations still state that young ladies shall not go to the railroad station to meet the night train without permission of the president. Yet when a housecleaning of outmoded legislation was proposed, the awful specter of a rigorous set of statutes, likened to the Napoleonic Code, appeared and faculty members quickly abandoned the project.

Technically, faculty meetings more recently have been designated as meetings of the university assembly. The president is the presiding officer. Professors who teach full-time are voting members. Administrative officers given faculty rank are also members. Since the 1960s, there have been eighteen students, representing not student government but the instructional colleges and schools of the university. There have been fifty-five committees of the assembly. A count in 1975 revealed that 553 persons had served on these committees: 307 faculty members, 127 students, and 119 administrative officers. It has been estimated that some committees meet as much as four hours a week; others may meet only an hour or two a year. There have been eight committees generally regarded as commanding the greatest prestige, power, and hard work, the objects of their study being academic requirements, student-faculty grievances, student conduct, protection of human subjects, teacher education, campus planning, curriculum, and library.

Not all faculty members have been eager to serve on committees. When the committee on committees has asked for faculty volunteers to fill 300 faculty places, perhaps as many as 250 have indicated a willingness to serve. Other faculty members must be "recruited" in order to obtain the necessary complement of faculty representation. When the nominations are finally submitted to the university assembly, approval is automatic.

In 1932 the university assembly voted to create an academic council which was renamed the faculty senate in 1937 and the university senate in 1974. In this last year the membership was increased from thirty-six to fifty-four members by the addition of eighteen students, the same students who serve in the university assembly. The senate does not enact legislation. Rather, it is a screening device for all committee reports and other matters concerning academic problems. If an issue appears to be one involving academic policy, the senate passes the matter along for consideration by the university assembly.

In addition, after 1937 the faculty by mail vote elected an advisory council of seven members to meet with and advise the president. In 1973 this council, by action of the assembly, was split into two parts: an advisory council and a committee on faculty personnel. This second committee advised the president on all faculty appointments, promotion, and tenure.

The University of Oregon experienced a considerable amount of student disorder and violence in the late 1960s, especially in 1968–69. The issues were familiar: the war in Vietnam, opening faculty meetings to student participation and public attendance, eliminating academic credit for courses in military science, abolition of ROTC programs, dirty words in the student newspaper, a boycott of grapes in the dining halls, increased student aid, the length of hair for athletes, communist speakers on campus. An ROTC building was bombed. Disruption and threats of other violence were widespread. Only slowly did the university assembly respond to student demands. Faculty governance was not governance geared to speedy and decisive action.

The whole machinery of faculty governance seemed to work tolerably well, except in a crisis. In spite of turbulence and the death of an acting president in tragic circumstances in the spring of 1969, the university assembly continued to function and gradually to make changes in the rules governing its meetings (they were opened to the public)', in degree requirements, and in the regulations for student conduct. Tradition dictated faculty control of matters academic, and the faculty at Oregon was willing to compromise with changing circumstances but not to abandon its powerful role in such areas as degree requirements, curriculum, and student behavior.

The Oregon State Board of Higher Education has delegated to the presidents of each campus the authority to "operate" the campus, and to the faculty the authority to determine educational policies. Presumably some authority of supervision has remained with the state board, but, unless the president asked the board to intervene in some matter, it has been careful not to do so. The president in effect has a veto over all legislation of the university assembly by refusing to take the legislation to the state board. One president did this on the subject of a one-margin vote to change the academic calendar from quarters to semesters. But in general presidents have worked closely with committees and the university assembly to avoid conflict. The president at the University of Oregon is more a creation of faculty will than a master of educational direction.

A relatively typical meeting of the university assembly would involve an agenda of about ten to fifteen major items. Almost all of these would be adopted but often with amendments from the floor. There would be efforts to return some items to committee or to table or postpone action. Such motions were more likely to be defeated than adopted. The major issues would be changes in the grading system, the general education requirements for a bachelor's degree, some restrictions upon intercollegiate athletics, and the addition of new instructional programs. In the late 1960s the university assembly acted to give "full campus citizenship" to students, removing almost all campus regulations governing student social and individual behavior.

By 1975 the day of the radical student had passed. The concerns largely remained the same, except that student conduct receded as an issue. Should students evaluate faculty instructional performance and publish the results? The university assembly approved student evaluation but disapproved publication as a threat to academic freedom.

The essence of faculty governance has been the committee structure. Here the real work of campuswide governance is performed. The most important single committee activity in recent years has been the work of the Hearing Panel on University Priorities appointed by the president. The president asked the panel to recommend budget cuts of more than $1 million. The president accepted some but disapproved other recommendations. The whole exercise created immense hard feelings throughout the faculty. The faculty was disposed not to wish to repeat this particular episode. Budget adjustment would have to fall to the president and the state board.

Although the faculty periodically at Oregon has considered some reform of its governance structure, any substantial change has been defeated each time it has been proposed. Faculty governance involving all the faculty has remained powerful at Oregon.

## New Mexico

In its 1949 constitution, the University Faculty of the University of New Mexico included in its membership a limited number of administrative officers, including the president, the vice-presidents, the academic deans, and a few others. Thus an administrative presence was officially sanctioned in the faculty body. From its formal establishment in 1889 as the state university but not the land-grant institution of the state, the University of New Mexico had slowly developed its mission, which was fashioned after that of leading state universities in the Middle West. Enrollment grew after World War II, and, thanks to the importance of New Mexico in the development of atomic energy, the university gained stature.

The faculty role at New Mexico was not essentially different from that at other universities. The faculty insisted that it should provide the decision-making voice in academic matters and expected the president and board of regents largely to acquiesce in these determinations. Along with the specification of faculty membership in 1949, an administrative committee was created, with a small group of faculty members included as members. Advisory to the president, this administrative committee was a consultative device for the president's use in formulating recommendations to present to the board of regents. Thus some degree of interaction between faculty and administration was sought by means of mixed participation in the university faculty and in the administrative council.

In 1963 the university experimented with still another arrangement, a committee on the university. The membership of the committee consisted of four faculty members nominated by the faculty policy council, four administrative officers appointed by the president, four undergraduate and two graduate students appointed by student government officers, and two alumni appointed by the alumni association. The charge to the committee was to study the aims and goals of the university and to present recommendations for change through established organizational bodies. In particular, this committee was to be concerned with efforts "toward improving the educational climate of the university." The charge exceeded the capacity of the committee. The record of the committee from 1963 to 1972 was unimpressive and it was disbanded in 1972.

As early as 1966 a group of students petitioned that faculty meetings be opened to students, but the faculty refused. Under continued pressure from students, the faculty a year later voted to permit students on specified occasions to be represented at faculty meetings in order to present their views on matters of concern to them. By 1969 the pressures were even greater. In a highly charged faculty meeting that debated the pros and cons of a suspension of two teaching assistants for the use of allegedly pornographic material in a freshman English class, the faculty voted to admit twenty-five undergraduate students, fifteen graduate students, ten representatives of the Black Student Union, and two newspaper reporters for the duration of this discussion.

Later in the spring of 1969, on recommendation of the faculty policy council, the faculty approved a proposal to admit fifteen student representatives with permission to participate in faculty discussions but without the privilege of making motions or voting. At the same time, the faculty agreed to include students on a number of faculty committees. But on two committees, those on faculty policy and on academic freedom and tenure, the faculty declined to include any students. Student contributions have been more notable in the committees than in faculty meetings.

In addition to the regular committee structure, ad hoc committees were created from time to time. An important one was the committee on aims and objectives, set up in 1948, involving faculty, student, and administration participation. This committee drafted a statement of mission that was eventually incorporated in the 1954 catalogue. The committee then turned its attention to the problem of rapidly increasing enrollment and issued a report on this subject in 1957; it then disbanded.

The University of New Mexico was racked by a succession of crises in 1968–69 and again in 1969–70. In addition to issues of national policy, localized matters fueled conflict. Should the university remain in the same athletic conference with Brigham Young University? Then an allegedly obscene poem read in a freshman English class set off a statewide furor, including reduction in the university appropriation by the state legislature. At the time of the Kent State and Jackson State violence, the student union building was occupied by a group of demonstrators who were then ousted in accordance with a court order obtained by the regents. The building was cleared by law enforcement officers and a contingent of the National Guard; those refusing to leave were arrested. These events triggered more excitement and student protest.

108                              New Structures of Campus Power

The crisis in student conduct in 1969 persuaded the board of regents to establish a committee on university governance made up of nineteen persons: six faculty members, six students (four undergraduate and two graduate), four administrative officers, and three alumni. The board decided not to be represented on this committee but to reserve the right to review fully any of its recommendations. At the same time the board established a special council advisory to the president composed of faculty, students, administrators, and alumni to assist in maintaining law and order on campus.

The committee on university governance submitted a report in May 1971 with recommendations under five headings: creation of a university community council; (2) recognition of a student voice in curriculum matters and quality of instruction; (3) creation of a faculty senate; (4) establishment of a university ombudsman; and (5) a grievance and disciplinary procedure. These proposals generated a great deal of debate and some action. The plan for a faculty senate did not obtain the necessary two thirds vote of the faculty until late in 1975. The community council was changed to a university community forum before it was accepted. The creation of an ombudsman was approved, but a reorganization of grievance and disciplinary procedures had not been accomplished as of mid 1976. In March 1972 the board of regents also authorized faculty and student representation at its own meetings in an advisory capacity.

The idea of a university community council was acquired from Princeton University. The New Mexico concept was that the council would be a forum rather than a legislature; the council would not displace or supersede any existing bodies of governance such as the university faculty, the associated students, or the graduate student association. The council was to consider any issue of communitywide concern, to investigate, and to recommend solutions to component parts of the university. With a change of designation to "community forum" rather than "council," the proposal was approved in December 1971 by the university faculty and by the board of regents.

Initially, the forum was composed of 49 persons: nineteen members of the faculty (two ex officio and seventeen elected); fifteen undergraduate students (three ex officio and twelve elected);

four graduate students; two alumni; three elected staff members; and six administrative officers (the president, the academic vice-president, two other vice-presidents designated by the president, and two deans selected by all the deans). The president became the presiding officer. Election procedures were not spelled out but left to the discretion of the various constituencies involved. In October 1973 the forum informally requested that the regents name one or more members to become a part of the forum, but the regents were not inclined to accept the invitation.

The university community forum began to function in 1972, but interest in the arrangement had already begun to wane by that time. The administrative officers were more consistent in their attendance than any other members. A great deal of time was spent in developing operating procedures. For a while a steering committee endeavored to determine the agenda, but the committee was abolished in 1973. Any item requested by any member was then to be included on the agenda. This arrangement led to long and short agendas, with too many items on some occasions. The forum agreed to meet monthly and to require a majority of the total membership as a quorum. Of a total of some twenty-five meetings between early 1972 and June 1975, over half failed to obtain a quorum. In 1975 the quorum requirement was repealed. Attendance did not notably improve in 1975–76.

The forum utilized no standing committees. It was intended to be a place to articulate and debate issues. But the role was never realized as intended. The lack of authority vested in the forum and the failure to develop any close relationship with faculty, student, and administrative organs of decision making proved to be ingredients of failure rather than success. In its early history much discussion centered around the issue of university purpose, but the forum never reached any consensus on the subject and did not contribute any new ideas. Other issues involved size and composition of the student body, instructional program planning, instructional effectiveness, university finances, and student affairs (such as the desirability of coed dormitories). At one time, the forum considered the possibility of its becoming the center of long-range planning interest in the university, but this interest never eventuated in any concerted effort or any results.

In 1973 the board of regents created a committee on university planning, some of whose faculty membership served in the forum. The university forum appeared to acquiesce in this arrangement and tried to schedule some discussion of planning problems and planning progress reports. The report of the committee on university planning was distributed in the summer of 1975. During 1975–76 the university community forum provided no reasoned comment about the issues or proposals presented in this report.

The community forum did devote a good deal of attention to the subject of admission standards and to the obligations the university might have to young people in the Albuquerque metropolitan area. A consensus seemed to develop that the university ought to admit all high school graduates, even though resources were not sufficient for their instruction or their remedial assistance. A resolution was introduced at one meeting stating that no decision should be made on admission requirements without further study of the impact of such action upon the students and school districts of New Mexico. The motion was passed by a decided majority of those present, although the number was less than a quorum. This unofficial action was the only one taken by the forum in its history through 1975–76. The university faculty and the board of regents ignored this position in voting to reestablish course distribution requirements in high school as a condition of admission, with satisfactory American College Test (ACT) scores regarded as acceptable substitutes for specific course requirements.

The university community forum engaged in desultory debate about campus parking, prices charged by the campus bookstore, and relations of the university with the state legislature. The one specific assignment to the forum ended in failure. The forum was supposed to recommend three persons from whom the regents would choose an ombudsman for the university. The forum undertook the task of nomination but became involved in controversy about the status of the position, the role of the official, and the desirable qualifications. Eventually two names were sent to the board of regents, but neither was acceptable to the board. Additional names were not provided the board, and the board failed to create the position and to staff it.

A bizarre episode in February 1973 complicated university

life. The governor appointed a man to the board of regents who was opposed by Navajo students. The man was abducted at gunpoint by an Indian student leader, who then committed suicide rather than surrender to the police. Student reaction on campus was intense and emotional. The forum tried to deal both with the matter of procedure in selecting persons to be members of the board of regents and with the whole subject of the problems of Indian students on campus. Neither concern produced subsequent action.

The university community forum was created as a campus-wide governance arrangement in response to two pressures, one internal and one external. Acute campus crisis had placed severe strain upon existing mechanisms for dealing with situations that demanded prompt action. Because various situations focused upon him as crisis manager, the president felt the need for an agency bringing together various campus constituencies. An informal mechanism for providing information about a situation as seen by participants and for considering various options of action was an essential part of crisis management. It was hoped that these informal arrangements might give way to more formalized arrangements suitable for long-term governance. In addition, the University of New Mexico was aware that campus governance on other campuses was undergoing considerable change and experimentation. The university was disposed to join in the creation of new arrangements.

When measured against its expectations, the university community forum was generally considered by 1976 to have been a notable failure. The fact that the forum was superimposed upon existing structures and replaced none of them may have contributed to its dismal record. By the time the forum became operational, the critical conflicts arising from the spring of 1968 to the spring of 1972 had subsided. The forum was not called upon to assist in crisis management. In the changing circumstances occurring after the spring of 1972, the forum found it difficult to create a role for itself in the university community. Apart from the abortive effort to assist in the establishment of a university ombudsman, the forum had not by the summer of 1976 recommended and transmitted a single formal proposal for action to another body of the university. Because of the circumstances attending its creation, the president was not disposed to assert a leadership role for the forum. In the absence of his leadership, no other leadership emerged. A new president, who came into office on October 1, 1975, had other priorities and did not push to make the forum a viable agency of campus governance. By the summer of 1976 the university community forum at New Mexico was in a state of suspended animation and appeared to be quietly expiring.

## Tennessee State University

Founded in 1909 primarily as a teachers college for blacks and located in Nashville, Tennessee State University in 1972 became part of the newly created State University and Community College System of Tennessee. Comprising six state universities and ten state community colleges, the system is headed by a chancellor and a state board of regents. Prior to 1972 these institutions reported to the commissioner of education and the state board of education. The state university system was paralleled by the University of Tennessee system of five campuses, each reporting to a president and a board of trustees with headquarters in Knoxville.

The state board of regents was vested by law with the authority to govern and manage each of the institutions in the system. The board appointed each president and fixed the terms of his or her employment and the salary. The board confirmed the employment of other administrative personnel and the faculty, determined instructional programs, approved degree requirements, fixed the operating and capital budgets, established policies regarding campus life, and generally assumed responsibility for the operation of each campus.

Campuswide governance at Tennessee State accordingly had to conform to directives and policies, previously of the state board of education and more recently of the state board of regents. The peculiarities of Tennessee State arose primarily because of its historical role. From 1912 to 1922 the institution was designated the Agricultural and Industrial State Normal School for Negroes. From 1922 to 1927 it was known as the Agricultural and Industrial State Normal College; in 1927 the word *normal* was dropped from the title. In 1941 the General Assembly permitted an expansion of activity to the master's degree level and in 1951 changed the name to Tennessee Agricultural and Industrial State University. In 1958 the university was recognized as one of two Morrill Act land-grant universities in Tennessee, along with the University of Tennessee, Knoxville. The designation of Tennessee State University was adopted in 1969.

Prior to 1966 the authority of campus governance at Tennessee State rested for all practical purposes in the hands of the president. There was no representative faculty body. There was an elected student council, but its role in the decision-making process of the university was by no means clear. Between 1966 and 1969 two documents were drawn up and approved by the state board of education, recognizing a limited role for faculty and students in presenting recommended actions to the president. During these same years there was considerable student activism and some disruption on the Tennessee State campus. It became apparent by 1969 that some further action was desirable in order to encourage various constituent groups on the campus to develop a sense of participation in and commitment to university operations.

As a consequence, a formalized arrangement was drawn up providing for a faculty senate, a student government association, a staff senate, and a president's council. This pattern was developed in large part by the president, who succeeded in obtaining approval of it by the state board of regents. The structure did not provide for an interrelationship among these four bodies except as this might be accomplished in the person of the president. With some minor modifications, the organization as established in 1969 was still in operation as of 1976.

The faculty senate was established as a "broadly representative body" for the purpose of "securing effective participation of the university faculty in the activity and development of the university." The senate consisted of twenty-five elected faculty members, five academic deans (arts and sciences, agriculture and home economics, education, engineering, and graduate), the vice-president for academic affairs, and the president. The twenty-five faculty representatives were apportioned among the five schools and elected by the faculty members of each individual school. In order to serve on the faculty senate, a person had to be a full-time member of the university faculty with the rank of assistant professor or above and must have served three consecutive years or more on the faculty. All full-time faculty members in the rank of instructor and above were eligible to vote in these elections.

With the establishment of the faculty senate came a period of determining just what its role might be. In May 1973 the recommendations of a study committee were accepted by the senate. These recommendations recognized the "primary function" of the senate to be legislative and defined the senate jurisdiction as that of "matters of policy, procedure, and regulations directly concerned with instruction, research, and guidance of the faculty." The recommendations further directed that certain university committees should report to the faculty senate; these were committees on academic affairs, faculty personnel, curriculum and instruction, library, meritorious awards, and the lyceum program. Most of the actions of the senate were acceptable to the president, and a substantial stride forward in the development of faculty governance was then achieved at Tennessee State. Later the senate modified its standing committee structure to include committees on academic affairs, student affairs, faculty research and planning, grievances and university relations, constitution and bylaws, and budgetary involvement and fringe benefits. The faculty senate elected its own chairman and controlled its agenda through an executive committee.

A student council of administrators and students had existed at Tennessee State for a good many years prior to 1969. Nonetheless, substantial student unrest on the campus in 1967–68 involved, among other issues, the participation of students in university governance. The existing informal arrangements for such participation were breaking down, and students wanted definite and prompt action to change the paternalistic point of view of the university. After the assassination of Dr. Martin Luther King, Jr., on April 4, 1968, all regular campus activities came to a halt. Consultation between the president, faculty leaders, and student spokesmen led to the belief that a new structure for student government was needed. The student government association emerged as the representative body for all students, with fifteen members elected by classes (three each by freshmen, sophomore, junior, senior, and graduate students), plus a president and vice-president elected by universitywide student voting. In addition, a judiciary system was created that involved faculty, student, and administrative participation. A separate student union board of governors served in an advisory capacity to the director of the union building. There was also a staff senate which served as an advisory body on matters concerning nonacademic personnel and as a court of appeal on nonacademic personnel grievances. This senate consisted of eleven persons, ten elected by the staff and one appointed by the president.

The president's council included the four vice-presidents of the university: for academic affairs, fiscal affairs, student affairs, and development. It was this council that advised the president about recommendations on all university matters to be presented to the chancellor and the state board of regents. The president's council had ever to be mindful that Tennessee State was part of a state university system, that the governing board was concerned with a system of campuses and not just with one campus, and that the state government was in effect the court of last resort on all matters affecting the university. These considerations necessarily influenced the decisions of the president's council, and the council appeared to be more attuned to external pressures than either the faculty senate or the student government association.

Tennessee State has had its full complement of issues to be resolved by faculty, student, and administration effort: access to higher educational opportunity by blacks, remedial or developmental activities to overcome deficiencies of precollege education, the administration of student financial aid (with as many as 70 percent of all students receiving such assistance), the processing of student payrolls ahead of other disbursements, traffic control and parking, campus security, the use of alcoholic beverages, open visitation in dormitories, the quality and cost of food service, the cost of the athletic program—all of these concerns brought about substantial discussion and some action by the state board of regents. The faculty tended to believe that inadequate compensation was its primary complaint, followed by a feeling that the administration still did not give faculty decisions on academic affairs the weight they deserved. There was also faculty dissatisfaction with the instructional workload. Yet these complexities could be resolved only if more income was forthcoming from the State of Tennessee.

Conscious of its black heritage and of the fact that 90 per-

cent or more of the student body, faculty, administration, and staff
was composed of blacks, Tennessee State has been more concerned
in recent years with its external status than with internal arrangements of governance. The development of a branch of the University of Tennessee in Nashville established an additional state
university presence in the Nashville area. For several years the state
government and both university systems had been under a federal
court mandate to develop an integrated public higher education
structure in Nashville. It proved impossible to achieve any agreement about how this objective should be accomplished satisfactorily.
Early in 1977 the federal court ordered a merger of the two institutions. Issues of internal governance seemed of little moment alongside of this more far-reaching, and to many persons more threatening, circumstance. Since 1968 and the beginning of court action, the
Tennessee State community has found it essential to work together
in an effort to determine the conditions for its own survival. Campuswide governance was subordinated to the larger matter of the
future public higher education structure to operate in the Nashville
area of Tennessee.

## Emory

Emory College was established by the Georgia Conference of
the Methodist Episcopal Church in 1836 and located at Oxford,
Georgia. Emory was moved to Atlanta in 1915 and acquired a university charter that same year. The university remains affiliated with
the Southeastern Jurisdiction of the United Methodist Church,
whose Quadrennial Jurisdictional Conference has confirmed the
election of trustees of the university. The university has an enrollment of around 7,000 students, an endowment in book value of
around $150 million, and an annual budget of around $75 million.
In addition to its college of arts and sciences, the university includes
a school of medicine, a school of law, a school of theology, a school
of dentistry, a school of nursing, a school of business administration,
a graduate school, three instructional divisions, and a related research center. The Woodruff Medical Center includes two university-owned hospitals and a clinic.

The board of trustees is composed of thirty-three members;

three are nominees of the alumni association but all are formally selected by the board itself. Final decisions about the university, including the right to review any internal decision making, are prerogatives of the board. The president is the chief executive officer for the board. The administrative staff includes an executive vice-president and six other vice-presidents. In addition, there are nine academic deans and two directors of academic divisions. For many years the faculty met as a single body to hear various reports, but this practice ended in the 1960s. Since then the faculty of each of the separate schools and divisions has held its own meetings and has controlled its own affairs. A university senate was established in 1950. In outline, the governance structure of Emory University as of 1976 was largely a traditional one.

As authorized by the board of trustees in 1950, the university senate was created, subject to the powers vested in the president and the board, to "consider and to act upon all educational matters which concern the university as a whole or which affect more than one college of the university." Initially the senate was composed of twenty-seven members representing the various academic components of the university and twenty-six administrative officers serving ex officio. Subsequently, late in the 1950s, the senate was reorganized in order to reduce its size to seventeen members; twelve were faculty members, one was a librarian, and four were administrative officers including the president and two vice-presidents ex officio. Of some twenty-one committees, fourteen were designated as committees reporting to the president and seven as committees reporting to the senate. A 1962 self-study of the university described the senate as the central deliberative body of the university but also reported that its prestige was not high. The major problem was identified as a lack of power; the implication seemed to be that power resided in the president and board, and nothing was said about the power residing in the individual faculties.

A new president as of 1963 endeavored to make the senate a more important agency in the university decision-making process, encouraging its more active consideration of issues prior to their presentation to the board of trustees. For a time he also encouraged the senate to meet with the entire faculty and to respond to questions. This last practice proved to be of little utility. In November

1968 the student government association passed a resolution recommending reorganization of the university senate with representation of faculty, students, and deans. In 1969 the senate added students to its various committees and invited a new class of "delegates" to participate in all discussions but without the right to vote. The delegates would include three nontenured faculty members, three students, and one teaching assistant. In addition, the senate created a committee on university governance to study desirable changes in structure and process.

The committee on university governance reported in April 1970, making it clear that, because of time pressures, it had concentrated its attention upon the structure of the university senate and had not considered the structure of the board of trustees or of the administration of the university. The committee recommended a reconstituted university senate with faculty members, students, professional staff representatives, alumni, and one member of the board of trustees. The total membership was to be thirty-four persons: seventeen elected faculty members; nine elected students; five special members (one librarian, two from the Employee Relations Council, and two alumni); and three ex officio (the president, a vice-president, and president of the student government association). Both the faculty representatives and the student representatives were to be elected from academic units of the university.

Although there was some criticism of the committee report, the new structure was approved by the university senate, the president, and the board of trustees effective in January 1971. There was some fear that the restructuring would emphasize political and social issues above academic matters, while others observed that the senate remained only an advisory body. The bylaws of the university specified that the university senate should consider and make recommendations concerning all matters of general university interest, as distinguished from those affecting a single school. The senate might consider matters referred to it by the president or the board of trustees or submit recommendations of its own initiative to the president.

In practice, decisions of the university senate, with the approval of the president, were considered to be final, unless or until the board of trustees took other action. When the president disapproved senate action, the subject was reviewed by the board of trustees or by the board's executive committee, which made the final determination. The chairman of the senate presented the senate's case to the board. A liaison committee of the senate, made up of the chairman of the senate, three faculty members, and two students, endeavored to build a close working relationship between the senate and the president. The president consulted this committee about agenda items to be presented to the board of trustees. And on occasion the board had met with the entire committee. Five faculty members of the university senate constituted the committee on faculty relationships, which reviewed personnel procedures and policies of each school and served as an appeals body in cases of termination of an appointment.

A university faculty advisory council was also established in November 1970; it was composed of all faculty members in the university senate plus eight additional faculty members appointed by the president. This council made recommendations to the president about the "academic affairs" of the university. Some members of the university community considered the council to be a mechanism for circumventing the university senate, while others considered the arrangement appropriate for handling issues of primary concern to the faculty. There was some ambiguity in determining the respective jurisdictions of the senate and the council. On occasions the same matters were considered by both bodies.

In the years since 1970 the major gap between expectation and performance in the work of the university senate has been in the area of long-range financial planning, budget priorities, and the allocation of income resources. These issues, of course, have occupied a great deal of attention, but the academic community appears to believe that the role of the senate has been less than effective. The budget timetable and the budget process are such that senate participation in any meaningful way has been lacking. A proposal in 1973 to create a faculty budget committee of the faculty advisory council was defeated. The president and other administrative officers did begin to discuss budget problems informally with the liaison committee of the senate, with the council, and with student leaders. The flow of budgetary information within the university substantially increased. But the university senate and the faculty advisory council continued to through 1976 find little that they were prepared to undertake to perform in connection with budget decisions.

For seventeen years preceding 1974, not a single classroom building or laboratory had been added to the campus for the arts and sciences. The Emory endowment had been largely held in common stocks with a relatively modest income yield. In 1974 and 1975, considerable attention was given to investment policies and performance, but the board of trustees considered such to be in its own decisional jurisdiction. Tuition charges doubled in many of the schools between 1965 and 1975, from $1,400 to over $2,800 per year. As a consequence there was a substantial concern that student enrollment could not be maintained. The student financial aid resources of the university were not considered adequate, especially for undergraduate students. The university senate, the faculty advisory council, and other bodies called attention to the need for more student financial aid but were not able to offer any practical advice about how to obtain the desired resources.

The level of faculty salaries at Emory was discussed frequently in the university senate and in the faculty advisory council. In order to achieve a balanced budget, faculty salaries were frozen during 1971–72. Since then salaries have been increased, but at less than the rate of inflation. Bodies within the university community have wanted increased salaries from endowment and gift income rather than from increases in tuition charges. Yet, here again, the sense of need was not matched by a corresponding sense of means to achieve the desired end. Emory University was slow to expand instructional or other output programs for fear that the resources to do so would have to be obtained from existing programs.

In the management of the central services of the university, the university senate and the faculty advisory council were mostly preoccupied with library matters and with plant operation. Faculty members tended to believe that library expenditures were inadequate. Faculty members in the arts and sciences were concerned about the adequacy of the instructional and research facilities, while students were concerned about the adequacy of university housing. No new residence halls had been constructed since 1962, and existing facilities were both old and not adapted to the changing lifestyles of students.

Since 1970 the most active area of university senate policy making has been that of student and faculty behavior. The president in 1963 delegated universitywide authority for the formulation of regulations on student conduct to the university senate. In 1965 a general code of conduct was adopted that was applicable to all schools of the university. This code was quite broad in its terms, calling for students to observe high standards of courtesy, integrity, and responsibility in all personal relationships within the university. Conflict arose about the interpretation of the meaning of "high standards": If a woman student became pregnant, what was the appropriate university action, if any? What about the use of alcohol on campus? What about women visitors to men's dormitories? In 1968 and 1969 the senate endeavored to write a more detailed code of conduct but was unable to agree upon the desired provisions.

In 1970 Emory experienced some campus disorder, including disruption of ROTC classes. These events increased the pressure for a new code of conduct. This time the administration prepared a general document, entitled "Student Conduct Standards and Procedural Guidelines," which was approved by the board of trustees and transmitted to each school with instructions to prepare their own more detailed codes. Each school proceeded to do so, and these were approved by the board in March 1971. Thus the administration and the various deans took over authority for handling student conduct. The faculty representatives appeared more relieved than upset by this development.

The most extended student demonstration at Emory arose in May 1969. In March the Black Student Alliance of one hundred black students presented a list of proposals to the president. These proposals involved creation of a black studies program, increased recruitment of black students, and employment of black faculty members and administrators. In May, while discussion of these proposals was still under way, black students interrupted a Sunday worship service on campus and then, with white students, blocked access to a university cafeteria. Further demonstrations occurred the next day at the cafeteria. The president and the board chairman then asked for a court restraining order, and considerable campus reaction followed. The conflict was resolved by withdrawal of the restraining order, by a commitment to eradicate racism at the uni-

versity, and a pledge that any demonstrations in the future would
be nonviolent and nondisruptive. Eventually, in 1970, the board of
trustees enacted a statement on freedom of expression and a strict
injunction that dissent must be orderly and peaceful.

In 1973 the board of trustees reaffirmed the Christian principles and church relationship of Emory, declared that admission
must be nondiscriminatory, ordered that students be dismissed only
with due process, asserted the right of students to participate in the
development of rules and regulations pertaining to their conduct,
and repeated the general standards of conduct expected of all students. Membership in student organizations was left to the determination of the organizations themselves. Some modification of this
position became necessary with the enforcement of the nondiscrimination provisions of the Education Amendments of 1972 of the
federal government.

As far as faculty rights and academic freedom were concerned, there was very little conflict between the faculty, the university senate, the president, and the board of trustees. In the mid
1960s there was considerable controversy about the alleged "heresy"
of a member of the theology faculty. The president and the chairman of the board of trustees issued statements about the importance
of academic freedom, the university senate enacted resolutions of
appreciation for the stand taken, and eventually the conflict appeared to die out. In 1969 the university senate refused to take a
position on the Vietnam war on the grounds that the issue was not
one directly affecting the educational program, the community, or
the immediate environment of the university. The university senate
and the faculty advisory council have been much concerned about
the extent of tenured status within the faculty but have devised no
alternative line of action. The board of trustees has declared it will
not impose any tenure quotas upon schools or departments.

The experience in campuswide governance at Emory University has been conditioned by the realities of a privately sponsored
institution struggling to achieve educational distinction within a re-
gion and a metropolitan area undergoing rapid change. In this
environment the board of trustees has played a major role. Neither
faculty nor students have been able to devise an alternative to the

board's role that would ensure survival and effectiveness for the university.

## Howard

Founded by an Act of Congress in 1876, Howard University was in large part the idea of General Otis Howard, commissioner of the Freedman's Bureau, who with his colleagues desired to establish an educational institution for newly emancipated slaves. Although officially classified as a "private" or "independent" university, Howard throughout its history has depended in large part upon an annual subsidy from the Congress of the United States. Located in the District of Columbia, Howard has always envisaged its mission as national in scope, as providing an educated national leadership for blacks and for the nation. Predominantly black in its student enrollment, Howard has in the past numbered the most distinguished black citizens of America among its alumni.

Howard University is made up of thirteen schools and colleges, including liberal arts, medicine, pharmacy, religion, dentistry, law, engineering, allied health services, and business administration. Its graduate program extends through the Ph.D. degree. With an enrollment of around 10,000 students, Howard has a faculty of some 1,300 persons, an administraive and operating staff of some 2,500 persons, and an operating budget of over $75 million. About one third of the total income is derived from a federal government subsidy.

The board of trustees of Howard University consists of twenty-seven members who are self-perpetuating in that they elect their own members. Board members normally serve three-year terms; in recent years it has been customary to elect to the board two students, who serve one-year terms, and two faculty members, who serve three-year terms. As is customary, the authority of government in the university was vested in the board.

Howard University is unique among the colleges and universities included in this study in its lack of any effort to construct an agency of campuswide governance based upon representation from multiple constituencies. Rather, when changes in the traditional structure of the university were undertaken during the 1960s, they moved in two directions. The addition of two students and of two faculty members to the board of trustees, a change accomplished within the ongoing structure of the university, was considered in effect to have added representatives of the student body and of the faculty to the top agency of governance within the university. The board of trustees thus became an instrumentality for campuswide governance. The second direction of change was to establish an advisory council of students and faculty members for each of the five vice-presidents of the university.

The president of Howard is assisted in the performance of his authority and responsibility by five vice-presidents: one each for academic affairs, health affairs, student affairs, business and fiscal affairs, and administration. Each of these vice-presidents is directed to establish an advisory council made up in equal numbers of administrative associates, faculty members, and students. The faculty members are nominated by the deans of the various schools; one from each school serves on each council. The student members are selected by the student councils as organized in each school. The advisory councils are expected to meet at least three times a year; they may meet more frequently upon call of a vice-president. The minutes of each council meeting are to be available for examination.

The vice-presidents are expected to discuss major issues of program and of policy with their advisory councils. The members are free to bring up any subject of concern. The record reveals that the councils have been quite active in recent years and have given some attention to almost all concerns of the university. It appears that the two most active councils were those for academic affairs and student affairs.

The minutes of the advisory council on academic affairs indicate that in recent years the council has considered new requirements for the bachelor of science in engineering, a new academic program in social work, a program of faculty awards and development, a new curriculum in architecture and planning, means for improving the library program, expansion of the Center for Academic Reinforcement (to improve verbal, quantitative, and study skills), the establishment of a social science research center, and the establishment of a center for the study of handicapped children. Among the policy issues receiving council attention are rules about incomplete grades, standards for admission, rules governing registration procedures, the fee structure for excess student course enrollments, factors influencing faculty preparation of grant proposals to be submitted to federal government agencies, faculty evaluation under student auspices, the scheduling of classes, and academic retention standards. All of these items have received careful consideration and it is evident that council advice tends to determine the recommendations submitted by the vice-president to the president.

The vice-president for health affairs has authority to supervise activities of four colleges (medicine, dentistry, pharmacy, and allied health sciences), the School of Nursing, the university hospital, and the university health service. In addition to the deans and a faculty and student representative from each college and school, the advisory council on health affairs includes the medical director of the hospital, the director of the university health service, and the president of the medical-dental staff of the hospital. A major concern of the advisory council has been the planning and operation of the new university hospital, completed in 1975. Other major program issues have involved the quality of service and the staff needs of the health service, a proposal for an animal farm, a proposal for a cancer institute, revision of the curriculum in pharmacy, review of the curriculum in dentistry, discussion of the desirability of an associate degree program in nursing, and creation of a new college of allied health services. Among the policy issues requiring a good deal of attention from the council on health affairs have been the extent of the university commitment to health care for students, the transportation of sick students, financial support of the health service, the desirability of professional liability insurance, and the scope of university housing, dormitory restrictions, and the privacy of student records.

The work of the vice-president for business and fiscal affairs is reviewed by the advisory council on budget and auxiliary services. This council consists of the dean, one faculty member, and one student from each academic division of the university. Council discussions tend to concentrate on the quality and cost of food service, the scope of bookstore operations, the crisis in fuel supply and energy costs, and the university budget system. The policy problems considered by the council involve the need for auxiliary enterprises to be self-supporting, the over- and understocking of textbooks, the location of book stores, the demand for larger and better portions of food, the desirability of a semester meal plan, the health standards of food service, the adequate maintenance and cleanliness of buildings, heating standards, increased theft of university property and supplies, salaries of technical and crafts personnel, needed improvements in personal security, and possible reductions in energy demands. In recent years both faculty and student members have wanted more information about the university budget system and process. A great deal of time therefore has been devoted to budget information.

The vice-president for administration presides over an advisory council on administration services, which includes the directors of various services (computer service, institutional research, security service, personnel management, building program development, and the auditorium) and a faculty and student representative from each college and school. The problems of the council involve mostly issues about the scope and cost of the various services, personnel requirements and standards, campus parking, use of the auditorium, affirmative action requirements, campus lighting, and the relationship of campus security officers to city police officers.

It is obvious that the five councils within Howard University serve a dual purpose: to ensure participation by faculty and students in the consideration of the various programs and policy positions of the university and to provide extensive information about the university to faculty and student representatives. On the one hand, the arrangement provides fairly extensive opportunity for faculty members and students to become involved in universitywide affairs. On the other hand, the arrangement tends to separate programs and policies into five fairly discrete categories or groupings. The interrelationship of all programs and policies has to be accomplished by the president and by the board of trustees. The president is guided in his decision making by recommendations from the five vice-presidents, who endeavor to achieve some consensus among the academic constituents of the university (deans, faculty representatives, and student representatives). In turn, it is apparent that the board of trustees is expected to ratify all major decisions within the university.

Howard University experienced only limited student disruption during the period from 1968 to 1970. The most critical situation arose at the time of the assassination of Martin Luther King, Jr., in April 1968. The riots that destroyed extensive property within certain areas of the District of Columbia were largely kept away from the campus itself.

Howard University's dependence on annual appropriations from the Congress serves as a continuing reminder to board, administration, faculty, staff, and students that the university can prosper only as it obtains that support. The governance of Howard University is performed under the continuing scrutiny of the media of mass communication and the elected representatives of the nation located in the District of Columbia.

## Syracuse

Syracuse University was founded in Syracuse, New York, in 1870 under the auspices of the Methodist Episcopal Church, North. In recent years, the university has been caught between the aspiration to be a university of regional and national recognition and the reality of the needs of a large urban area for higher education service. Limitations of financial support from a relatively small endowment and from relatively modest annual gifts have compelled the university to give more attention to the metropolitan community than might otherwise have been the case. And in the course of events the university has found it useful to assert its nonsectarian status, even though the resident United Methodist bishop of the Syracuse area continues ex officio to be a member of the board of trustees.

With a total enrollment of around 15,000 full-time and part-time students, with an operating budget of around $85 million, and with a wide variety of instructional programs, Syracuse University has endeavored to achieve distinctive scholarship and professional competence in such diverse fields as education, engineering, architecture, business, law, public affairs, music, library science, and nursing. A medical school was transferred to the State University of New York in the 1950s. Perhaps internal uncertainty about basic purpose helped to provide the university with a unique experience in governance during the 1960s.

As an independent, nonsectarian institution, Syracuse University is governed by a board of trustees of sixty-eight persons. This board includes twenty-eight self-perpetuating voting members serving six-year terms; another twenty individuals were designated as nonvoting life members; and two ex officio and eight nonvoting honorary members, including the chancellor of the university, the governor of New York, the mayor of Syracuse, the resident bishop of the United Methodist Church, and certain additional public officials. The board asserts an active interest in the university and is disposed to insist that, through its chief executive officer, who is the chancellor, it should exercise a pervasive authority in decision making.

Syracuse University experienced considerable turmoil in the years after 1966. Both the nature of the university and its structure of governance came under serious attack. As elsewhere, national political and social issues had much to do with the extent of student and faculty activism at Syracuse, but these issues served to encourage an introspection about the university and its operation. As a consequence, campus governance was given careful and lengthy scrutiny. For a time a kind of student-faculty coalition in favor of "democratic self-government" emerged; after 1974 faculty self-interest reappeared as a dominant factor in university affairs.

For some 27 years, from 1942 to 1969, Syracuse University had been led by a single individual as chancellor, William P. Tolley. Although criticized for his paternalistic attitude toward faculty and students and his "old school" educational philosophy, Tolley was also widely admired as the institutional leader who had built Syracuse into a university of national visibility. Tolley was well known for his "hip pocket" style of management; he carried within himself an amazing array of detail about the personnel and the finances of the university. A clergyman by background, Chancellor Tolley took pride in his informal relationships with faculty members and students. Every autumn for many years the chancellor invited a select group of student leaders to a retreat in the Adirondacks. Here frank and full discussion took place between administrative officers and students about the affairs of the university. At the same time a kind of ethos was developed about the role of the Syracuse student.

Nominally, faculty interest in the university was expressed

through the faculty senate, a body comprising 180 representatives of the faculty with the rank of instructor and above. The committee structure of the senate was revised in 1953 to provide for nine standing committees: agenda, instruction, research, appointments, promotions and salaries, library, students, faculty, and academic planning. The agenda committee sought to oversee the work of the senate and nominated the individuals to serve on all committees. Its chairman was considered to be one of the most influential faculty members. Although the work of the senate was performed within the various committees and although the faculty elected all members of the committees, the relationship between the committees and the administrative officers of the university was close and generally cordial. The principal issue addressed by the senate in the early 1960s was the question of comparability of Syracuse faculty salaries with those at other major universities. Educational development was largely the province of individual faculty departments and chairmen. Indeed, one senior faculty observer noted that the genius of campus governance at Syracuse during the Tolley years was the absence of any campuswide governance or planning.

Then, in 1965, circumstances began to change. The social climate for students perhaps had lagged behind developments elsewhere. Suddenly, football weekends, fraternity and sorority social activity, and beauty-queen contests disappeared from the center of campus interest. A new student generation brought with it a new life-style. In April 1965 the student newspaper published a series of highly critical "letters to Dr. Tolley." A study of the control of alcohol on campus had been sidetracked in 1964, and the university continued to insist upon its right to dismiss a student because of "unbecoming" conduct. These and related issues provided fuel for criticism. Suddenly the chancellor found himself out of touch with students and with a considerable number of younger faculty members. "Teach-ins" to consider the state of the world quickly became teach-ins to consider the state of Syracuse University.

In 1967 the president of the student government association publicly drank beer at a dormitory party in the presence of the dean of men. The student court refused to act in the case, claiming that a student senate "bill" on possession and use of alcoholic beverages was the legitimate regulation of the university rather than that of the administration. When the dean of men took disciplinary action on his own authority, the battle lines were drawn. The board of trustees set up a committee on student affairs, and from this effort emerged a new council on student life with representatives from the faculty, student body, and administration. But it soon became apparent that the council was simply an advisory body to the chancellor. Efforts of the faculty senate to become involved with student affairs were resisted by the chancellor. Students began to attend meetings of the faculty senate and then to demand participation in senate meetings. In 1967 a resolution was introduced to deny academic credit for ROTC courses.

Beginning with the academic year 1967–68, student and faculty activism gained ground. Student dissatisfaction was voiced about tuition increases, the failure to liberalize social conduct rules, and the quality of food service. By March 1968, student antiwar protests were numerous and vociferous. The crescendo of criticism reached still further volume in 1968–69. Chancellor Tolley decided to retire in 1969 rather than in 1970, and a joint faculty-student-trustee committee was named to assist in finding a successor. In the meantime, black students began to express their dissatisfaction with their life at Syracuse. An ad hoc committee of the faculty senate presented a report in March 1969 advocating "meaningful campuswide participation" in university decision making. The report proposed that the 180-member faculty senate become a university senate of ninety faculty members, forty-five students, and forty-five administrative and staff officers. The committee asserted that the student protest on campus was not the work of a destructive, misguided small minority but rather was an expression of widespread and justifiable dissatisfaction with the university. Almost simultaneously the faculty senate voted to abolish academic credit for ROTC courses and to ban military drill from the campus. And the action of the council on student life to permit dormitories to determine their own rules was disapproved by the chancellor. A two-day "April revolution" followed, in which faculty members joined students in demanding a "new" university. A boycott of classes was ended when various actions were taken by the administration to meet accumulated grievances, including approval of dormitory autonomy in setting rules about access and visitation. By the end of the summer of 1969 students had played a major role in the selection of Chancellor Tolley's successor, had achieved representation in the faculty senate, had obtained control over the allocation of a part of the university fee, and had forced abandonment of almost all university restrictions on social conduct.

With a new chancellor in office, with student members added to the faculty senate (now in fact a university senate), and with the dormitories free to set their own social rules, the academic year of 1969–70 opened with the promise of an end to campus strife. It was not to be so. The issues of ROTC and racial discontent were still at hand. A student group called for investigation of the Syracuse University Research Corporation. Another student group wanted the provision of birth control and gynecological services from the student health service. On February 19, 1970, the new chancellor announced that he had intervened in the ROTC controversy and had decided to create a new academic division under which ROTC courses would continue to receive academic credit. The next day the student government president led a student occupation of the administration building. Meetings and forums were held across the campus. Various proposals were put forth for further changes in campus governance. A campus referendum on March 6 revealed a student majority in favor of a transfer of trustee power to a governance structure to be devised by a constitutional convention; a faculty majority endorsed the addition of faculty and student members to the board of trustees. The senate then established an ad hoc committee on governance, which in turn called for the convening of an assembly on university governance in the autumn of 1970.

After further demonstrations, the idea of an assembly on university governance was accepted and began to function in 1970–71. For two years this assembly heatedly debated all areas of university policy and considered various proposals for restructuring the governance of the university. In 1970–71 the university senate met almost weekly and enacted various "radical" reforms, some of which, with modifications, were accepted by the chancellor. There was also a bitter dispute in the autumn of 1970 about black athletes on the football team. Then in the spring of 1971 the chancellor announced his departure from the university to become president of the University of Illinois. The vice-chancellor for academic affairs and a former prominent faculty leader became acting chancellor and then chancellor. The university senate continued to put forth its own ideas about university governance while the assembly on governance continued to meet. In the meantime, financial stringency emerged as the foremost problem of the university and the new chancellor necessarily began a number of actions designed to reduce the budget deficit. In November of 1971, a freeze on all employment was announced, and efforts were started to increase enrollment. While extensive informal consultation preceded these decisions, the formal machinery of governance was largely ignored.

As the academic year 1971–72 proceeded, the work of the governance assembly began to occupy more and more campus attention. The new chancellor made it clear that he would not support a university council on any basis other than advisory. A proposal to restrict the autonomy of schools and colleges in academic governance and management sparked new controversy. Student activism continued high, including occupation of the administration building again in April 1972. Student demands included clarification of housing policies for undergraduate and graduate students, the establishment of coed housing alternatives, clarification of the dormitory autonomy concept, restoration of previous budget levels for Afro-American studies, the inclusion of students on the affirmative action committee, and disaffiliation of the Syracuse University Research Corporation.

The work of the assembly on university governance was completed in June 1972. The assembly had seen as its objective some check upon executive power, as represented by the chancellor and the board of trustees, in the name of "the governed." The political theorists in the assembly envisaged a shifting away from a corporate/hierarchical model of governance toward a mixed structure of shared power with a campus representative democracy. The goals committee of the assembly encountered unending difficulty in trying to arrive at a consensus on university goals and purposes. After lengthy debate, the initial report of the committee proposed that the university should be a democratically governed community in which individuals could develop "enlightened social and personal values." The university had an obligation to prepare its members "for significant participation in any society" and to challenge the values of society. This report was attacked as a "flowery essay" about moral authority that taught, in effect, that there were no moral standards. The goals statement that finally emerged as the preamble to the governance proposal began by asserting the "pursuit of knowledge" as the major purpose of the university, but it went on to endorse a governance process by which "authority to make decisions derives from the consent of the members of the community."

In the discussion of the structure of the university, the assembly appeared to accept the legal and financial power of the board of trustees but tended to be critical of the board for its lack of initiative in augmenting the financial resources of the university. The budgetary process was criticized as too secretive and too highly concentrated in the hands of the administration. The assembly early became committed to the idea of a university governing council, representative of faculty and students. Conflict arose about the status and structure of this council. At one time a committee called for all "legislative power" to be vested in it, and for the chancellor to be selected by it and accountable only to it. The proposal was deemed idealistic and unworkable by the assembly as a whole. In the end, the proposed university governing council was given powers to determine policy and legislate on all matters concerning the university, but the chancellor was given the power of veto, to be overridden only by a two thirds vote. The right of the board of trustees to take "final action" after the action of the governing council was to be limited to: (1) the amount of the budget; (2) investments; (3) physical assets; and (4) the endowment. The budget process was specified in some detail. The chancellor would prepare an annual operating budget in consultation with a university governing council committee. He would then submit the budget formally to the council, which could adopt any amendments and then transmit its decision directly to the board of trustees. The assembly rejected any suggestion of adding faculty and student members to the board on the grounds that the board should not become an "action group."

As far as the structure of the university governing council was concerned, the council was to be composed of one hundred members: forty-five faculty members, forty-five students, and ten staff representatives. The faculty-student parity in representation was included at the insistence of student members of the assembly over substantial faculty misgivings. All faculty and student representatives were to be elected by their respective colleges or schools. Each college and school would have at least one faculty and one student representative, and the additional members were to be apportioned according to the number of faculty and of students. The council was to have an executive committee and four standing committees: academic affairs, administrative operations, student affairs, and university relations. The chancellor was to be selected by a procedure to be mutually agreed upon by the board of trustees and the council, but vice-chancellors could be appointed by the chancellor only with the advice of the standing committees and the consent of the council. The charter declared that the faculty and students of each college or school should retain jurisdiction over the "internal affairs" of each unit, but that any decisions might be overruled by the university governing council.

The governance proposal also called for creation of the office of an ombudsman, a judicial system, an elections commission, periodic review of the governance structure, initiative and referendum on governance structure, and a guarantee of academic freedom. In order to become effective, the change of governance would require the approval of a simple majority in each of three constituencies: of students, of faculty, and of the board of trustees. A negative vote by any one of the three groups could prevent adoption of the new instrument of governance.

When the plebiscites were held early in October 1972, the student body in a slim turnout approved the charter by a vote of 2,208 to 672; the faculty disapproved the charter by a vote of 364 to 149; and the trustees rejected the charter unanimously. The Syracuse University experiment in constitutional drafting for internal democracy thus came to an end.

After the autumn of 1972 the university settled back into the mold of the "advisory participation/executive model" advocated by the chancellor. Although many faculty members have continued to assert that it would be a mistake to view the university as a hierarchical corporation, they have appeared to be equally opposed to any idea that the university can be governed as a representative democracy. The chancellor has continued to emphasize openness, communication, and meaningful participation in university decision making on an advisory basis. The university senate has continued to function with faculty and student participation. Various changes have been made in academic policies involving grading, women's studies, curriculum changes, and independent study. The Syracuse University Research Corporation was disaffiliated from the university under a phaseout decision of the board of trustees in 1973. A review of graduate programs has also been undertaken, but it became clear in a short time that the senate would not be able to agree on particular programs to be terminated. The administration has developed a close working relationship with the senate's committee on budget and finance. In 1971 an office of institutional research was created which has continued to provide data about enrollment trends, financial circumstances, and general management performance. But universitywide discussions of zero-based budgeting and income-based budgeting are rare. Conflict about student-conduct regulations had largely disappeared by 1976, because the regulations themselves had largely disappeared. Some conflict remains about the control of funds for student organizations and activities. The student newspaper has separated from the university after a libel suit was filed against the paper, and some difficulty has arisen about the showing of pornographic films by student organizations. Student interest in the financial affairs of the university focuses on tuition charges, health services, and student activities.

Participation and advice have become the basic ingredients of campuswide governance at Syracuse University. The structure and the process appeared to be functioning with reasonable satisfaction in a vastly changed environment as of 1976. There are still some conflicts, and very real fears about the future have emerged about enrollment and income reduction, with attendant requirements of university retrenchment and academic redirection. It appears uncertain whether or not the university senate can or will have a role in making the hard decisions that lie ahead.

## Roosevelt

Roosevelt University is an independent, nonsectarian, coeducational institution located primarily in downtown Chicago and

serving the Chicago metropolitan community. With an enrollment
of 7,500 students and an operating budget of $12 million, the uni-
versity includes five colleges (arts and sciences, business administration, education, music, and continuing education) and graduate
programs through the master's degree. Roosevelt evolved from the
Central YMCA College of Chicago and was founded in April 1945
largely through the determination and courage of its first president,
Edward J. Sparling.

Sparling had been president of the Central YMCA College
but resigned precipitately because of a conflict with the board of
trustees about academic freedom and nondiscrimination in the admission of students. Supported by some faculty and a small inter-
racial board, Sparling determined to create an institution that was
militantly and unabashedly egalitarian and democratic. Originally
intending to designate the institution Thomas Jefferson College,
Sparling and the board changed the name to Roosevelt University
after the death of Franklin D. Roosevelt on April 12, 1945. The university was avowedly integrationist. It began instruction in September 1945 with 1,300 students and temporary facilities. The university had no endowment and depended on student tuition for
operating income, including rent and debt service on any available
facilities. In its second year the university purchased and occupied
the historic Auditorium Building at Congress Street and Michigan
Avenue.

Campuswide participation in the governance of the university was encouraged by Sparling and became an important part
of the institution's ethos. Sparling recommended that there be
faculty members on the governing board, and eventually it was
agreed that 25 percent of the board membership should be faculty-
elected representatives. The faculty of the university rejected the
idea of majority membership because the board was expected to be
concerned with fund raising. Other board members became self-
perpetuating; all served for three year terms.

At the outset of the university in 1945, the faculty met as a
body in town-meeting style. "The Faculty" was presided over by an
elected chairman rather than by the president. All full-time and
part-time faculty members were voting members of The Faculty, as
were almost all members of the professional and administrative staff.

Two students participated in meetings but without a vote. It was decided that while the president and the deans would be appointed by the board, they should be confirmed by a two thirds vote of The Faculty and should submit to a vote of confidence every three years. Department chairmen would be elected by the executive committee of each college. A grievance procedure was established for both faculty and students. The concern for constitutional perfection that characterized Roosevelt in 1945 has remained a characteristic of the institution as of 1976. Many hours have been spent in debating details of university governance.

In 1943 a senate was established to supersede The Faculty, which nonetheless continued as a whole to conduct triennial votes of confidence and to vote on referenda concerning constitutional amendments. By 1966 votes of confirmation in the selection of the president and deans were abolished. For a time, additional faculty members were added to the board as its membership increased. When the board of trustees expanded to forty members, however, faculty representation remained fixed at seven. A budget committee was established in 1951 consisting initially of six faculty members elected by the senate and six administrative officers, including the president as chairman. This committee reported directly to the board. Although the president retained for himself the right to submit a minority report to the board, in practice the reports almost always have been unanimous. Created when a budget crisis confronted the university as veterans' enrollment declined, the budget committee has continued to function through the years and has become one of the most powerful bodies within the university.

As of 1976 the senate of Roosevelt University consisted of eighty-nine persons: sixty-nine faculty members elected by their respective academic departments, one person elected by the library staff, one person elected by the administrative staff who are voting members of The Faculty, one person elected by administrative associate members of The Faculty, two students and fifteen administrative officers ex officio (the president, nine deans, the treasurer, the librarian, and three others). The senate meets monthly. Initially, agenda were prepared by the president in consultation with the chairman and the deans. In recent practice, agenda items are submitted to the president's office by the senate chairman and placed

on the agenda without exception. Every monthly meeting begins with
a report from the president, followed by questions. The next item
is a report from the faculty members of the board of trustees. After
these reports come the items from standing committees.

The standing committees of the senate include an executive
committee, a graduate council, a student activities board, the student senate, the academic conference, and committees on curriculum, budget, planning, and faculty tenure review. This last committee, established in 1975, serves as a grievance committee on issues
involving tenure denial when violations of academic freedom or of
due process were alleged. The student activities board reviews matters concerning student organizations. A report from the student
senate was included at student request as a means whereby the student senate could obtain faculty attention. The academic conference, composed of academic deans and student personnel administrators, serves to integrate academic and student concerns.

The senate acts without challenge on curricular and academic matters affecting more than one college. It can propose
amendments to the constitution of the university, but these have to
be ratified by the board of trustees. On some other matters it is
recognized that the senate's action is simply advisory to the administration, as in its recent recommendation in favor of an extension
of fringe benefits to the survivors of deceased faculty members. On
occasion there are disagreements between the senate and the administration about the need for senate action on some issue or, if action
is taken, whether or not it is binding.

Roosevelt University has been proud of its actions to achieve
racial and ethnic integration within the academic community, although this stance gave the university an undeserved image of political radicalism in its early years. When the University of Illinois
opened its Chicago Circle campus in 1965 and thus presented the
question whether or not there was a continuing market for Roosevelt University's services, the university senate had to struggle with
the question of the basic purpose of the university. A new president
(as of 1965), a consulting group named by the chairman of the
board, and a senate committee all sought to find a satisfactory
answer to the question of mission. In addition to an integrated academic community, the statement of mission eventually accepted

within the university spoke of research and scholarship, public service, and—although emphasis was placed on education for economic and social mobility—a liberal education for its own sake. The planning committee of the senate found a broad formulation of purpose, including traditional as well as emerging functions, as the most acceptable to a large proportion of the faculty.

Within the context of this statement of mission, the committees of the university senate sought to ensure that programs undertaken by the university had objectives compatible with basic purpose. One major issue arose in 1967 in the decision to offer a new program leading to the degree of bachelor of general studies. In this program student competencies rather than units of course credit were to be the primary basis for award of the degree. The program became the first nontraditional adult degree program in the Chicago area and one of the first in the United States. In 1971 extensive debate was devoted to the issue whether or not to reconstitute the department of education as a College of Education. After four months of discussion the proposal was approved by a referendum vote of The Faculty, required on constitutional matters when the senate was closely divided, and was then ratified by the board of trustees.

A new president in 1965 inherited a large accumulated deficit. Under instructions from the board to eliminate this deficit, the president proposed a three-point effort: (1) increased fund raising, (2) tighter control of expenditures, and (3) more conservative budget making. The third part of this endeavor proved especially difficult to implement. The president decided that a major difficulty was the composition of the budget committee, especially with its membership of the various deans. The planning committee of the senate was asked to study the issue, and the committee recommended a budget committee of six rather than twelve members: three elected faculty members and three administrators—the president, the dean of the faculty, and the controller. After lengthy argument, the senate approved the recommendation in 1967. The revised arrangement appears to have functioned successfully, and as of 1976 the university had completed ten years with a balanced budget.

In recent years the budget committee has had to grapple

with the problem of declining enrollments in some departments and colleges, while enrollments were increasing in other departments and colleges. No simple solution has yet been found for this situation. In 1972 the senate voted to establish a special committee to study the budgetary process. The committee proposed only modest adjustments in the process: more time for deans to present their case to the budget committee and more prompt notice of impending budget reductions. In addition, the president began the practice of making a formal report to the faculty as a whole on the decisions of the budget committee. In practice, the board has accepted the budget recommendations of the budget committee. With 85 percent of the operating budget continuing to be derived from tuition, Roosevelt must raise student tuition in order to generate additional income. Such action must always be cautious, lest it leads to a decline in enrollment. One response of the administration to this situation was to develop an expanded program of satellite campuses in the suburbs of Chicago.

For the most part, faculty members tend to think of enrollment expansion and income development as administrative functions, and program development and academic standards as faculty functions.

Similarly, the Roosevelt University Senate has given very little attention to issues of instructional procedure; these matters were considered to fall within the province of the individual colleges and departments.

Most Roosevelt students entered with some prior college work. In 1969 the senate agreed that transcripts of college performance elsewhere should not be used as the sole criteria for admission of students who had been out of college for five or more years. On the other hand, the senate twice rejected a proposal to confer junior-year status upon every student entering with an associate degree.

Student activism occurred at Roosevelt as elsewhere during the 1960s, but it remained somewhat muted because of the commuting nature of the student body. A group of students picketed the trustees' meeting in 1966 when the acting president was appointed president, protesting the exclusion of students from the selection process. In 1969 a group of black students disrupted a number of classes to accent their demand for an expansion of the black studies program. The university declared a general moratorium of classes in May 1970 following the death of students at Kent State and Jackson State. An earlier demonstration protested "cooperation" with the Selective Service System. As a result of these conflicts, the administrative council revised both the student code of conduct and the judicial review procedure in order to protect the university. Both student and faculty leaders were consulted extensively in the process of change, although the senate was not asked to take formal action.

Beginning in 1966 the student senate pushed for increased student representation in the university senate and on various senate committees. Some additions in the number of students on senate committees were agreed to, but since 1972 the student senate often has failed to fill these committee slots. The participation of students in departmental meetings was approved in principle in 1970, with the provision that student voting strength should not exceed 25 percent of the faculty voting strength of a department and that students should have only an advisory role on personnel matters and on elections. Faculty rights and obligations within the university are specified by the faculty constitution.

The university senate has given only sporadic attention to issues of program reporting, evaluation, and accountability. Administrative officers have prepared extensive reports that are circulated throughout the university and deposited in the library. The administrative council in 1974 agreed to a system of management by objectives. Faculty committees have participated in self-study and accreditation activities. The senate in 1968 voted to recommend to all faculty members that they place copies of their course syllabi and course examinations in the library, but compliance has been entirely voluntary.

Roosevelt University has had a unique history in campuswide governance since its founding in 1945. It is evident that this governance structure has been more active in some areas of operation than in others. Although scarcely intended as such, the university senate has thought of its competence primarily in terms of perfecting constitutional provisions relating to governance and academic affairs. Other issues have largely been left to the discretion of administrative officers and the board of trustees, such as faculty and program evaluation. Always in the background has lurked the question of how to survive and flourish in a large metropolitan area in competition with a public multicampus community college, a state university campus, and several other public institutions, as well as with other independent colleges and universities.

## Conclusion

The nine universities whose experience in campuswide governance has been summarized in this chapter have had little in common in terms of history and tradition; their locations, which undoubtedly have substantially influenced their behavior, are geographically distinct. There can be no question but that pressures of an external environment as well as the force of various internal assumptions determined the response to various challenges of governance.

The accounts of governance experience as summarized here in some detail have certain common features: faculty insistence upon determination of those matters clearly identified as academic in nature, presidential leadership in institutional affairs, student activism in various degrees in the years from 1966 to 1972, the gradual and then precipitate retreat from institutional control of student social conduct, and some diminution of interest in campuswide governance since 1972. All nine of the universities found it either expedient or essential to revise their internal arrangements for governance during the years 1966 to 1972. The pressure for further change tended to disappear after 1972.

Roosevelt University was founded in 1945 with the explicit idea of constitutionalism and democratic participation in campus governance. The thirty-one years of its history are distinguished by some modest retreats and some more pronounced practical changes, in recognition of the realities of institutional viability. At the University of New Hampshire and at Syracuse University occurred the most comprehensive efforts to create a formalized structure of campuswide governance. The procedure and the product at Syracuse University are especially instructive. Here was the most intensive effort to bring about far-reaching change. The ratification procedure by separate constituencies brought about rejection of the new charter by faculty and by trustees (who also reflected the administration point of view). The year of the voting, 1972, undoubtedly had much to do with the voting results, but so also did modification in administration behavior.

# CHAPTER FIVE

◇◇◇◇◇◇◇◇◇◇◇◇

# Governance in General Baccalaureate Colleges

◇◇◇◇◇◇◇◇◇◇◇◇◇◇◇◇◇◇◇◇◇◇◇◇◇◇◇◇◇◇◇◇◇◇◇◇◇◇◇

In addition to the fifteen universities included in this study, the experience with campuswide governance of fifteen general baccalaureate colleges was also reviewed. Of these fifteen colleges, seven operate under public sponsorship (all but two of these as units of a multicampus system) and eight operate under private or independent sponsorship. At the time of the study, the public general baccalaureate colleges ranged in enrollment from 2,000 students to 13,000 students. Their operating budgets varied from $2 million to $17 million. The eight independent colleges ranged in enrollment from 450 to 3,500 students, and in current operating expenditures from $2 million to $20 million.

These fifteen colleges have been grouped into five categories: two elite independent colleges; two distinctive independent colleges;

144

four church-related colleges; four transitional public colleges; and three new public colleges. This grouping is intended simply as a convenience to presentation and understanding. At the same time, however, it must be emphasized that the classification utilized here has a certain internal logic. Varied as general baccalaureate colleges are in sponsorship, in mission, and in operation, certain comparisons of experience among institutions sharing one or more common characteristics are useful. The effort at comparison in this study proved to have the hoped-for utility.

A few words of definition are in order. By *elite colleges* I mean colleges that are highly selective in their admission of students in terms of academic promise and their potential for intellectual achievement. For some persons the word *elite* connotes undemocratic, snobbish, or socially indifferent behavior. In this context an elite college is simply one committed to academic excellence of a high order, and it seems to me that such a commitment calls for no apology in any society. By *distinctive colleges* I mean colleges with a special kind of mission. Here, one such college was committed to a particular outlook (conservative) in intellectual discussion and in expected social behavior; a second distinctive college was one committed predominantly to the education of black students. By *church-related colleges* I mean colleges whose ties to a religious denomination are more than nominal and whose behavior patterns are influenced by a sense of responsibility to a church body. By *transitional public colleges* I mean public institutions that have been in the process of change from a limited mission (a teachers college or a community college) to a more general undergraduate mission. By *new public colleges* I mean public institutions established during the 1960s in order to accommodate the tidal wave of students that descended upon the public sector of higher education during that decade. These definitions should suggest the peculiar or unique characteristics of each grouping of these fifteen general baccalaureate colleges.

## Two Elite Colleges

*Vassar.* For more than one hundred years (1861 to 1969) Vassar College built a reputation as a small, high-quality, presti-

gious liberal arts college for women. In 1969, following the termination of negotiations for merger with Yale University, Vassar admitted its first male students and became coeducational. At the
same time, the college changed its fairly rigid curriculum in order
to create more flexible and innovative degree programs. As of 1975
Vassar had an enrollment of 2,250 students, of whom about one
third were male. With an endowment currently valued at nearly
$76 million and an operating budget of nearly $18 million, the college has had budget difficulties since 1968. From 1969 through
1976, Vassar was a college in transition, and this circumstance in
turn influenced the experience with campuswide governance.

Legally and formally, the authority of governance of Vassar
is vested in a self-perpetuating board of trustees of twenty members;
five members were nominated by the alumnae and alumni association. In addition, the board provides that two trustees be recent
graduates who would serve a two-year term that may be renewed
for a second period. All other trustees serve an eight-year term, final
except under unusual circumstances of need for the service of a particular trustee. The president's immediate administrative associates
were a dean of the faculty, a vice-president for student affairs, a
vice-president for administration, a vice-president for development,
and a secretary of the college.

Vassar College was one of the first institutions of higher education in the United States to develop (in 1922) a comprehensive,
written document on governance. Because a small group of trustees
were opposed to the progressive policies of the college president in
1918, the alumnae association called for a joint committee of trustees, faculty, and alumnae to review the arrangements for governance, including the method of election, terms, and authority of the
board of trustees. As early as 1915, a faculty report had recommended the desirability of a written constitution. From these initiatives emerged, in 1922, a new set of bylaws of the trustees and a
statute of instruction. In 1942 these two documents were combined
in a single publication and the term *governance* was employed for
the first time as the title for the whole. Beginning in 1922, the board
of trustees limited the term of service for all its members and acknowledged faculty participation in the selection of a president and
dean. The primacy of the faculty in "academic affairs" was ac-

knowledged. The statute established the right of the faculty to a "formal conference" with the board on matters of mutual concern. The thrust of the 1922 changes, and of later developments as well, was to clarify and strengthen the role of the faculty in relation to the board of trustees.

Vassar experienced some student agitation during the 1960s, mostly concerned with the rules governing student conduct in the residence halls. In 1969 the document on college governance was revised to include for the first time a chapter on student rights and responsibilities, including the right of formal conference with the faculty and with the board of trustees. At the same time the faculty committee system was restructured to include student membership in addition to faculty and administration. A proposal to create a campus senate of faculty, administrators, and students was never given serious consideration, because its need was not readily apparent. Thus, a committee system along with various ad hoc conferences and commissions became the Vassar approach to campus-wide governance as a result of the experiences of the 1960s.

Since 1923 Vassar has come to think of the conference arrangement as a satisfactory mechanism for resolving issues of college policy and program. In a series of conferences from 1968 to 1970, trustees, administrators, faculty, and students considered at some length both the college mission and the governance structure. It was apparent from these conferences that there was little disposition within the academic community for changes other than those completed in 1969. The committee structure was expected to generate proposals for action, which might then be referred to the faculty or student senate for action. The final decision might be still made by the board of trustees, but an adverse decision would not be made without a conference discussion involving either faculty and board members or student leaders and board members.

Three faculty committees are composed exclusively of faculty members: the appointments and salary committee, the compensation committee, and the policy and conference committee. Other committees have joint faculty, student, and administration representation: the committee on curricular policies, the committee on the library, the committee on admission, the committee on scholarships and financial aid, the academic panel (concerned with charges of student academic dishonesty), and the appeal committee. These committees report to the faculty. Other committees (master planning, all-college events, campus regulations, and financial planning) report to the president and board of trustees. In other instances, ad hoc committees are appointed to consider special issues: a comprehensive plan, graduate education, the education of minority students, the quality of residential life, campus security, and other subjects.

The major problem of institutional mission to arise in the 1960s was that of Vassar's future as a single-sex college. An ad hoc Committee on New Dimensions, created in 1966, focused its attention on coeducation, graduate study, and off-campus study. Suddenly the president announced that Vassar had agreed to study with Yale University the possibility of affiliation. The issue seriously divided administrative officers and faculty; students generally were disposed to favor the idea. Neither the faculty nor the student body was asked to render a formal recommendation on affiliation. The study of alternatives to affiliation became the rallying point of those opposed to a merger. Eventually, the trustees terminated further discussion with the Yale corporation, and the faculty voted in May 1968 for coeducation, 103 to 3. Only afterwards were voices raised questioning whether or not something important in the historic Vassar mission had been lost by the decision in favor of coeducation. This concern found expression in the creation of the Trustee Committee on the Education of Women at Vassar, which issued a report in 1973 pledging continued effort to meet the special educational needs of women in the context of coeducation.

The Joint Committee on New Dimensions in its 1967 report also recommended that Vassar develop several specialized graduate programs. Some administrative officers and some faculty members believed that Vassar could not retain its commitment to academic excellence if it remained an undergraduate liberal arts college for women. The committee recommended that the college develop several special graduate programs geared to college strengths and the special geographic needs of the area, particularly the needs arising from the presence of the IBM Corporation in the vicinity. The idea of a graduate program in science and technology generated a good deal of campus controversy. Some students were quite hostile to the idea, and faculty members in the humanities and social sciences were generally opposed. After extensive study by various committees and after considerable negotiation with other universities, a proposal in 1970 to establish a graduate center in science and technology to include the study of the relationship between human values and technology was narrowly approved by faculty vote. The board of trustees then began to have doubts about the financial feasibility of the endeavor, and the project was allowed quietly to die in 1971. It was apparent that student pressure had a great deal to do with the final action.

Other problems occupying a good deal of faculty, student, administration, alumnae, and board attention included the education of black students and the establishment of a black studies program, black student housing, tenure, revision of degree requirements, the establishment of interdisciplinary majors, student social regulations, and location of structures on the campus. Probably the most controversial issue of the past ten years was that of budget priorities. The board jealously guarded its power to fix the college budget, although the faculty, through the compensation committee, enjoyed the privilege of presenting the faculty salary budget ahead of any other budgets. The final stage of budget preparation was handled by a budget review committee (committee on financial planning), consisting of faculty, student, and administration membership, with trustee observers. These procedures were time-consuming and enmeshed individuals in a multitude of details rather than in broad or long-term budget strategy. In 1974 a proposal by a faculty committee for a joint commission to study budget procedures and priorities was rejected by the board of trustees. In 1975 a consultative procedure was established by the board as an experimental arrangement in obtaining faculty and student advice about budget priorities.

It is obvious that campuswide governance at Vassar College during the past ten years has been generally adequate to handle the major issues which arose. Campuswide governance has been founded upon committee and conference arrangements for bringing together faculty, student, and institutional interests. The faculty and the student body have retained their own separate identity and organization, but at the same time have found a satisfactory practice for interrelating their interests with those of administrators and board members. Vassar alumnae, both formally and informally, also have had a considerable impact upon the decision-making process.

*Carleton.* Founded in 1866 in Northfield, Minnesota, Carleton College grew slowly in enrollment decade by decade until it reached 1,650 students in 1975–76. The values of a small academic community have competed with considerations of intellectual viability, an expanding national population, and finances. In the process of slow growth, Carleton committed itself to standards of academic excellence, and this commitment has dominated the consideration of all other issues.

Before 1962 the governance structure of Carleton tended to be hierarchical. Led by extremely able presidents with an average tenure of twenty-four years, both faculty and board of trustees were inclined to follow. A strong academic program developed after World War I attracted attention first in the upper Midwest and then throughout the country. Increased diversity in faculty and students, along with the changing family and intellectual background of students, encouraged a new look in the 1960s at how decisions were made in the college. Because of the prestige of two long-term presidents, Donald J. Cowling (1909–1945) and Laurence M. Gould (1945–1962), there was little disposition to question existing arrangements. The presidents informally and formally involved faculty participation in decision making on academic matters, and the board of trustees was vigorous in defending academic freedom within the college. The "understandings" of earlier years began to unravel after 1962.

In the first year of a new president, 1962–63, a proposal was introduced in a faculty meeting for the faculty to elect a five-member committee on faculty policies and practices to advise the president officially on appointments, tenure, dismissals, promotions, and compensation. After lengthy discussion in the faculty, the matter was referred to the executive committee of the faculty, and this committee decided to serve as the desired faculty agency. Other issues arose in rapid succession. In 1964, instead of by appointment by the president, an elected committee on committees was set up by faculty vote to choose the membership on all faculty standing committees. That same year a student-faculty-administration council of four members from each group was established under pressure from the student association to handle revisions in social rules and regulations. In 1967 students were added to all standing committees of the faculty except three and were included thereafter on all ad hoc and special committees as these were created. Informal meetings between students and trustees and faculty and trustees began about the same time.

By 1969 the time had come for a comprehensive consideration of governance structures. The chairman of the board of trustees at a faculty meeting in June recommended the creation of a committee of students, faculty, administrators, alumni, and trustees to review the mission of Carleton College. The proposal was accepted, and a planning committee began work that summer. The attention of the committee was quickly turned from purpose to process, from mission to governance, and the device of the planning committee itself became the model for a new structure of campuswide governance. The result was the creation in 1970 of a college council as a central decision-making body with faculty, student, administrator, alumni, and trustee membership. The council was to consist of twenty-four members: seven faculty, seven students, three trustees, two alumni, and five administrative officers, including the president as presiding officer. The council was to have three standing committees: an educational policy committee (of seven faculty, four students, and three administrators); a social policy committee of six students, three faculty, and three administrators); and an administrative policy committee (of five administrators, three faculty, and three students). These three standing committees might create subcommittees and special committees as they deemed necessary.

All college council decisions were subject to review by the board of trustees. The faculty by majority vote might challenge a decision of the council, and students through the student senate and a referendum might question a council action. A presidential right to challenge preserved the president's unique role of leadership. A challenge required council reconsideration and a two thirds vote for renewed approval. Board rejection of a council decision was considered most unlikely.

The Carleton faculty was not entirely satisfied with the 1970 structure, for they were not happy to have students and administrators so heavily involved in "faculty" affairs. Although the faculty was continued with its own elected chairman, faculty members perceived that a major shift had now occurred in the decision-making process about faculty affairs. Yet for the most part, academic planning after 1970 produced no definite or clear conflicts between faculty, students, and administrators. Degree requiremnts were made more flexible, physical education was continued as a requirement, some distribution requirement remained, and various kinds of experimental courses were authorized. Various foundation and government grants helped immensely in strengthening instruction and in encouraging innovation in instructional practices. Because administrative officers were instrumental in obtaining these grants, their influence in curricular matters continued to be substantial. In the 1970s it became increasingly evident that the college could not afford gifts that committed it to continuing future expense. In general, student impact upon educational policy and practice was apparent but by no means controlling.

The three policy committees struggled throughout the 1970s with the question of how to distinguish policy issues from administrative details. The effort was made to have subcommittees and special committees deal with matters of administrative details, while the parent committees undertook to examine policy issues. In practice, the policy committees found themselves involved with issues on which there was considerable confusion or conflict about the desirable course of action. In addition, the educational policy committee, on a four-year cycle, engaged in a review of all departmental and interdepartmental programs. Departments were asked to list all changes in courses during the four-year period, the purposes of the changes, the effects of the changes upon the quality of the program, the allocation of resources within the department, and the direction of future anticipated change. This review process proved to be burdensome to departmental chairmen and to make too little use of outside evaluators. The procedure was changed to a seven-year cycle and to involve the use of peer judgment from other institutions.

A major issue after 1963 was that of achieving increased racial, economic, and cultural diversity in the student body. The objective met almost no opposition, but no one was prepared to estimate the cost involved. The objective soon became entangled with the question of intellectual standards expected of the Carleton student. Beginning in 1965 a concerted effort was made to recruit black students. A foundation grant in 1964 sparked the new endeavor. The next several years produced change but also caused confusion, bitterness, disillusionment, and some second thoughts. What appeared to be a gesture of openness by whites was viewed by blacks as tokenism, continuing racism, and an attempt to assimilate the black minority out of existence. By 1967 there were as many as forty black students; to the blacks the number remained too small. In early 1976 conflict between black students and white youth in the town developed. Continuing consultation between students, faculty, and administrative officers helped to meet, if not resolve, most issues. The board of trustees also added four black members to its number. But the college discovered that it lacked both the financial resources and the support resources to achieve its black student objective.

A faculty-administration-student committee during the 1960s and later the social policy committee of the college council struggled with the issue of student social life. Increasingly, students were given responsibility for the quality of dormitory life, while the college endeavored to strengthen academic and personal counseling. Each year there was a gap between what students thought ought to exist and what administrators considered to be the meaning and shape of responsible freedom. In 1969 students established, on their own, one floor of a dormitory on a coed basis. The next two months were spent in intensive discussion, and, finally, in February 1970, Carleton became coeducational in yet another way. A college council decision not to offer a single-sex housing option to men as well as to women was overruled by the board of trustees. A proposal to liberalize the rules on use of automobiles in Northfield was defeated in a student referendum. Continuing debate was still going on in 1976 about the scope and cost of gynecological services by the college, the increased costs of food service, and the position of the college on student cohabitation.

The decision-making process was further tested after 1970 in consideration of the desirable relationship between tenure and the evaluation of teaching. No matter how much lip service had been given over the years to the importance of teaching as an institutional purpose, Carleton, like other institutions, had done little to determine how to evaluate teaching or to decide the appropriate steps by which to advance teaching effectiveness. In 1968 some funds were set aside in the budget for curriculum research and development. In 1970 a decision was made to publish an extended course-description book, with detailed information about each course. Then, in 1971, administrative and trustee concern was directed to the question of the financial implications of a highly tenured faculty. Rather than establishing a collegewide rule on faculty evaluation, certain "understandings" about evaluation emerged, including the use of student evaluation, and the actual conduct of evaluation was left to the operation of each department.

Prior to 1970 the president, his administrative associates, and the board of trustees controlled the budget process and made the vital budget decisions. With the creation of the college council and its three policy committees, access to information about income, expenses, cost projections, and development expectations was diffused among faculty, students, and others. The administrative policy committee became in effect the budget committee, and the college council became a forum for budget discussion. Informal channels have continued to influence decisions as before. The president directed department chairmen utilizing various assumptions to project expenditure patterns five years in advance. The administrative policy committee reviewed all budgets in order to bring them into realistic relationship to revenues, and to each other. In 1974 the critical confrontation occurred in the committee and the council: how to increase faculty salaries without increasing student enrollment or tuition. Faculty and student representatives took opposite positions, and in April 1975 the president created a college priorities committee of eleven faculty members, students, and administrators to review the long-range financial circumstances of Carleton.

Various solutions appeared. Some budgets, as for public events, were drastically reduced. A summer session was established, and Carleton decided to enroll, on a part-time basis, high school teachers and older students. Other proposals remained under active consideration at the end of 1976: elimination of small classes, a ceiling on student aid grants, enrollment of more students from Minnesota because of the state grant, limitation upon the credits accepted from other institutions, and analysis of enrollment shifts among departments. Even with its capital gifts campaign more than half way toward its goal, Carleton had reason to continue to be fearful about its financial future.

Since 1970 Carleton has undertaken to operate a structure of campuswide governance both centralized and federated. While an increasing number of decisions are now shared by faculty, students, administration, and trustees, many decisions have remained the province of the constituent groups of the college. The arrangement has meant a substantial involvement of time for many persons. Many discussions become repetitious. In spite of the availability of minutes, reports, and open meetings, many persons have continued to say that they are uninformed about decisions or lack an opportunity to participate. The claims of the nonprofessional staff of the college have not been recognized. Participation in various meetings has tended to decline. Administrators, and presidents in particular, have tended to perceive the structure as unresponsive to leadership and as delaying the decision-making process. Yet the structure has had its strengths as well. It has encouraged the development of a sense of community. It has encouraged long-range planning. It has set requirements for better data upon which to base decisions. It has handled change in a systematic and considered way. And it has advanced the learning process itself in the experience of students, faculty, and administrators.

## Two Distinctive Colleges

*Tuskegee.* The Tuskegee Normal and Industrial Institute was established in 1881 under the leadership of Booker T. Washington; initially, it was a private vocational high school for blacks. In 1927 the institution assumed college status, and the name Tuskegee Institute was formally adopted in 1937. The institute has an enrollment of 3,500 students and a budget of around $20 million. It consists of a college of arts and sciences, a school of applied science, a school of education, a school of engineering, a school of nursing, and a school of veterinary medicine.

Of the twenty-five members of the board of trustees, five

were appointed by the governor of Alabama, the state superintendent of education served ex officio, and the remaining individuals were elected by the board itself for three-year terms. Tuskegee has had a tradition of strong presidential leadership. Predominantly comprised of blacks as faculty members, students, and administrators, the institute has emphasized its mission of instruction, research, and public service regardless of race, religion, nationality, or socioeconomic status. Tuskegee receives an annual subsidy for operating purposes from the State of Alabama.

The emphasis in instruction, research, and service at Tuskegee from the beginning has been placed upon practical results: skilled competencies for students and needed services to blacks and others in an originally rural economy more recently become urban. The institute offers instruction in agriculture and in a variety of professional fields. It provides a health and hospital service for rural people. It early adopted both work-study and cooperative educational opportunities, as well as special educational services to overcome deficiencies in high school preparation. This emphasis upon practical achievement tended to reinforce presidential leadership; the governance structure arose not from some concept of desirable arrangement but from a practical concern to expand services to blacks and to obtain the income essential for operation and capital plant.

Early in the 1940s the president of Tuskegee added student membership to an executive council that was advisory to the president. In the 1950s an educational council was added as a second advisory group to the president, but this council was composed entirely of faculty members and administrative officers. In the middle of the 1960s, student leadership at Tuskegee demanded active participation in all phases of academic and social life on the campus. An additional student member was added to the executive council, two students were added to the educational council, and the board of trustees created a committee on student affairs. A committee was appointed to study and recommend further student participation in the educational council and in various council and school committees. As a result, in 1967 student membership was expanded to eleven out of thirty-four persons on the educational council and to nine of thirty-seven persons on the executive council.

In the spring of 1968, after the death of Dr. Martin Luther King, Jr. and after a white charged with murder of a black student had been acquitted in Alabama, students expressed their accumulated frustrations by occupying the administration building, locking the trustees in their meeting room, and otherwise hampering the operation of the institute. Tuskegee was closed for two weeks. Upon reopening, a committee of faculty, students, and administrative officers was appointed by the president to consider various student grievances. Library hours were extended, and a request to faculty members to provide course outlines at the beginning of a semester, to explain grading standards, and to clarify course requirements for a degree was approved by the educational council. The requirement that all male students enroll for two years in ROTC was eliminated. But one demand of the students was not acceptable, largely because of faculty opposition. This demand was for a university senate composed equally of faculty and students, with a small proportion of administration participation. Faculty members perceived this arrangement as a threat to their own status and indeed to continued external support of the institute.

The statutes of Tuskegee Institute were revised in 1969 to reflect the increased participation of students in the work of the executive council, the educational council, and various standing committees. At the same time, both bodies continued to be advisory to the president. Some faculty members have pressed since 1969 for complete faculty control of appointments, tenure, promotion, and salary. Faculty members have also argued that they should have complete control of all degree requirements, grading standards, standards of academic freedom, and standards of student conduct. Faculty members have wanted a definite role in the selection of department chairmen, deans, and top administrative officers, including the president.

The Tuskegee faculty has continued to meet as a whole on a periodic basis. Many faculty members believe that only an elected faculty senate would be able to speak effectively on behalf of faculty interests within the institute. Although committees had been appointed in the early 1970s to draft proposals for both a faculty senate and an institute council composed of students, faculty, and administrators, as of late 1976 none of the proposals had been acceptable to both faculty members and the board of trustees. Indeed, the faculty disapproved the proposals upon the grounds that no decisions of a faculty senate should be subject to review by a campuswide council. In the meantime, previous governance structures have continued to operate, with strong decision-making authority exercised by the board of trustees.

*Rockford.* Founded in 1847, Rockford College is an independent, coeducational, predominantly residential general baccalaureate college. It enrolls 1,100 students in twenty-one fields of undergraduate study, including the arts and sciences, the fine arts, and education. It offers a modest program leading to the master's degree in teaching. From its beginning, the college's governance has been vested in a self-perpetuating board of trustees of not more than forty-five persons. Board members serve for lengthy periods of time; half the membership in 1976 had been members in 1966. The number of alumni on the board doubled in this same period.

The unique character of Rockford College is based on its conscious and articulated philosophy of educational and social traditionalism. With the same president, John A. Howard, since 1960, the college has insisted that the ultimate judgments about the objectives of the institution and the ways in which the institution is to serve society can best be made by the board of trustees. The board's bylaws clearly indicate that the president is the "principal agency" through which the board carries out its policies and decisions. All personnel decisions, in both educational and business activities, are made by the board on advice of the president.

The president has made it clear that there is only a limited role for either students or faculty in the governance of Rockford College. Student advice and criticism about courses, about degree requirements, faculty performance, and social regulations have been welcomed and given serious attention, but it has been made clear that final decisions on all these matters will be made by the board of trustees. The unique and essential competence of the faculty has been fully acknowledged. Within the limits of the objectives of the college as defined by the board, the faculty has been expected to develop a curriculum, to establish and maintain standards of academic performance, to propose and carry out educational innovation, and to assume responsibility for instructional and research activities. Faculty advice has been welcomed in decision making about student life, community relations, and long-range planning. The board of trustees has retained the authority to make final decisions about all important or major issues concerning the college.

In the governance structure of Rockford College, the role of the president is a primary one. The president is expected to be "the first scholar" of the faculty in articulating the purpose of the college, to be the spokesman of the college in interpreting that purpose to external communities, and to be the administrator responsible for ensuring that purposes are fulfilled. The president is the principal adviser to the board in all decisions made by the board. When a board of trustees expects to be involved in any and all aspects of college operation, the role of the president is critical in presenting recommendations for action and in ensuring that decisions of the board are fully implemented.

A number of arrangements have been developed at Rockford College to facilitate communication between faculty, students, president, and board. At two board meetings a year, in November and February, representatives of the faculty and of students are invited to present matters of current concern directly to the board members. Informal communication through dinners and other social occasions has also been quite frequent. Administrative associates of the president are in close contact on a daily basis with faculty and students. Committees of the board of trustees have met frequently on campus to discuss academic affairs with faculty members and student affairs with student leaders. After 1966 some of these arrangements were more formally structured than had been the case in earlier years.

The faculty of the college has been recognized as having a corporate existence for many years. Through various committees, the faculty has had a major voice in admission requirements, degree requirements, curriculum, special academic programs, and other matters. In 1966 student representatives were invited to meet with the educational policy committee of the faculty, and in 1967 the faculty voted to invite student representatives to attend the meetings of all committees except five (appointments, tenure, admissions, financial aid, and graduate study). The status of students as voting members was left to the discretion of each committee. By

1968, students had been made voting members on nine out of eleven committees, including three of the five committees at first exempted from student participation. For a time, especially from 1969 through 1971, there was a good deal of discussion at Rockford about the appropriate role of students in campus governance. The practice in response to this interest continued to emphasize student participation in the work of faculty committees. Students were quite influential in a study of curriculum revision during 1970–71 that reestablished the bachelor of science degree in addition to the bachelor of arts degree and rearranged the distribution requirements for both degrees. For a time this student role was a very active one, but it tended to decline after 1973.

In 1968 the student government at the college recommended the creation of a board of review in order to give students a further voice in campus governance. The proposal was accepted in principle by the faculty, the president, and the board of trustees. A board of review of nine members was authorized, to be composed of three faculty members, three students, and three administrative officers. Two nonvoting members of the board were the president of the college as chairman and the president of the student government. The student and faculty members were elected by their respective constituencies. The role of the board of review was to reconsider any policy position of the college upon request of any member of the academic community. If the policy was held to be inconsistent with the basic purpose of the college, the board's decision was final unless vetoed by the president. In case of a veto, the decision was then referred to the board of trustees for final action. In 1971 the name of the board was changed to Community Review Board, the decisions were made advisory to the board of trustees, the president withdrew from membership, and petitions for review required signatures from 10 percent of the students, 25 percent of the faculty, or 25 percent of the administrative staff.

In practice, the device of the review board was used quite infrequently. A petition questioning the new policy of establishing freshman dormitories was submitted in 1970 but was later withdrawn. Another petition questioned the escort requirements for residence-hall visitations, and another desired a revision in the campus speaker policy. Revisions were made on both matters by the usual machinery of the college, and it appeared thereafter that the review board arrangement would be of little usefulness in the governance of the college.

The governance of Rockford College has been founded since 1964 upon a statement of purpose approved by the board of trustees on June 6 of that year. The development of this document resulted from action by a group of students who, in the autumn of 1962, wished to invite a Communist to speak on campus. A policy on campus speakers was then devised by the board of trustees in 1963 that led to considerable student and faculty protest. Eventually it became clear that a policy on campus speakers needed a broader framework. As a consequence, a committee of two faculty members, the president, and the dean of the college was set up to draft a statement of purpose. Eventually the statement thus prepared was approved by the educational policy committee, by the faculty, and by the board of trustees. The statement of purpose reads as follows:

> The fundamental purpose of Rockford College is to provide an educational program which will assist the student to develop the full use of his intellectual capabilities and to call into play his highest motives so that he may be a creative, courageous, and constructive member of society.
>
> The educational program presents, through formal studies, a broad range of theoretical knowledge, attempting to give the student an understanding of himself, of society, of the natural universe, and of the world of art and humanities. The college further includes in the experience of learning a diversified program of activities permitting the student many informal opportunities to augment, test, and apply the knowledge obtained in his studies.
>
> The philosophy of the college is based upon these premises:
>
> Man is a thinking and feeling being. Therefore, the college seeks to confirm in each student a concern for truth, a respect for fact, the habit of inquiry, the practice of intellectual discipline, and the art of creative expression.
>
> Man is a social being. Therefore, the college nurtures in the student a belief in the inherent dignity and worth of each individual. It seeks to help the student dis-

cover the attitudes and conduct which will lead him to exercise that integrity and responsibility which are vital to a free society and provide a basis for mutual trust among persons, communities, and nations.

Man is a spiritual being. Therefore, the college proposes to each student the importance of finding significance in life in religious terms and the necessity of discovering a hierarchy of personal values to which he will commit himself.

Finally, Rockford College seeks to improve and refine the educational process so that its program will be valid and vital for each generation of students.

This statement of purpose did more than help to resolve the conflict about the speakers policy, which was resolved in terms of insisting that outside speakers advance the purposes of the college and that the president should make the decision on behalf of the board of trustees in cases of doubt. The statement became the fundamental yardstick by which all educational and social issues within Rockford College were to be resolved.

In the autumn of 1973 several forces combined to suggest the desirability of a review of the statement of purpose. One factor was the need to decide what kinds of student records to retain. Another factor was a concern whether or not the religious commitment was in fact being realized. An evaluation of the college was undertaken by means of the Institutional Goals Inventory of the Educational Testing Service, along with the use of a locally prepared instrument. The results of these surveys were presented in a report in July 1974. Separate committees were set up thereafter for students, faculty, alumni, and administrators to examine the survey responses about the current state of the college, to suggest the priorities for future college endeavors, and to propose particular lines of action. The committee reports were completed by the spring of 1976, and the year 1976–77 was expected to be a critical one for decision about future direction of Rockford College.

## Four Church-Related Colleges

*West Virginia Wesleyan.* Founded in 1890 by the West Virginia Conference of the Methodist Episcopal Church, the institution operated as an academy or preparatory school for fourteen years. In 1904 the college assumed its current designation and collegiate status. In essence, the conference owns the land of the college but a separate corporation operates the institution. The authority of the corporation has been vested in a board of trustees whose members are elected for four-year terms by the Annual Conference upon nomination of the conference board of higher education and ministry. At least three fifths of all board members are required to be members of the United Methodist Church. It is possible for the Annual West Virginia Conference of the United Methodist Church to remove any trustee by majority vote "for cause deemed by it to be sufficient." Controversy and deeply felt emotional issues involving the college could lead to removal of board members; although such a move was considered in 1974 and 1975, none has ever taken place. For thirty years the number of trustees has been forty, half of whom are ministers and half laymen.

A serious strain in relationships between the college and the Annual Conference developed over the issue of the possession and consumption of alcoholic beverages in the college dormitories. Because of student pressures, the administration with the assistance of certain trustees developed a new statement of policy that prohibited the possession and consumption of alcoholic beverages in the public areas of residence halls but omitted any reference to dormitory rooms. In fact, the new policy recognized an existing practice, which was not to search student quarters. The policy statement was widely interpreted, however, as an encouragement to student drinking and led to extensive debate in the Annual Conference. The conference even refused to approve any new trustee appointments. Only gradually did the conflict appear to recede.

West Virginia Wesleyan has had a traditional form of governance. The faculty met as a whole to approve various academic matters and student conduct regulations. The faculty was not consulted, however, about the new policy on possession and consumption of alcoholic beverages, although the faculty would probably have been in favor of the statement. Collaboration of faculty and administration depended in large part upon continuity of leadership. In the absence of continuity and mutual trust, a continuing struggle for power seemed to take place, arraying faculty against administration and trustees. Until the 1960s students had little part in this conflict. Student unrest was generally muted during these years. Only the issue of alcohol use emerged to test relationships within the academic community, and the consequence was considerable argument about the role of the United Methodist Church in relation to the college.

A formalized faculty constitution did not exist at the college until 1970. The resulting structure provided for a faculty assembly of all faculty members presided over by the president, a faculty council of eight elected members with the vice-president for academic affairs as a nonvoting member, and various faculty committees. The council was a kind of executive committee for the faculty assembly. Decisions of the council were final unless revoked by a majority vote of the assembly. For the most part faculty actions on degree requirements, courses, and academic standards were accepted by the president and the trustees.

Also in 1970 the board of trustees decided to create three trustee councils: one on academic affairs, one on student affairs, and one on financial affairs. Faculty, student, and administrative officers served on these councils, which began to involve themselves increasingly in various campus issues. At the same time the existence of the councils tended to encourage increased decision making by the board. The major issues of the college were enrollment growth, financial stability, and program development. A nursing program was begun in 1976. Some general education courses were especially designed and approved, new majors in interdisciplinary studies were introduced, and two language majors were dropped. A faculty evaluation procedure was adopted, including student participation. Faculty concern about operating budget deficits was considerable, but there was no faculty action. The president resigned early in 1976 to run for governor of the state, and the college has not been disposed to resolve any issues until a new president was appointed.

*Augustana.* Augustana College in South Dakota came into existence in 1918 when several predecessor institutions that had moved westward from Illinois through Wisconsin and Iowa were consolidated in a new, single location. The college was an expression of interest on the part of families of Norwegian ancestry who belonged to the Norwegian Lutheran Church of America. Ownership of the college was separated from the church in 1925 through a device known as the Augustana College Association. The association was made up of members of the American Lutheran Church living in the upper Mississippi valley. The college did not experience any substantial growth, however, until after World War II.

From 1943 to 1965 the college had only one president, Lawrence M. Stavig. A structure of governance devised in these years reflected both the personal warmth of the president's leadership and the needs of a rapidly developing college. The faculty acquired a reasonably well-defined role in academic affairs, while the administration "managed" the institution. Students were recognized as having some vague control over their own activities, although student conduct regulations remained the province of the faculty and board of regents. The board itself heard reports and was generally supportive of presidential initiatives.

A new president selected in 1965 was the first to be a nonclergyman and of solely academic background. The administrative structure was reorganized under three vice-presidents (academic affairs, financial affairs, and development). Although faculty members were somewhat concerned about what they regarded as a "bureaucratization" of the college, it was also apparent that a more highly formalized process of leadership was necessary. In the ten years from 1966 to 1976, Augustana College reached a period of substantial maturity. The curriculum was revised, a new calendar introduced, the physical plant greatly expanded, enrollment sustained, and financial solvency maintained. The student activist traumas of the years 1969 to 1972 produced no irreparable damage.

The Augustana College Association is a corporation of church members. All church members in a specified geographical area belong to it. The association acts through elected delegates, who meet annually and select the board of regents of the college. The board of regents is the governing agency of the college and elects the president. Although the faculty is organized by divisions rather than by departments, the faculty operates through four councils (personnel, planning, curriculum, and cocurriculum). Each council in turn has spawned a number of committees. The faculty meets as a whole to approve any formal actions emanating from one of the councils. Student government is based upon a student association. Various committees are organized to reflect student concerns with campus living arrangements, student activities, and academic affairs.

Augustana College had not seen fit, as of 1975, to organize any community council or college council. There was more disposition in 1975 than in 1965 to share information throughout the college, to have more extensive discussions about policies and programs, to consider various points of view, and to understand the budget problems of the college. These changes were achieved by personal contact, by the leadership style of the president, and by informal arrangements rather than by a formalized structure of campus governance. Moreover, the common religious heritage of most students, faculty, and administrators tended to provide a mutual respect and trust that permeated all operations of the college.

The issues that agitated campus governance in the late 1960s were the desirability of having an ROTC unit on campus, modification of institutional purpose to acknowledge the presence of and need for professional educational programs, curriculum revision to reduce distribution and other course requirements, and regulations governing student behavior. The issues were largely resolved by recognition of changing circumstances.

The students at Augustana College are the group most inclined to express dissatisfaction with existing arrangements. Confrontation is apt to seem more attractive than negotiation. Students seem to feel that they should have a voice in all college matters, and they appear to believe that conflict can be resolved by votes. Faculty members and members of the board of regents are willing to listen to student points of view but are not willing to accept student decisions about various matters affecting the work of the college. The regents tend to see their role as that of ensuring sound fiscal management and the employment of competent personnel to carry out the purposes of Augustana.

*Aquinas.* Aquinas College in Grand Rapids was founded in 1923 as a Catholic college. Initially a junior college for women, the college admitted men in 1931; in 1940 it began to offer four-year instructional programs. In 1969 the state-granted charter was amended to permit laymen to serve on the board of trustees. As of 1975 Aquinas had reached an enrollment of 1,000 full-time equivalent students, and the board consisted of ten Dominican sisters, thirteen lay persons, and one priest. As of 1976 two students participated as voting members on the board's committee on student affairs and three faculty members were members of the board's committee on academic affairs.

Throughout the 1960s there was a continuing debate at Aquinas College about the relative roles of administrative officers, the board of trustees, the faculty, and the students. This debate necessarily took place within the context of a college with strong ties to the Catholic church, but it also took place in a period of rapid social and religious change. The structure of the college was perceived as inhibiting, in various subtle ways, the progress of change, and much of the discussion turned upon the legalism of organization rather than upon the substance of change itself.

As of 1964 the president was regarded as the source of authoritative decision making, reinforced by a board of trustees made up of members of the Dominican order. The role of the faculty was modest, involving degree requirements, course offerings, and student academic standards. Moreover, faculty decisions on these matters were made by a two-thirds vote. Ostensibly the faculty operated through nine committees: admissions, studies, discipline, student welfare, faculty welfare, library, scholarships, athletics, and budget. The president was ex officio a member of all committees, and he named committee members except in the case of faculty welfare. The committees were not very active. As the faculty increasingly became composed of laity, new pressures arose for recognition of preponderant faculty influence upon "academic" matters.

In 1968 the board of trustees approved a faculty constitution. The idea for such a constitution had been under discussion since 1966, largely encouraged by the work of the local chapter of the American Association of University Professors. The president appointed an ad hoc committee on a faculty constitution in 1967. The draft document circulated at the end of the year asserted that the faculty had "full legislative responsibility and competence" in regard to the curriculum, methods of instruction, student grading, admission requirements, degree requirements, rights and duties of faculty members, and the general conduct of students. This draft document encountered both faculty and trustee opposition. Eventually, the 1968 constitution, as approved by the trustees, recognized trustee authority to review faculty decisions and established faculty "responsibility and competence"—the word *legislative* was dropped—as a delegation of authority from the trustees. Under this constitution faculty committees became generally elected, and a committee on rank and tenure became the voice of the faculty on personnel matters.

In 1969 Aquinas College named its first lay president. The president insisted upon an extensive self-study of the college, which proceeded over the next fifteen months. In the meantime, in March 1970, the faculty approved a statement on rights and freedoms of students that was intended to prevent the arbitrary dismissal of students. A procedure was also devised for considering student grievances against alleged faculty tyranny. The self-study was organized to consider five broad areas of concern: governance, faculty rights and responsibilities, student rights and responsibilities, teaching resources and theory, and learning resources and theory. The committee on governance proposed separate faculty and student agencies rather than a single collegewide assembly. An academic assembly composed predominantly of faculty would be responsible for "policy making" about academic affairs, while a community senate composed predominantly of students would be responsible for policy making about student life. A new constitution embodying these proposals was then drafted and approved by faculty vote and student referendum in 1970.

The principal issue that emerged during the consideration of this constitution was whether or not the actions of the academic assembly and of the community senate were advisory. The president ruled at the time that the actions would be considered to be legislative, subject to veto by the president and final decision by the board of trustees. In performance, the community senate since 1971 has been somewhat disappointing. Participation in elections and in meetings has involved less than half of the students. A sharp conflict did arise in 1972 between the community senate and the academic assembly on the subject of student publication of a guide evaluating individual faculty members and individual courses. Under strong protest from the chairman of the academic assembly, the student leadership backed down from its plans for student-initiated evaluation of faculty performance. Another conflict arose in 1975 about the reorganization of academic departments into divisions. The initiative for this structural change came from the council of deans; the issue was whether or not the academic assembly and the community senate should have approved the proposal. The issue was considered then by a committee of the assembly, the assembly did not act, and a divisional structure was made effective in May 1975.

As of 1976 the structure of 1971 was still operative, budget and educational questions had emerged as the primary concerns for the future, and a growing realization was developing at Aquinas College that campus governance required a conscious determination, common sense, and good will if it was to work effectively.

*Albertus Magnus.* Founded in New Haven in 1925 as a Catholic liberal arts college for women, the college had an enrollment of 456 students in 1975. As of 1976 the board of trustees consisted of six lay members and six sisters from the sponsoring group, the Dominican Sisters of St. Mary of the Springs. The president was a member of the order and of the board. The principal administrative associates of the president were an academic dean, a dean of students, the business manager, and the director of development. The college budget was around $1.7 million a year.

In 1969 the college created a faculty assembly and a cooperative council, the one concerned with academic affairs and the other with student affairs. All of the teaching faculty comprised the faculty assembly; administrative officers and students might serve on faculty committees but have no vote in the assembly. The faculty assembly was delegated "primary responsibility" by the board of trustees on matters of admission, degree requirements, curriculum, faculty status, the library, the instructional budget, and general academic development. Major issues of policy still had to be approved by the board of trustees. The cooperative council consisted of three students, three faculty members, and three administrative officers. The student government association elected the student members, and the faculty assembly elected the faculty representatives. The cooperative council, subject to the reserve power of the board, was given authority to make regulations governing student behavior and residential life and to establish and supervise a judicial structure. In addition, the cooperative council might advise the president and board on any issues affecting the welfare of the college community.

The arrangements instituted in 1969 represented the culmination of nearly ten years of campus debate about governance. Prior to that time, decision making in the college was centralized, for all practical purposes, in the person of the president. Early in the 1960s, faculty discontent surfaced over the issue of the faculty teaching load. At that time there were ten trustees, all members of the Dominican order. Five of them were resident in Ohio and seldom met in New Haven; the other five trustees included three administrative officers of the college (the president, the academic dean, and the librarian). The perceived need to reorganize the board of trustees encouraged faculty insistence upon a faculty decision-making role in academic affairs. Two student disruptions demonstrated the further need to provide for student participation in campus governance.

Agreement about the scope and nature of changed relationships since the late 1960s has not come readily at Albertus Magnus. Some faculty members were strongly antiadministration; others emphasized the need for common endeavor and compromise. Eventually all but three administrative officers were excluded from the faculty assembly, and the president was excluded from all but the two faculty committees on which the president had no vote. The faculty insisted upon naming its own chairman of the assembly. In practice, however, the faculty assembly brought about a better communication and a closer working relationship between faculty and administration at the college. In 1967–68, student unrest was quite evident on the campus, the underlying cause appearing to be the exclusion of students from the decision-making process. Students boycotted classes, and student leaders demanded authority to interpret all administrative and academic regulations. This last proposal produced faculty opposition, of course. Out of this conflict emerged the cooperative council, a tripartite representative body.

The record of the cooperative council after 1969 at Albertus

Magnus was somewhat disappointing to all concerned. Students felt that student conduct regulations were altered too little, too slowly. Housemothers were replaced by student coordinators. Each house (freshman houses excepted)' was permitted to fix its own curfew. A proposal for each house to determine all social regulations was withdrawn when it became evident that a majority of students did not support it. Subsequently, visiting hours for male guests were extended after lengthy debate about social regulations versus the transmission of values by personal conviction and example. In 1970 debate arose between students and faculty about the role of a college in society. In later years student activism began to recede.

The key issue to emerge in the 1970s has been survival and how to survive well. The faculty assembly took the initiative in raising the issue. In short order the faculty was confronted with questions about the meaning of *Catholic, liberal arts,* and *college for women.* Discussion became rampant; agreement proved elusive. For example, in the discussions of the catholicity of the college, some faculty members believed that this character was reflected in the visible witness of Catholic members of the faculty (especially the Dominican sisters) and in an active campus ministry. Others argued that it meant giving the highest priority to competent departments of religious study and philosophy. Still others saw it as a commitment to the Christian view of man and society; that is, the dignity of the human person and education of the individual as a "whole" person. Yet others interpreted catholicity in the light of Vatican II, as an ecumenical spirit encouraging dialogue between individuals of differing religious and social convictions. It is admirable, however, that these discussions were held without conjuring up visions of religious domination or of a loss of academic freedom. The concept of the liberal arts was broadened to emphasize the vocational or applied dimensions of the various academic disciplines. The college also began to move toward a new student clientele.

In budget matters the faculty assembly and its committees were reluctant to assume any considerable authority. College economics appeared to inhibit faculty discussion and decision. The budget remained the province of the president and board. The faculty

was acutely aware only of income stringency and the need to econo-
mize in expenditures. At least a sense of shared community had
been enhanced in the struggle for survival.

## Four Transitional Colleges

*Armstrong.* Armstrong State College in Savannah was
founded as a junior college in 1935. Originally housed in a downtown mansion, the college has built or acquired five additional
buildings. It became part of the University System of Georgia on
January 1, 1959, and by authorization of the board of regents began
conversion to a four-year state college in 1964. In December 1965
the college moved from downtown Savannah to a 200-acre sub-
urban site. Enrollment increased from 800 full-time equivalent students in 1965 to over 2,500 full-time equivalent students in 1975.
While the college offers programs in the arts and sciences, the professional programs in business, nursing, criminal justice, and education have drawn the most students.

Over 90 percent of the students come from the Savannah
area, and the student body has been basically conservative. The
college was not affected during the 1960s by the student dissension
and disruption experienced elsewhere. When a small group of student activists sought to establish a local chapter of Students for a
Democratic Society in 1968, the student activities committee, composed of four students, five faculty members, and one administrative officer, unanimously rejected the petition. Efforts to excite student protest over this decision proved futile. A student government
organization has worked for change in some student regulations
through established channels, and some change has taken place.

Governance on the Armstrong State campus has had to
operate within the context of a highly centralized state system controlled by a single multicampus governing board—the board of regents—and directed by a state chancellor. Thus, some academic
requirements (those for general education) are centrally prescribed,
and all degree programs must be approved by the board. Although
there is some flexibility and discretion available to the college administrative staff and faculty, the scope of this authority is limited.
Local initiative in establishing governance arrangements is subject

to central scrutiny and approval. The contents of the statutes and bylaws of Armstrong State were dictated in large part by a 200-page document on policies, published by the board of regents.

Initially, in Armstrong's history as a four-year college, matters of academic program and policies were recommended to the president by a faculty council comprising the academic dean, all department chairmen, and elected faculty members. An administrative council included one department chairman and one faculty member. In 1967 the structure of governance was revised to include the administrative council, a student government association, and a faculty with various committees, the most important of which was the executive committee, replacing the former faculty council. This executive committee, presided over by the dean of the college, included six elected faculty members. Students served on eleven of the sixteen faculty committees and might attend faculty meetings but might not vote. The faculty as of 1975 numbered 160 persons, including administrative officers with faculty rank. The executive committee nominated persons for membership on all committees. All actions of the faculty, the administrative council, and of the student government association were subject to veto by the president, an arrangement required by the board of regents.

As a junior college, the Armstrong instructional program was entirely oriented toward academic disciplines. As a senior college, Armstrong developed professional programs. This change caused some controversy within the college but was confirmed by the faculty in 1971 when a statement of college purpose, drafted by a committee of five faculty members and two students, was approved. Other faculty debates concerned the admission of older students and the extent of the "core courses" in professional programs. Budget issues were left entirely to the president. A proposal in 1973 to establish a faculty finance committee to advise the president was defeated in the executive committee. Instructional practices at Armstrong have been left largely to departments and individual faculty members. The faculty did support development of an academic skills program for students of limited academic competence. The faculty also sought to provide various forms of encouragement to the most gifted students. Student evaluation of instruction was developed within the faculty. National censure of Armstrong State by the American Association of University Professors arose out of a conflict over nonobservance of prescribed procedures for consideration of a faculty grievance.

Because the college had almost no residential students, the problems of residence-hall life were not present. The most troublesome student conduct issues were the honor code and a procedure for considering student grievances about course grades. Student interest in campuswide governance was only lukewarm, and faculty members did not encourage it. Faculty and students appeared to be generally satisfied with the structure of student representation on faculty committees.

To some extent there was a kind of adversary relationship between faculty and administration at Armstrong State, but for the most part the faculty saw itself as dominant in academic affairs insofar as the rules of the board of regents permitted and was not disposed to involve itself with administrative affairs lest control of academic matters might somehow be jeopardized. The small size of the college encouraged internal communication, and there were frequent informal contacts between faculty, students, and administration. Within the governing structure of the university system, these arrangements remained generally acceptable as of 1976. The principal faculty concern for the future was the relationship of Armstrong State to Savannah State College, a predominantly black institution. Since 1971 Armstrong had been under mandate from the board of regents to develop joint master's degree programs with Savannah State, but relationships between the two state colleges remain fragile and fraught with complexities.

*Central Connecticut State.* Established as a normal school in 1849, Central Connecticut State College in New Britain is the oldest public institution of higher education in the state. In 1933 the normal school was redesignated a teachers college, and in 1959 the institution became Central Connecticut State College, a multipurpose general baccalaureate college. Since 1955 the program offerings have included the master's degree in education. Programs in the arts and sciences were expanded to the master's degree level in 1968. The enrollment at Central Connecticut expanded from some 8,200 students in 1966 to over 13,000 students in 1975. More than 8,000 students were enrolled full-time, almost all of them at the under-

graduate level. Some 5,000 part-time students were largely commuting students enrolled in the late afternoon and evening; half of
such students were candidates for the master's degree. By 1975–76
the annual operating budget was around $20 million. The college
was organized into four schools, each under the general supervision
of a dean: arts and sciences, business, education and professional
studies, and graduate.

Central Connecticut was one of four state colleges (and the
largest) under a board of trustees of sixteen persons, fourteen appointed by the governor and two students elected by students of the
colleges. The board was served by an executive secretary but had
delegated substantial authority to the president of each college as
administrative agent of the board. Campus governance was necessarily constructed and operated within the structure of policies and
expectations of a multicampus governing board. The board of
trustees replaced the state board of education as the governing board
of Connecticut state colleges only in 1965, and the following ten
years were years of some centralization of authority. These were
also the years of maximum growth at Central Connecticut.

A faculty senate was organized at Central Connecticut only
in 1970. Prior to that date the faculty had endeavored to transact
business as a whole. A college senate functioned as a kind of executive committee but had no substantive authority. The town-meeting
tradition was so strong within the faculty that various proposals
prior to 1970 to create a representative body to transact faculty
business were defeated. The establishment of a faculty senate was
strongly supported by the president of the college and by some faculty leaders and was finally accepted by faculty vote in April 1970.
The membership of the faculty senate was based upon one senator
for every fifteen full-time members of the staff. The resulting membership consisted of sixty-one persons: forty members elected by
thirty-two academic departments, two elected by the laboratory
school, two elected by the library staff, four elected by the department chairmen and division directors, five elected by the administrative staff, and eight members ex officio (president, two vice-presidents, and five deans). The formal authority of the faculty senate
was that officially vested in the college president: to develop bylaws
for the college consistent with the personnel and other policies of

the board of trustees. Legislation by the faculty senate was subject to veto by the president. The senate met twice monthly, and elected its own presiding officer. The senate operated through a steering committee and various standing committees.

Of 137 actions taken by the faculty senate between 1970 and 1975, three were disapproved by the president, four were modified, and one deferred. The measures disapproved involved creation of an FM radio station and of a sabbatical leave committee with faculty membership; both were disapproved for budgetary reasons. Another proposal called for a standing budget committee to expand senate participation in the budget process; the president held that existing procedures, including an advisory senate committee on the college budget, were preferable. Measures modified by the president and his administrative colleagues concerned a faculty evaluation form, procedure for making an annual distinguished faculty service award, new faculty personnel procedures contrary to board policies, and arrangements for establishing a summer educational opportunity program for disadvantaged students. The president deferred implementation of senate action to abolish the laboratory school. Frequent informal consultation between senate committee members and administrative officers ensured consensus on most senate actions.

The quantitative record of the faculty senate at Central Connecticut is substantial; it translates into an average of two major actions per meeting. Moreover, the work of the committees and the debates of the senate have encouraged a widespread sense of faculty participation in institutional decision making. The Central Connecticut faculty has expressed concern that the systemwide personnel policies and other regulations developed by the board of trustees tend to decrease institutional autonomy and to negate the role of the faculty senate in resolving issues of importance to the campus community. F. Don Janes, the first new president in forty years when he took office in 1968, has stressed from the beginning his desire to share authority and responsibility with the faculty. This initiative greatly encouraged the collaboration between faculty senate and president that occurred in the years from 1968 through 1976.

Students, however, were excluded from the faculty structure

developed as of 1970. The issue of shared governance was continually brought up in meetings of the faculty senate, but a majority of the members were not willing to include student representatives on committees or in the senate. In 1975 by law the Connecticut General Assembly added two students to the board of trustees and specified that two of the members appointed by the governor must be alumni of the colleges. At Central Connecticut the faculty senate and the student senate created a liaison committee to keep both bodies informed about the activities and concerns of each.

Senate leadership had been greatly tempted on various occasions to seek to by-pass the president and to deal directly with the board of trustees. On matters of personnel policies, budget priorities, and pending state legislation, senate members were disposed to go directly to the board. Only firm insistence by the board upon working with the college through the president had prevented this practice from developing. Nonetheless, faculty members perceived that an increase in faculty authority could only emanate from the board of trustees and not from the president; as a result there remained this inclination to "woo" the board. Governance has remained in many ways an unresolved issue at Central Connecticut because of uncertainties in 1976 about faculty collective bargaining, the role of the president in a multicampus system, and the future organization structure of public higher education in Connecticut, which was under active debate. For some faculty members the real issues of the future were job security, salaries, and fringe benefits. They seemed to feel that these critical issues could be resolved only by faculty collective bargaining and that a senate structure could be left in place to resolve such remaining educational issues as academic standards, curriculum changes, and student behavior.

*Eastern Montana.* Established in 1927 by act of the Montana legislature as a two-year normal school, in 1946 Eastern Montana became a four-year college of education. The college has had master's degree programs in education since 1954, and in 1966 it was authorized to offer programs in the arts and sciences. Since 1966 Eastern Montana College has operated as a multipurpose general baccalaureate college, adding programs at the associate degree level in 1972. As of 1975 the college enrolled 3,400 students.

Eastern Montana College is one of six colleges and univer-

sities comprising a multicampus system under the governing authority of the Montana Board of Regents of Higher Education. The
board was established by the Montana State Constitution with "full
power, responsibility, and authority to supervise, coordinate, manage, and control the Montana University System. . . ." The
board's staff work was headed by the commissioner of higher education. The board delegated administration of the college to the
president of the institution, who was expected faithfully to execute
all policies of the board and to exercise "local authority and responsibility" for campus operations. The president of the college thus
became the central authority of campus governance.

Since 1959 the principal agency serving in an advisory capacity to the president has been an academic council. This council
expanded from fourteen members in 1966 to twenty-eight members
in 1970, but was cut back to thirteen members in 1973. The academic vice-president serves as chairman, and the other members
are three elected faculty members, three elected students, and three
appointed administrative officers. In addition, there are some twenty
standing committees, made up usually of faculty, students, and administrators, which report to the academic council. The committees have such assignments as general education, teacher education,
graduate study, admissions, financial aid, student affairs, registration, library, Indian education, operations, and athletics. A committee on rank and tenure and an administrative council report
directly to the president and not to the academic council.

For the most part the standing committees have evolved into
policy-making committees. Only on rare occasions has either the
academic council or the president believed it necessary to modify
or to veto a proposal from a standing committee. This trend is most
noticeable in matters of academic affairs: faculty promotions, faculty appointments, recommendations for tenure, approval of new
courses, and exceptions for individual students from degree requirements. The president as of 1966 felt that in the transition phase of
Eastern Montana, which continued during the next ten years, widespread participation of faculty, students, and administrators, through
an elaborate committee structure, was desirable. In 1969 a North
Central accreditation team visiting the campus noted that Eastern
Montana College had an administrative structure and a committee
system "appropriate for an institution three times its size."

Student behavior standards on the Eastern Montana campus were generally fixed by the academic council, with advice from the standing committee on student affairs. In 1970, because of student agitation on several campuses, the Montana Board of Regents issued a reminder that students were subject to federal, state, and local laws as well as to institutional regulations. Each campus, in consultation with faculty and students, was directed to review and restate standards of student conduct. The academic council established a committee of six faculty members, seven students, and the dean of students to establish these standards. The result was a document on rights and responsibilities of the campus community, based largely on a report of the Carnegie Commission on Higher Education, of which the president of Eastern Montana was a member. This document was approved by the academic council in 1973.

The academic council has been concerned with academic policies and programs within the college. It has also been involved with such "gray" areas as the use of college facilities, intercollegiate athletics, student publications, publication of a faculty and staff handbook, and general rights and responsibilities of the campus community. A faculty rank and tenure committee recommends appropriate action to the president on promotion and tenure. This committee, composed of six full professors elected at large, the deans of the two schools of the college, and the academic vice-president as chairman, has had a record of long hours, hard work, and little appreciation. At one point, in 1972, the committee voted to dissolve itself, but the faculty refused to concur.

The corporate faculty at Eastern Montana meets each academic quarter to perform primarily routine matters: to elect faculty members to the academic council, the committee on rank and tenure, and the faculty senate; to hear reports from the president and others; and to discuss occasional matters relating to faculty welfare. The faculty senate of twelve members serves as a kind of executive committee of the faculty representing faculty viewpoints to the president and presenting issues to the faculty as a whole for endorsement. Matters considered by the senate are not usually debated extensively by the faculty. Often the senate is also asked by the president to nominate faculty members to serve on ad hoc committees. By 1975 faculty collective bargaining was under way, and it seemed evident that the faculty senate might well recede in importance, especially since the senate had never had a decision making role in the governance structure of the college.

The major problem issues from 1966 to 1975 at Eastern Montana included: summer session programming and budgeting, academic council structure and membership, sabbatical leave policy, student participation in standing committees, general education requirements, student evaluation of faculty, establishment of a faculty committee on budgeting, faculty salaries, administrative organization, faculty promotion standards, and faculty role in the appointment of deans and other academic administrators. One of the positive accomplishments of the period was the development of a program in Native American studies, which could serve as an academic minor in both arts and sciences and teacher education. As the decade proceeded, it was evident that faculty expression tended to become more strident, moving from advice to position papers to demands. During this same period more and more decisions appeared to fall to the academic council. At the same time it was apparent that the president was more and more caught in the middle, between faculty aspirations on the one hand and the board's policies and budgets on the other hand. Faculty collective bargaining appeared to be the faculty's choice in response to the realities of a multicampus system and the state government's declining interest in higher education. As of 1976, the outline of the future was obscure.

*Frostburg State.* Founded in 1898 in the western panhandle of Maryland as a two-year normal school, Frostburg State College became one of six state colleges removed from the governing authority of the state board of education in 1963, placed under the jurisdiction of the Maryland Board of Trustees of State Colleges, and assigned a multipurpose mission. Frostburg shared much of the history of traditional teachers colleges, a history that recently has meant a transition from hierarchy to community of internal campus authority. The academic program of teachers colleges was largely prescriptive, determined by the requirements of teacher certification. The administrative style of teachers college presidents was modeled on superintendents of schools rather than on presidents of liberal arts colleges and of comprehensive universities.

With transition from a single-purpose to a multipurpose

mission, academic planning and administrative style also underwent transition. This story was well illustrated at Frostburg. The president as of 1963 was unable to bridge the change, an acting president from 1963 to 1965 was the center of considerable controversy, and a new president in 1965 began to lay the groundwork for faculty preeminence in governance of academic affairs. When the president resigned to become president of another college in 1969, faculty, students, and staff were consulted by the board of trustees in selecting a new president. Since 1969 the effort to achieve faculty preeminence has given way to an effort to achieve community governance.

Under the statutes of Maryland, it is clearly evident that the authority for operation and management of the several state colleges was vested in the board of trustees and the individual presidents. The board of trustees in turn specified only that each college should include in its faculty handbook a written statement concerning the role of faculty members in the governance of the college and that each college should determine those college committees on which "student representatives can serve effectively." In 1975 the Maryland legislature directed that a student member should be added to the board of trustees. Much of the character of campus governance depended on the inclinations of the college president and on the forces at work on each particular state college campus. The state personnel classification system, however, did much to draw a sharp line of distinction between faculty and administrative officers, including the president.

Experience in Maryland under statutory provisions and in state governmental expectation indicates a preference for a campus structure of authority by which the president is clearly "in charge." Governors and legislators tend to ascribe institutional successes and failures to the president. On occasion, a president has been chided about some decision with the comment: "You are the president, how did you ever let that happen?" Or a state official might say: "You spend too damn much time asking faculty members what they think!" Moreover, administrative controls exercised by the governor's office in Annapolis and by other state agencies make no essential distinction between executive departments and higher education institutions.

Student and faculty attitudes toward administration at Frost-

burg have been fairly traditional. Although many students are
largely indifferent to campus affairs, a few student leaders and publication editors have watched presidential leadership closely and
have expected this leadership to be supportive of student interests
as student leadership defines them. Students assume that the president has power to do whatever he sees fit and pay little attention
to state government power in Annapolis or to faculty power in
Frostburg. Older faculty members have tended to be deferential to
presidential authority, while younger faculty members have tended
to be critical. The development of a sense of community, of common
interest, has been difficult to achieve in this environment. Only
gradually has the realization dawned that the "enemy" may not be
sitting in the president's office but might be located in the state
capital. The board of trustees in Maryland has performed only a
minimum role of governance. The board has been largely concerned
with common procedures for budgeting and fiscal management,
with admissions, and with record keeping. State government, on the
other hand, has been omnipresent.

In 1965 the president at Frostburg established the practice of
monthly faculty meetings. The president insisted that the faculty
establish a considerable number of standing committees on such
matters as admissions, curriculum, academic standards, athletics,
student affairs, and buildings and grounds. A proposal for a committee on promotions and tenure engendered considerable controversy that ended in a decision to have no such committee. After
extensive discussion the faculty decided it did not wish to establish
the needed standards of student conduct but wished to leave them in
the hands of the president. Students and student personnel officers
then began lengthy negotiations to arrive at an acceptable code of
expected student behavior. The faculty increasingly, however, accepted authority for decisions on academic affairs. Then, around
1970, students demanded a voice in campus governance. Students
were first admitted to faculty meetings as observers. Then a college
forum was created, and this in turn gave way in 1971 to a college
senate. Student demands received greater support from administrative officers than from the faculty, partly because of the generally
conservative and responsible behavior of student leaders. The college senate consisted of ten students elected by the student associa-

tion, ten faculty members elected by the faculty assembly, four department heads elected by all department heads, and five administrative officers elected by the administrative staff. The senate elected its own chairman. In addition, students were added to all committees. Both alumni and civil service staff were excluded from the college senate.

The college senate at Frostburg has wrestled with a number of issues since 1971. These issues have included residence-hall arrangements for some 2,800 undergraduate students in a town of just 7,000 inhabitants; the development of graduate instruction and its relationship to undergraduate instruction; institutional planning (as directed by the governor in 1974); adoption of a statement of institutional goals; faculty productivity; the location of an environmental laboratory of the University of Maryland on the campus; student financial assistance; campus cultural activities (Is a rock concert "cultural"?); budget priorities; student fee increases; the summer school budget; faculty evaluation; library usage; and use of campus facilities. The college senate was not able to resolve all such issues; no decision was made on faculty evaluation, and decisions about budget priorities were too general to be of much administrative usefulness. But the communication achieved in the consideration of these problems did much to acquaint the academic community with its own complexities, as well as to help develop some sense of the need for a common interest in the resolution of issues. Campuswide governance has had some success at Frostburg in clarification of instructional program objectives and in the development of new academic programs. It has been least productive in clarifying the objectives of support programs, in clarifying budget priorities, in establishing standards of faculty and student behavior, and in program evaluation. For all the efforts at community involvement, both faculty members and students have had interests and points of view that are narrowly rather than institutionally focused.

## Three New Institutions

*Evergreen State.* Evergreen State College was established by an act of the Washington State Legislature in 1967. The board of trustees held its organizational meeting in August of that year, and the first president began his duties of office in August 1968. By September 1970 an administrative and support staff had been assembled, and in the autumn of 1971 the college opened with a faculty of fifty-five persons and an enrollment of 1,100 students. As of the autumn of 1975, enrollment had risen to 2,500 students and the number of faculty members to 125.

From the outset, Evergreen has been governance-conscious. Conceived and organized at the end of the turbulent 1960s, Evergreen had to develop a governance structure unfettered by tradition but related to a college that saw its mission as the creation of a responsive and relevant educational program reflecting a humanistic rather than a behavioral theory of learning. A model of governance was devised that was both idealistic, placing considerable trust in an open evaluation system, and realistic, recognizing that a state college cannot be an independent democratic community. The governance structure thus devised was representational and consensual. While there was more "power" near the top or center of the structure than at the base, the proper exercise of that power was the condition for its exercise. Some have referred to the governance of Evergreen as that of a benevolent dictatorship. It might more accurately be termed a government of benign autocracy.

From the beginning, the faculty has been expected to be the center of decision making. The faculty is not organized into departments and divisions. A faculty member operates as an individual or as a participant in a small group of from three to five persons. These groups hold together for only one academic year and offer interdisciplinary "coordinated" studies. Faculty groups may devise written or unwritten understandings about their instructional objectives and their sharing of activity. Students also may become a party to these understandings or covenants. In any one year, as many as 60 percent of all faculty members have entered into these groupings. The remaining 40 percent function individually, entering into individual contracts with students to consider a common subject or a project-oriented endeavor. Faculty organization has thus been intended to emphasize the primary function of the faculty, which is to teach rather than to administer a campus. A clear dichotomy has been sought at Evergreen between governing the learning process and governing the campus as an enterprise.

Evergreen has four academic deans designated by letters of the Greek alphabet. Faculty members are assigned to one of the academic deans more or less at random. Deans have considerable power: to hire and retain faculty members, to allocate budget resources, to determine office and program space, to make assignments to instructional groupings. Faculty members meet with the dean once a week, and all decisions are discussed in these meetings. Deans are faculty members and serve three-year terms. The faculty members assigned to a particular dean may be reassigned the following year. The deans in turn meet regularly with the vice-president and provost of the college.

The directors of support services at Evergreen do not rotate in their positions but are recognized as "permanent" heads of services, such as the library, the computer center, and the business office. Deans are encouraged to work directly with these directors and not to seek the assistance of the top administrative officers. Deans and directors have a weekly breakfast meeting in order to encourage informal communication and consultation. Decisions are made by deans and directors, not by groups. But decisions are expected to be made only after considerable discussion. The vice-president and provost and the administrative vice-president confer frequently with deans and directors and with each other in order to ensure the continuing flow of essential information. In turn, the two vice-presidents necessarily work closely with the president.

The board of trustees consists of five persons appointed by the governor and confirmed by the state senate for five-year staggered terms. The board has final responsibility for all operations of the college as delegated by state government. The board has been generally supportive of the thrust of all college decisions; from the beginning, Evergreen was planned to be different from other state colleges, and the board approved this decision. At the same time, the board gave a great deal of time to the college in an effort to ensure some adjustment between internal aspirations and external expectations.

Evergreen has no student organization; the students have periodically discussed the desirability of some kind of organized student government arrangement but have rejected all such proposals. The college has made extensive use of ad hoc committees to resolve issues of campuswide dimension. Such committees have always consisted of faculty members, students, staff members, and administrative officers. Committees have often been selected on a random basis from computer listings. The composition of a committee is made public, as is the committee's mission, and the reports are circulated throughout the campus community. The committees may be named by any decision maker: the president, one of the two vice-presidents, the directors of service, an academic dean. The final decision is that of the responsible policy maker. There were only three permanent advisory boards within the college as of 1976, one on student publications, one on the broadcasting station, and one on professional leaves. Information flow has been facilitated within the college by organization of an information center, by establishment of the "Sounding Board," and by periodic convenings of a college forum.

The Sounding Board is an arrangement of thirty-six persons presided over by the president. Ten are appointed by each vice-president and fifteen are students selected by fellow students, usually by volunteering to serve. Participation is limited to three academic quarters. The sounding board is a device for considering reports of ad hoc committees or for discussing any current campus issue. Grievances are handled by mediation or by appeal to a campus hearing board of three members (one faculty, one student, one administrative officer). If a formal hearing is held, two temporary members are added, one each from the peer group of the two disputants.

The governance structure thus outlined was originally set forth in a document titled "Governance and Decision Making at Evergreen." The document was written by a committee on governance and was accepted by the board of trustees in the autumn of 1971. It was reviewed and revised by an ad hoc committee in 1974; the committee chairman was a member of the clerical staff. Some ambiguities were clarified, but the original document was retained essentially unchanged. Two doctrines underlay the decision-making system. Decisions must be made closest to those who would be affected thereby. Those responsible for decision making must be locatable and accountable: they must be identifiable, and they must bear the responsibility for action. In general, between 1971 and 1976 the structure of decision making and the decisions resulting therefrom appeared to be generally satisfactory to the community. The college had to grapple with and resolve issues involving facilities, academic programming, self-study assessment for accreditation, budget development within a state government formula, reduction in force as mandated by the governor because of state financial difficulties, affirmative action organization (which went all the way to the board), and other problems. The emphasis throughout was upon participation: participation in academic planning, in academic operation, in academic standards of conduct. Evergreen College has made its difference visible and generally acceptable to those who have voluntarily joined the community. To many persons outside the campus community, the difference may appear strange, even bizarre, and has been the basis for considerable criticism.

*Northern Kentucky.* Northern Kentucky State College was created in 1968 by act of the state legislature to meet higher education needs in the most rapidly growing part of the state, the Kentucky side of the Cincinnati metropolitan area. The name was changed to Northern Kentucky University in 1976.

The state already had two major universities (Kentucky and Louisville) and five regional universities when Northern Kentucky was founded. There had been a community college in the northern Kentucky area since 1948, administered by the University of Kentucky. This community college was dissolved by the 1968 legislation, and its programs were taken over by the new state college. The new board of regents selected a president in the autumn of 1969. A new campus site was selected in Highland Heights, about five miles from downtown Cincinnati, and classes were started on the new campus in the autumn of 1972. Enrollment had passed the 6,000 student head-count projection by the autumn of 1975, and still further growth is anticipated. Construction of a campus concurrently with instruction created some confusion and disruption. As of 1975–76 the campus consisted of two classroom buildings, a library, and a gymnasium-auditorium. Construction of a student center was under way, and another classroom and physical education building were in the planning stage.

With an operating budget of approximately $10 million in 1975–76, Northern Kentucky offers fourteen associate degree programs, thirty majors at the baccalaureate level, and a master's degree in education. The college has also acquired by gift an independent law school previously located in Cincinnati; the law school uses the former community college campus. The organizational structure of Northern Kentucky is fairly traditional: a board of regents, a president, two vice-presidents, and directors of various staff and support services. The university was to be organized into four colleges (including law) as of 1976–77. The first president has shown much interest in involving faculty and students in the decision-making process.

The device established in 1971 for campuswide governance was the administrative council, composed of thirteen administrative officers, thirteen department chairmen, four faculty members, and two students. The vice-president for academic affairs serves as chairman and appoints the other members. The administrative council is the final body to recommend desirable policy to the president and board. It might receive policy proposals from the faculty senate, standing and ad hoc committees, and department chairmen. In essence, three constituent groups are expected to submit proposals to the administrative council: the faculty senate, the student government, and the inter-organizational council (a group of delegates from student organizations).

The faculty senate is composed of one representative from each department and ten faculty members elected at large. The senate meets monthly. All faculty members belong to the faculty assembly, but the assembly meets infrequently to consider issues decided by the senate about which there might be considerable controversy. The senate has three standing committees selected by it and reporting to it: academic affairs, student affairs, and faculty affairs. At one time the faculty senate gave serious consideration to withdrawing from the administrative council on the grounds that the council was not a proper body to stand between the senate and the president and board. This action was not taken. Another issue was whether or not the administrative council might modify proposals from the faculty senate. In 1973 the council agreed to accept or reject proposals, although, in one subsequent action relating to sabbatical leaves, the council did reduce the amount of the stipend.

The administrative council at Northern Kentucky has had a full agenda. From 1971 to 1973 the council met weekly; by 1975 the number of meetings had been reduced to twice monthly. The agenda is not distributed in advance, but the practice has arisen that items introduced for discussion at one meeting will not be voted on until the next meeting. The council has considered a variety of issues: the development of a statement of college purpose, a statement on institutional role and scope prepared for the Kentucky Council on Public Higher Education, the approval of all degree programs submitted by the faculty senate, the recruitment of students from the Ohio side of the river, the encouragement of part-time enrollment, the encouragement of faculty research, faculty involvement in off-campus consulting activity, the evaluation of faculty, general education requirements, noncredit courses, the expansion of support services such as a student health service, the imposition and use of a student activity fee, student advising, and class scheduling. Proposals on all of these subjects originated from outside the council. The council has served as a vehicle for expressing varying points of view about the needs and resources of the college and has ensured some degree of internal communication before decisions are made by the board upon recommendation of the president.

The most divisive issue to emerge at Northern Kentucky has been that of tenure. When Northern Kentucky was created, it acquired the faculty and facilities of Northern Community College. Early in 1972, the administrative council, after some debate, adopted a proposal that the usual probationary period for faculty members would be three years. Then the faculty doubled in size in the autumn of 1972, and all of these faculty members became eligible for tenure in 1975. An ad hoc committee was appointed in 1974 to develop new criteria and procedures for awarding tenure, but this action was widely interpreted as a move to delay tenure status for all the faculty members who considered themselves eligible for tenure in 1975. The committee recommended with slight modification the procedures formulated by the American Association of University Professors (AAUP), including a probationary period of six years. The faculty senate endorsed the recommendations, but in the administrative council the procedure was modified to shorten the time required for advance notice of nonreappointment. This action by the administrative council resulted in faculty objection to the board of regents, which restored the original AAUP procedure. The entire episode brought about strained faculty-administration relationships at Northern Kentucky.

A large number of younger faculty members hired at Northern Kentucky have expressed dissatisfaction with the arrangement of the administrative council and the lack of an adequate faculty role in its deliberations, as they viewed the situation. Relationships between faculty and administration deteriorated steadily during the calendar year 1975; the tenure issue was only one part of a mounting controversy. Ill-founded charges were made of administration efforts to spy upon faculty activities. The administration proceeded to bring action to terminate the appointment status of one faculty member, and this caused still further conflict. In September 1975 the president resigned. A new president was not selected until the summer of 1976. A review of campus governance structure is expected during the new president's period of service.

*California State College at Bakersfield.* Opened in September 1970, California State at Bakersfield was the newest, the second smallest, and in many ways the most innovative of the nineteen campuses comprising the California State University and College system. When the college faculty assembled for the first time in September, the members heard a presentation by Lewis B. Mayhew of Stanford about the stages and complications of college development. Many of his predictions were to be borne out by experience.

The basic structure of the college's academic program had been set forth in a master plan prepared in the spring of 1968 by the academic dean. The plan was approved by the board of trustees of the system in July of that year. The plan called for a three-course, three-term calendar, a general education seminar for sophomores and for seniors in the bachelor of arts program, an integration of living and learning through residence centers for freshmen and sophomores and through "living-study" centers for upperclass students, the encouragement of interdisciplinary programs and courses, and student involvement in academic planning. The faculty senate, as at all other campuses in the system, was expected to be influential in translating these broad outlines into specific degree requirements, course offerings, and other academic practices.

Because of experience on other campuses, including those of

the California state system, the president in 1970 decided to encourage the development of a college council, the membership of which would be drawn from students and staff as well as from faculty members. As established in September 1970, the college council consisted of twelve faculty members, four students, one representative of the nonprofessional staff, three deans, two division chairmen, and certain designated heads of support services. The academic vice-president was selected by the president to be chairman of the council. This arrangement, begun in 1970, was still in operation in 1976. The membership had increased from twenty-seven to thirty-six voting members, with sixteen members from the faculty, seven from the student body, and two from the nonprofessional staff. The college council became advisory to the president and the chief agency for approving instructional programs, appraising curricular innovation, and recommending policy decisions. The council was also recognized as the principal mechanism within the college for providing for communication among all segments of the academic community.

The survival and the apparent stability of the college council in the early history of Bakersfield was real enough, but also could easily be misunderstood. The fact was that a very substantial proportion of the decisions affecting the Bakersfield campus were not made on the campus but were made by the chancellor's office and the system's board of trustees. In addition, in the years since 1970 the presidential style of leadership and faculty attitudes have changed. Nonetheless, in the autumn of 1975 there was some faculty sentiment in favor of keeping all "academic" affairs in the jurisdiction of the faculty senate rather than putting them before a multiconstituency council. Both a faculty forum and a staff forum had grown up as devices for single-constituency discussion, but formalized advice to the president was transmitted only through the college council.

The California State University and College system, as it was designated in 1972, provided only limited autonomy to each campus. First, various governmental agencies in Sacramento exercised considerable control over system operations, more so than for the University of California system. Secondly, as the board of trustees expanded its control over the system, more and more decisions were made by the chancellor's office. The chancellor's office had grown by 1976 to include a professional staff of over 200 persons. In some instances the chancellor's office was simply cast in the role of carrying out directives from Sacramento. In other instances the chancellor's office made systemwide policies, such as a policy that all community college courses were to be accepted in fulfillment of requirements for the bachelor's degree. The chancellor's office ruled, in another instance, that Bakersfield might not offer a physics major but might offer a physical science major with a physics option.

The first president at Bakersfield believed in strong presidential leadership and was perceived as not attaching major weight to advice from the college. In 1973 this president was moved by the board of trustees to the presidency of San Francisco State University. The second president, named in 1974, had had no prior experience in the system and spent most of the first year learning about the restrictions imposed upon the college. In 1975 he sought the assistance of each faculty department, the principal administrative officers, and the college council in assessing institutional performance and program objectives. The president asked in particular: What qualities should the college seek to instill in its graduates? What instructional programs should the college be offering? What organizational arrangements would best enable the college to utilize its resources in the accomplishment of its objectives?

The college council was uncertain about the usefulness of this endeavor, but decided to accept the challenge lest the president alone endeavor to answer his own questions. A response to the first question was completed by December 1975. The response to the other two questions was then taken up in 1976. The response to the third question was in effect an invitation to reexamine the structure of governance at Bakersfield. It was clear by the summer of 1976 that the future of the college council really rested with faculty and student sentiment on the Bakersfield campus. Some administrators considered the council an interference with administrative authority. Student interest in the council clearly declined in the years after 1972. And, increasingly, the faculty preferred a faculty senate to decide academic affairs rather than a college council. Yet at the end of 1976 the college council was still in existence and still working.

As California State College at Bakersfield grew, it became

increasingly evident that its mission was not that of a residential college but that of a public higher education institution serving the Bakersfield area. Departments, schools, and the college had slowly adjusted to the understanding of this change. The college council became an agency for approving this change; it never was the leader or instigator of change. The most controversial issue was development of an acceptable program in law enforcement and corrections administration. Faculty ideas of an acceptable program differed from those of the potential clientele. Eventually, after two years of argument, a major in criminal justice was finally approved and established. A similar but somewhat less heated conflict centered around a program in child development. The organizing and offering of courses, especially master's degree programs, to teachers in the area also occasioned debate. Both schools and departments tended to be defensive of vested interests, and, as more and more programs of applied knowledge were put forward, fears about enrollment loss began to appear in the academic departments of the humanities and behavioral sciences—often in the guise of concern for maintaining standards and the eternal verities of higher education. The college council had to wrestle with these and similar issues, with little appreciation from the rest of the academic community.

Enrollment growth in 1974 and 1975 was below that projected, so the size of the faculty had to be reduced. The college council created a special committee on program review to assist the president in making necessary faculty cutbacks, and the recommendations of the committee were carried out in January 1975. The council also acted to slow down an interest in the development of a program of intercollegiate athletics. The college council found it necessary to decide that faculty personnel matters were not appropriate for student participation, and special procedures were devised involving only faculty and administration review and decision on matters of appointment, tenure, and promotion.

The college council appears to have made substantial contribution to the development of Bakersfield as a new campus in a multicampus system. At the same time its power base has been slowly eroding. Faculty members continue to think of academic affairs as distinct from administrative and student affairs. The system of community governance has served the college well in its formative years.

## Conclusion

The fifteen colleges whose experiences have been reviewed in this chapter are characterized by a variety of structures, procedures, and consequences. In many respects the experience of each college has been unique, yet certain similarities are observable.

The two highly selective colleges developed their instruments of campuswide governance under quite different circumstances and at different times. Both colleges have had a pervasive involvement of trustees in internal affairs; and campuswide governance at Carleton, by its arrangement for challenges to decisions of the college council, established the possibility of further trustee involvement. The two distinctive colleges are very different from each other in their mission, but both have had strong presidential leadership.

The four church-related colleges are widely scattered geographically, with the two Catholic colleges in large urban areas and the two Protestant colleges in small towns. All four have had some difficulty in defining their relationship to their church affiliation, especially as student conduct expectations departed from traditionally accepted norms. Moreover, the existence of alternative educational opportunities that were no longer as suspect as in earlier periods afforded prospective students a choice of educational environments. Enrollment considerations thus became a major factor for all four institutions to adjust to.

The seven state colleges in our sample make up two distinct groups, a transitional group and a new group. One state college has evolved from a community college, and three are former teachers colleges in various phases of more comprehensive development. At the time of this study, all four were experiencing complexities of adjustment to a state system in addition to a changing mission. Of the three new state colleges, two were created from new beginnings and one was created from a state university branch. All three have had difficulties growing out of newness; two have had the further concern of attempting to be innovative.

The independent colleges are relatively small in enrollment size and have endeavored to achieve a community consensus through personal relationships among students, faculty, and administrators. These personal relationships have been strained by different perspectives about roles and values. The two innovative state colleges have not had the enrollment growth expected for them; the other state colleges have had sustained enrollment expansion and, in two instances, have had rather spectacular expansion.

Perhaps the most evident common characteristic of these colleges is they experienced less student disruption than did the leading research and other universities. The priority given to undergraduate student instruction seems to have made a difference in the campus experience of the 1960s.

# CHAPTER SIX

◇◇◇◇◇◇◇◇◇◇◇◇

# Campus Governance in Action

◇◇◇◇◇◇◇◇◇◇◇◇◇◇◇◇◇◇◇◇◇◇◇◇◇◇◇◇◇◇◇◇◇◇◇

In the preceding three chapters, we have summarized the experience with new structures and processes of campuswide governance at thirty colleges and universities. Our concern primarily has been with events that helped to bring about changes in campus governance, with arrangements for involving two or three different groups in the structure of campuswide decision making, with issues that agitated campuswide governance in the decade after 1965, and with performance in helping to resolve these issues.

In general, it is accurate to say that campus governance underwent change after 1965. The ostensible cause, the precipitating event, in almost every instance was student activism and disruption. In some cases, students on residential campuses were especially eager to eliminate residence-hall and other conduct regulations deemed particularly restrictive of student behavior. In some instances, students desired to use the college or university as a base to protest the war in Vietnam, continued evidence of racism on or off campus, or higher education involvement in war-related recruitment and research. In a few instances, students wanted to be involved in decision making about student instruction and institutional priorities. Whatever the ostensible cause of student protest, the existing decision-making structure of the college or university was called into question.

Because of this student unrest and because of a desire to strengthen the faculty role in deciding administrative matters, faculties in some instances approved the reorganization of faculty governance without accepting the proposition of increased student participation in the decision-making process. This trend was especially noticeable at both Madison and Berkeley. In both instances, faculty domination of academic affairs was by no means to be surrendered to others, while faculty influence in relation to administrative officers was expected to be enhanced. In other universities and in general baccalaureate colleges with a tradition of strong presidential leadership, campuswide governance emerged as an advisory arrangement to influence that leadership without necessarily altering the actual locus of power within the campus structure. In many instances, presidents sought to broaden the appearance of legitimacy in the exercise of their own authority by consulting faculty members and students on campus issues.

In the light of the experience summarized in the preceding three chapters, it is appropriate to ask, What difference did campuswide governance structures make in institutional decision making? This question is obviously difficult to answer. As outlined more fully in the preface, we established eight areas of decision making with which to measure the performance of campuswide governance:

1. Clarification of institutional purposes
2. Clarification of program objectives
3. Clarification of budget priorities
4. Development of institutional income
5. Development of program technology and program management
6. Determination of degree requirements and of instructional outcomes

7. Determination of faculty and student behavior
8. Evaluation of program accomplishment

All of these areas of institutional concern deserve comment.

## Clarification of Institutional Purposes

Campuswide governance played a role in clarifying the educational purposes of the institution. This role was less evident in research universities than in other types of institutions. It appears that faculties and administrations tended to regard the mission of a leading research university as self-evident and were not particularly self-conscious about defining that role in general or specific terms. Even in the face of undergraduate student criticism that the research university was more interested in research, public service, and the instruction of graduate and graduate professional students than in the instruction of undergraduate students, neither faculty members nor administrative staff were inclined to be defensive about institutional priorities. A leading research university by definition did accept the priorities that undergraduate students complained about; if undergraduate students disliked this particular kind of learning environment, the faculty-administration attitude appeared to be that students had made a mistake in their enrollment choice and could always transfer someplace else.

Institutions other than the leading research universities tended to be more concerned about setting forth their formulation of educational purposes. The occasion for this formulation was most likely to arise in connection with a self-study preceding a periodic accreditation visit by a regional accrediting association. Since the focus of accreditation in recent years had shifted from so-called objective standards of quality to evaluation of performance in relation to specified purposes, a statement of mission then became an integral part of the accreditation process. As a consequence, some formulation of instructional, research, public service, educational justice, and other purposes became indispensable to institutional evaluation.

When confronted with the need to set forth a statement of mission, colleges and universities in the past decade or so have usually included campuswide governance as a major participant in developing such a statement. The day when a president, on his own or with the assistance of an administrative associate, would dare to prepare a statement of mission is gone. In an era of campuswide governance and of participation by various groups in institutional affairs, a president could no longer be the custodian or the articulator of institutional purposes. The entire academic community, through a representative body of some sort, expected to participate in the formulation of a statement of mission.

To be sure, a statement of mission developed by a representative body of campus constituents was likely to be primarily a rationalization of existing policies and programs. Experience demonstrated that a campus representative body was scarcely disposed to be innovative or forward-looking. Rather, the tendency was to accept the known and the familiar and to accommodate various points of view as fully as possible. By resorting to general and somewhat vague phrases, organs of campuswide governance endeavored to set forth purposes that could be subject to varying interpretation.

The student revolution in the 1960s did raise some very real questions about the social role of colleges and universities. In essence, these questions were as follows:

1. What is the role of higher education in relation to research needed to improve or develop weapons of national defense, including weapons for the war in Vietnam?
2. What is the role of higher education in the professional education of officers to serve in the armed forces of the United States?
3. What is the role of higher education in facilitating recruitment of degree recipients by industries heavily involved in producing weapons of war?
4. What is the role of higher education in providing community services to the disadvantaged, poor, minorities, and consumer groups in urban areas?
5. What is the role of higher education in overcoming or mitigating practices of racial or minority discrimination in society?
6. What is the role of higher education in overcoming or mitigating the existence of poverty in society?

7. What is the role of higher education in ensuring access to higher education by students of minority and disadvantaged status?
8. What is the role of higher education in investing endowment funds in relation to industries that are involved in defense production, or in production in South Africa or Rhodesia, or in production in nations with dictatorial regimes?

There is very little evidence that organs of campuswide governance, after they were established, were particularly effective in resolving these issues. Students, especially undergraduate students, were disposed to raise these issues from time to time, but faculty members, presidents, and administrative officers were not inclined to debate such questions at length or to formulate new positions on them. The traditional posture of colleges and universities has been apolitical, a posture of social neutrality in return for social acceptance of the practice of academic freedom. Students, in their attack upon the social neutrality of higher education, argued that neutrality was a pretense, in reality merely an alignment with the powerful and the wealthy in society.

The real issue, however, was financial support. Students had no answer to the question about how the programs and activities of higher education should be financed; some student spokesmen wanted a political and social alignment with the disadvantaged and continued or enlarged financial support from the advantaged. The contradiction in this position was apparent to administrators, who in turn communicated their concern to many faculty leaders. In their desire for financial advantage, faculty members could scarcely afford to be indifferent to the sources of income for the college or university of which they were a part.

Among the experiences examined here, the most extensive discussion of institutional purpose occurred in the "constitutional" convention at Syracuse University. This discussion was so lengthy and so intense that, for a time, the immediate objective of framing a charter of governance was almost completely submerged. Only a last-minute effort by a few individuals succeeded in producing a charter at all, and then the document was satisfactory only to students; the charter was rejected by faculty vote and by vote of the board of trustees.

Many organs of campuswide governance after 1968 found themselves involved in debates about Vietnam, Cambodia, draft resistance, and similar issues. Resolutions of opposition to various governmental actions were often approved with few, if any, dissenting votes. But apart from external publicity and internal indifference, these resolutions did nothing to clarify institutional purposes. Moreover, such resolutions suggested that colleges and universities were more interested in criticizing the behavior of other social institutions than in changing their own behavior. The campus senate or council became a forum for debate about society rather than a forum for debate about higher education or institutional performance.

Moreover, campuswide governance seemed singularly inept in providing any interpretation or specification of institutional purpose. Faculty members were generally reluctant to decide, through a campuswide organ of governance, the curriculum or course requirements for the general education component of an undergraduate education. There were too many vested interests to protect at the departmental level for faculty members to wish to involve students and others in this kind of central decision making. As administrators and others became more interested after 1972 in pushing career and professional education programs in order to maintain enrollment, campus senates and councils were not prepared to advance or to oppose these efforts. Faculty members in the arts and sciences were unhappy about the expansion of career and professional education and tried to delay or hamper such expansion as far as possible. But these same faculty members had no answer to the problem of changing student preferences in course or program enrollments. And even faculty members in the arts and sciences were not convinced that the campuswide organ of governance was the appropriate place to defend their interests.

Presidents who sought to involve campuswide governance in planning for the changing circumstances of the 1980s were usually disappointed in the results. Presidents pointed out the demographic fact of a substantial decline in the eighteen-year-old age cohort in the American population after 1978. Presidents spoke about nontraditional student enrollment and about new forms of educational service, such as continuing general education and continuing professional education. But these reminders and suggestions fell upon deaf ears; there was no manifest enthusiasm in campuswide governance for preparing for a new era.

The defense of academic freedom, along with an articulation of faculty rights and responsibilities, was largely fought out in American higher education during the 1950s, before the student revolution and before experimentation in campus governance occurred. The faculty's right and responsibility to criticize society was not a major campus issue in the late 1960s or early 1970s. The organs of campus governance were not generally called upon to defend academic freedom.

The purpose of educational justice did demand attention from campus governance, but here again the problem soon emerged as one not of intent but of implementation. Faculty members and students favored access for black students and other minority students, developmental student assistance, and student financial aid. The complication was how to pay for these endeavors; students were no more enthusiastic about increased charges to themselves than faculty members were about a slowdown in salary increases. And while students and faculty members were inclined to support open admission for minority students and affirmative action in institutional personnel appointments, they were loath to consider the impact of these programs upon institutional quality. It was assumed that institutional excellence was a basic purpose, even if no one was fully prepared to give it an operational definition. Quality was both a purpose and a commitment. No one was willing to urge that qualitative standards be sacrificed. There is no evidence that any campuswide organ of governance ever debated, let alone approved, any proposal to reduce the standards of educational quality then believed to be in existence. It was generally believed, without inquiry or fact-finding, that access for minority students and affirmative action could be accomplished without sacrificing institutional standards.

Some institutions found that their commitment to quality was impaired by their concern for black students. Institutional funds that had helped to enroll well-prepared students with $1,000 stipends suddenly reached fewer students when many poor black students, well-prepared or not, needed $3,000 or $4,000 each in order to be financially able to enroll. The result was some deterioration in the academic quality of the overall enrollment. Moreover, students who expressed the most vociferous concern about ROTC programs tended to ignore the contribution of these programs in providing financial assistance to students and in raising the quality of student enrollment. Educational justice as a purpose might dictate using financial aid funds for minority students, but, to some faculty members and administrators, this use tended to hamper the recruitment of students of the quality previously enrolled. Of course, such effects of new uses of student aid were more severe on independent campuses, where tuition charges were continually increasing and were substantially larger, than at public colleges and universities.

Campuswide governance made no notable or particular contributions to the clarification of institutional purposes. The opportunity for such clarification was present, but the disposition to seize it was not.

### Clarification of Program Objectives

Campuswide governance has demonstrated only a very limited interest in reviewing program objectives. The language surrounding program classification and identification evolved into a jargon somewhat condescendingly deemed appropriate to computer types and efficiency-minded administrators. The matter was not a deep, abiding concern for either faculty members or students. Indeed, faculty members tended to be distrustful of any procedure considered to be administrative gimmickry, and program classification and program objectives smacked of just such an inclination.

The National Center for Educational Statistics might promulgate a taxonomy of instructional programs, and the National Center for Higher Education Management Systems might issue a program classification structure, but these were matters of no substantive interest for campuswide governance. Suppose there were "primary" or output programs in a college or university (instruction, research, and public service)', and suppose there were support programs as well (academic support, student service, plant operation, and institutional support); what difference did these groupings of activities make for faculty and student representatives in a campus senate or council?

The evidence of this study overwhelmingly supports that campuswide governance had almost no impact upon the determination of program objectives in instruction, research, public service, hospital operations, independent operations, or student financial assistance. The prevailing organizational pattern of colleges and universities was one of departmental decentralization. Program objectives were set by departments, with occasional or routine review by aggregations of departments called colleges. In order for each department to preserve its autonomy of program formulation and development, it was necessary to respect and defend the autonomy of every other department.

On occasion, campus governance had an impact upon research. In three instances, a university was persuaded to divest itself of a research institute involved in national defense contracts. In another instance, a university withdrew from participation in a consortium of universities doing defense studies. These actions tended to be more cosmetic than substantive. In two or three instances, certain standards of research practice, such as a decision that no one in the university should be involved in sponsored research classified as secret, were adopted as policy formulations by campuswide governance. All such actions were an expression of disapproval within the academic community for the conduct of the Vietnam war, but they did not substantially alter the conduct of research within the university structure.

The one important program change introduced by campuswide governance was in the operation of support programs. Support-program organization and operation in colleges and universities have been substantially different from the organization and operation of "primary" programs. Whereas academic departments (or colleges within a university)` have controlled instruction, research, and public service on a decentralized basis, support programs have been administered on a centralized basis, serving the college or university as a whole. Thus, the library has been the library for all departments and colleges, even when there have been separate specialized libraries. The student health service has been a health service for all students; the student counseling service has been a service for all students; the recreational and social facilities have been facilities for all students; the cultural program has been a program for all students. The operation and maintenance of the physical plant has been a service for all facilities of the campus. The bursar's office has collected the accounts receivable from all students. The accounting department has maintained accounts on an institutionwide basis; the disbursement function has handled all accounts payable for the entire institution; the purchasing office has bought all supplies and equipment; the personnel office has employed all nonacademic personnel. The president has been president for the whole institution; the board of trustees has exercised the authority of governance for the campus as a whole (or even for several campuses).

The establishment of campuswide governance suddenly provided an instrument for campuswide concern, even intrusion, into all campuswide support programs. Previously, the president, in effect, had been manager-in-chief of all support programs. The only check upon the president's role as manager-in-chief was whatever interest was voiced by the governing board. Beginning with the events of the 1960s and the emergence of campuswide governance, this situation underwent considerable change. Now faculty representatives and student representatives in a campuswide senate or council demanded a voice in the policy making and operation of support programs.

The effort of campuswide governance bodies to direct and manage support programs was especially far-reaching at Cornell University. For some reason, the charter of campuswide governance divided authority for the day-to-day management of campus life between the university senate and the president. That this organizational arrangement should have remained in existence from 1970 to 1977 was more a testimony to mutual restraint on the part of both the senate and the president than an indication of organizational effectiveness. The senate took control of "campus life" apparently in the belief that presidential direction of these services had been a failure or had inadequately expressed institutionwide concerns and values. The position of vice-president for campus life, appointed by the president and approved by the governing board, continued in existence, but this officer was expected to obtain policy

guidance from a university senate committee on campus life. Except
for a close surveillance of parking regulations and the issuance of
parking permits by the committee, little basic change took place in
the operation of campus-life programs under the new organizational
arrangement. But the authority both to prescribe campus-life
policies and to manage campus-life programs remained uncertain
and a subject crying for change.

At no other institution did the intrusion of campus governance into support-program operation go quite so far as at Cornell.
Yet in every instance presidents found it necessary and desirable to
discuss important issues about support program operations with
committees of a campus senate or council. It can be argued, of
course, that this change was a desirable one, that support programs
should be operated under policies established by the principal
users—the faculty and the student body. This position could certainly be justified if it could be demonstrated that presidents and
boards of trustees had in the past operated such programs with
indifference to faculty and student benefit. What the new arrangement accomplished, above all else, was to guarantee that a substantial amount of faculty, student, and administrative time henceforth would be devoted to extensive discussion of the adequacy of
the service and the costs of various support programs.

## Clarification of Budget Priorities

In no part of institutional operation has campuswide governance been less effective than in the clarification of budget priorities. A college or university contains a substantial number of budget centers: all academic departments, various interdisciplinary
programs, colleges, research projects and research centers, public
service projects and centers (or services), hospitals, independent
research or service operations, student assistance funds, and many
different support programs. In addition, current income falls into at
least two important and distinct categories—unrestricted funds and
restricted funds. The latter consists of income available only for
specified purposes and may not ordinarily be used for any other
purpose. Even unrestricted funds may very well have implied re-

strictions; for example, athletic income earned from intercollegiate athletics is usually expected to be used for benefit of the athletic program. The same expectation arises from income earned by clinics, testing facilities, theatrical performances, musical events, hospital operations, farms, dining halls, residence facilities, and many other budget centers.

As colleges and universities expanded enrollment during the 1950s and 1960s and as income grew, incremental funds could be allocated to new programs, and services and overhead (support) costs need not be proportionate with enrollment and output expansion. In the 1970s this situation changed. Enrollment growth slowed down or disappeared; income surpluses became income deficits. More and more concern was voiced not about the allocation of an expanding income but about reallocation of a stabilized or even declining income.

It was possible that campuswide organs of governance might have evolved into legislatures reviewing and approving appropriation and income recommendations formulated by the president. In not a single instance among the thirty institutions studied did this evolution take place. Although presidents endeavored to involve senate committees in some discussion of budget problems, they were uncertain about the level of detail to provide and about the particular issues to raise. At such a campus as the University of California at Berkeley, with a long tradition of faculty involvement in budget decision making, the new governance arrangements of the 1960s made little difference. Other circumstances conspired to make the chancellor's role in budgeting more important than in earlier times. At such a college as Carleton, the budget did become a community concern. But, in general, campuswide governance did not produce a new budget procedure.

The explanation for this situation is fairly evident. The new mechanisms for campuswide governance were scarcely in place before the new depression descended upon higher education financing. The rate of income growth began to slow down, while inflation and other rising cost pressures continued their assault upon budget expenditures. College and university faculty members wanted increased salaries and job security. Students wanted more student aid

and some stabilization in student fees. Administrators were in the
the middle, and both faculties and students backed off from a direct
confrontation about budgets in favor of decision making by administrators and governing boards.

The budget-making process returned to or remained an act
of governance exercised by presidents and governing boards. The
authority of budget decision making was to remain certain and
clear-cut. Thus faculty members and students were left free to com-
plain separately and bitterly about whatever decisions were made.
And if faculty members were sufficiently bitter about budgetary
events, they tended to see faculty collective bargaining, rather than
direct changes in the operation of campuswide governance, as the
appropriate response.

## Income Development

Campuswide governance had no visible impact upon the
generation of additional income for financing the operating and
support programs of colleges and universities. Even though 60 percent of the income of all higher education for instruction, research,
and public service was derived from governmental sources, and
even though two thirds of institutional income for student financial
assistance came from governments, the internal structures for campus governance tended to give but little attention to the implications or the obligations of these circumstances. Income production
was a task gladly left to administrators.

Faculty members, of course, had considerable talents as entrepreneurs in the fields of research and public service. But these
talents were exercised individually or in small groups; they were
not exercised by faculties collectively. Moreover, students tended to
take very little interest as a group in how colleges and universities
were financed. It is of interest that the student government association at Berkeley had joined with other state campus student organizations to create a student lobby in Sacramento. The first objective
of this lobby was apparently to maintain low tuition charges at the
state universities: incidentally, it had also supported increased state
appropriations for higher education.

The most noteworthy event in organized effort involving campus income occurred at Madison in 1976, after the conclusion of our study of campus governance there. This occasion was the establishment of PROFS, the Public Representation Organization of the Faculty Senate. Incorporated as a nonprofit corporation supported by compulsory faculty dues, PROFS was formed primarily to undertake a public relations program on behalf of the faculty. With a statewide governing board and a statewide executive officer for all public senior higher education in Wisconsin, and with a legislature disposed to favor "equal" support among the various campuses of the state system, the Madison faculty felt that its unique contribution and role within the state was being misunderstood and neglected. Since the Madison administration necessarily had obligations to the state system, the faculty senate came to believe that it needed to take heroic measures to prevent irreparable damage to the flagship campus of the system. PROFS was the faculty senate response to a deteriorating situation. The ability of this new effort to present, and represent, the case for a campus heavily involved in research and public service in addition to instruction remained to be demonstrated. As of late 1976 there was no evidence that student leaders at Madison were disposed to support or assist the faculty endeavor.

Instances of outstanding faculty financial support of institutions on a personal and individual basis have been apparent. At one state university included in this study, three faculty members had individually contributed 40 percent of the total value of an endowment fund; two of these faculty members had published very successful textbooks and the other had successfully invested inherited funds. These faculty members had shared their personal wealth with the university of which they had been a part during their entire academic careers.

Research grants within a university are largely obtained on an individual basis—by the preparation of grant proposals for submission to governmental agencies and private foundations. The status of the leading research universities in this study had been achieved, in large part, by able and motivated faculty members who prepared research proposals and who could be expected to carry out the proposals if funds were granted. Other universities also depended upon the competence of faculty members to obtain research grants. Similarly, public service projects were in many instances the undertaking of an individual faculty member or of an individual faculty committee. Here again, the successful generation of income from such projects depended upon the abilities of individual faculty entrepreneurs.

There is no evidence that campus senates or councils were particularly helpful—or harmful—in developing projects to obtain income for institutional endeavors. Sometimes senates or councils endeavored to put some limitations upon research or public service proposals, and students (mostly undergraduate) were disposed to regard research and public service activities as competition with instruction for the time and attention of faculty members. In general, however, campus governance simply did not see itself as involved in the generation of institutional income.

It is difficult to understand how campus governance bodies could claim an institutionwide decision-making role and ignore the entire subject of where the income to finance campus programs was to come from. Campus governance remained lopsided when it devoted its attention to how available funds were to be spent and omitted attention to how available funds were to be obtained. Campus senates and councils could scarcely pretend to deserve equal status with presidents, or influential status with governing boards, until they demonstrated both a concern and a capacity to develop institutional income. This demonstration had not occurred on the campuses of this study, with the possible exception of the two highly selective colleges.

## Development of Program Technology and Management

On every campus issues involving the technology of work performance and the management of work resources needed to be resolved. As mentioned earlier, campus management organization differed substantially between that for operating programs (instruction, research, public service) and that for support programs (libraries, computer centers, student services, plant operation). At none of the institutions studied was there evidence that campus governance had become involved with issues of program technology or management.

Program technology is the work process by which desired outputs in instruction, research, and public service are produced. In the field of instructional programs, technology involves such processes as lectures, seminars, tutoring, independent study, work-study, computer-assisted instruction, competency-based instruction, laboratory instruction, research projects, visual aids, and other procedures as the appropriate method or methods of learning. Program technology in research involves research design and procedure. Program technology in public service involves the method of conducting or operating public service projects. The determination of appropriate program technology evidently is made by the individual instructor or faculty member. If higher approval is required, it comes from the department chairman or possibly of the whole academic department. Program technology is a decision to be made by academic specialists, and almost never has it become a matter for campuswide determination.

The most obvious issue in instructional technology is that of the student-faculty ratio, or instructional work load for faculty members. Here is the single most important issue to be resolved in terms of the management of instructional resources. The evidence accumulated in this study clearly indicates that faculty members and academic administrators considered the management of instructional resources a budget problem rather than an output problem. The issue of the desirable student-faculty ratio was not approached in terms of the ratio needed to produce a desired instructional output. This issue was almost never raised, apparently because departments and colleges had acquired no empirical data on it through experimentation. The management of faculty personnel resources was approached as a question of budgeted income. Presumably, the more income a department or college enjoyed, the lower the number of students per faculty member would be.

Faculty members were not disposed to bring questions of program technology and management to the attention of campus governance, and students and administrative officers avoided the campus senate or council as the appropriate forum for considering these issues. Even where program technology and management were actually articulated as subjects for discussion, they were not considered within the campuswide governance structure.

## Determination of Degree Requirements and Instructional Outcomes

Faculty members have long considered that the requirements for awarding degrees in terms of credit hours of course work completed, for course distribution and concentration, for prescribed and elected courses, and for grade point average were matters for the faculty to determine. Academic administrators have participated in this decision making in their role as faculty members rather than as administrators. Where administrative concerns have intruded upon such decisions, they have had to do with cost and income, enrollment, and institutional image.

As structures of campus governance developed, new senates or councils were almost always exempted from determining matters considered entirely within faculty jurisdiction. Within research universities and other universities, degree requirements were fixed by college faculties. The usual prescription in a university charter for campus governance was that matters solely within the competence or jurisdiction of a single college were not to be considered by a campuswide body.

Some distinction must be drawn here, of course, between universities and smaller general baccalaureate colleges. The smaller the institution in enrollment, the greater the number of issues considered to be of campuswide interest or concern. Smaller colleges tend to be more collegially inclined and more disposed to discuss all issues as campuswide issues than are the larger universities. In such an experimental college as Evergreen, the degree requirement of 180 quarter credit hours can be completed by a combination of courses and of individual instructional contracts to which the student was a party. In most other institutions, degree requirements are fixed by the faculty in the light of some implicit or explicit philosophy of the curriculum appropriate to a particular degree.

Faculties responded to student dissatisfaction with instruction during the 1960s mostly by increasing student choice in the selection of courses, even modifying or eliminating various course distribution requirements. Increasingly, students were left to decide for themselves the courses desirable for a bachelor's degree. This tendency was evident almost exclusively in liberal arts colleges and evidenced the bankruptcy of any faculty concept of a general or liberal education. In the general baccalaureate colleges, student representatives were inclined to discuss the meaning of an undergraduate education in the arts and sciences, but the interest fell short of any sustained effort at intellectual discourse. And the interest was evident primarily in the highly selective colleges rather than in other colleges.

A few universities did have an all-university set of general education degree requirements for the baccalaureate that extended across college boundary lines. This situation existed at Miami University. But the reconstruction of these requirements was assigned to an ad hoc committee rather than to the university council. The council subsequently demonstrated its inability to arrive at some reasonable reconstruction of the general education requirements. Many different special interests could not develop a general interest, at least on this subject.

The concept of instructional outcomes is too new an idea, perhaps, to have played any part in the deliberation of campus senates or councils. Faculties thought of instructional outcomes in traditional terms—of so many credit hours or so many course units with a minimum prescribed grade point average. Instructional outcomes in terms of certain prescribed student competencies or certain prescribed bodies of knowledge were not usually expected, at least beyond the confines of a single course. In none of the case studies was there evidence that campuswide governance had given attention to the possibility of defining instructional outcomes in a comprehensive way for individual degree programs.

Along with degree requirements, colleges and universities may set certain institutionwide rules for academic probation, suspension and dismissal; set forth penalties for academic dishonesty; establish the practice of course credit based upon examination; enact standards for the transfer of credits from other institutions; and legislate grading standards (including pass/fail and credit/no credit). When a university senate or council was established with student and other representation, the new body became the agency for enacting such rules and standards. One of the faculty complaints about campuswide governance was that the new body had displaced a former all-faculty body for making these decisions. It may be argued that students have an interest in these matters, even as do faculty members and academic administrators. Faculty members are likely to believe, however, that their exclusive judgment should prevail in these areas of decision making.

Student representatives in the late 1960s and early 1970s did press for a pass/fail option in various courses, often at the discretion of the student. As faculties responded by making this option available, within certain limits, student interest began to decline in academic affairs.

Two institutions in this study did undertake in the early 1970s a formal survey of student attitudes in an effort to obtain information about satisfactions and dissatisfactions with instructional programs and the learning environment. The results of these surveys were used by academic administrators and by student service administrators to bring about some changes. In some instances, the information was utilized to encourage faculty members to change traditional patterns of behavior. Only rarely were the results the basis for initiating new legislation governing degree requirements or instructional outcomes.

## Prescription of Faculty and Student Behavior

A major student objective in the dissatisfaction and disruption of the 1960s was a change in institutional regulation of student social behavior. At residential campuses, twenty-four of the thirty institutions studied here, the conflict centered around regulations concerning residence-hall life. Student representatives pressed for free access of men and women at all times of the day and night to all residence facilities. This demand was commonly referred to as the privilege of open visitation. In addition, student representatives pressed for residence halls of mixed occupancy rather than single-sex occupancy. Regulations on the use and possession of alcoholic beverages and drugs on campus also became a pressing issue at most institutions. Students insisted that colleges and universities should no longer exercise any controls of individual conduct based upon the doctrine of *in loco parentis*.

There were some other issues as well. Students argued that they should have control over the allocation and expenditure of so-called student activity fees. Students wanted the use of college or university facilities to organize off-campus political and other activities and expected political or social allies to have free access to all campus facilities. Students wanted a "no penalty" policy for engaging in disruptive activities; disruption was their accepted method of gaining attention for their "nonnegotiable" demands.

The organization of campuswide governance necessarily provided a forum for considering these issues. As soon as a university senate or a college council was established, student representatives began to insist that the institution, as an institution, should no longer prescribe standards of student behavior. In the past, faculties had exercised the legislative authority to enact regulations governing student conduct. Sometimes boards of trustees had delegated this authority to a faculty body; in a few instances, state law had vested such authority in "the faculty" of a state college or university. Now students insisted that they should be a party to this legislative process and should have a voice in the decisions about acceptable standards of student behavior.

Administrative officers were generally reluctant to change rules of student conduct quite as rapidly as students seemed to expect. Students professed to be indifferent or hostile to public attitudes voiced by the media, by indignant citizens in letters to the editors, by alumni and benefactors, and by state and national legislators. Faculties in many instances were prepared to abandon all student-conduct rules in the face of strong student opposition. Administrative officers were concerned about public reaction to student "license" and the impact of such reaction upon available income. Boards of trustees, as the link between campus and public, shared the concern of administrative officers. This situation emerged repeatedly in the case studies of campus governance.

In large part the story of campuswide governance in the years from 1966 to 1976 is one of almost endless discussions about student-conduct regulations and of a slow process of institutional adjustment to most, if not all, of student demands for control of campus life. The very rapid adoption of the Twenty-sixth Amendment to the United States Constitution between March 10 and June 30, 1971, hastened the process of change. Although the amendment simply forbade state governments to deny the right to vote to any person eighteen years or older on the basis of age, the amendment encouraged state governments to lower the age of majority for all persons from twenty-one to eighteen. With legal sanction for the proposition that all eighteen-year-olds were to be considered by society as adults, colleges and universities found themselves unable to maintain that students must be treated as minors.

Faculties soon tired of the seemingly endless arguments about acceptable student behavior. One solution was to revise, and indeed sometimes to eliminate, student-conduct regulations. The solution of Miami University was for the university council to encourage that a student affairs council be created to handle all student regulations, subject to approval by the president and the board of trustees. In this way the never-ending debate about student conduct was transferred to a different forum.

Another concern of campuswide governance in this decade was to define faculty rights and responsibilities. Almost all of the institutions in this study had accepted at an earlier time the 1940 Statement of Principles on Academic Freedom and Tenure formulated by the American Association of University Professors. In 1969 the AAUP had issued a Statement on Professional Ethics, encouraging faculties to formulate their own individual statements of rights and responsibilities. The colleges and universities of this study paid a good deal of attention to developing standards concerning political activity by faculty members, grievance procedure, policies and procedures for terminating a faculty appointment for cause, and campus obligations of the faculty member. To some extent this attention resulted from the participation of some faculty members in student demonstrations and disruptions. It also expressed a faculty determination to codify informal practices of the past and to place limits upon the discretion of academic administrators in handling faculty disciplinary cases.

The whole subject of faculty rights and responsibilities was another area of concern in which faculties tended to resent the intrusion of students. The prevailing faculty viewpoint evident in this study was that students had an inadequate or partial understanding of the faculty role in a university. In addition, faculties professed an interest in self-government rather than in institutional government. The approval of governing boards for faculty statements of rights and responsibilities was sought more as a matter of form than as an acknowledgment of board authority. Where campus senates and councils became involved in the process of approving standards of faculty behavior, the procedure resulted from the absence of other direct lines of communication between faculties and governing boards. Faculty members were usually unhappy about the lack of other approaches.

Faculties also desired direct means of negotiation about faculty grievances or about faculty disciplinary action with academic administrators and boards. A committee on faculty affairs was considered to be a faculty committee rather than a campus committee. The difference was one of composition. A faculty committee was composed only of faculty members; a campus committee would include student members and perhaps one or more academic administrators. Wherever campus senates or councils had been created, usually some way was found to have a committee on faculty affairs composed exclusively of faculty members. At one university with a campuswide university council and with student and other members of the university senate, the committee on faculty rights and responsibilities was an all-faculty committee. Department chairmen, academic deans, students, and members of the university council were ineligible for membership on this committee. This organizational arrangement was by no means unique but represented the prevailing practice.

Students at a number of institutions, especially the smaller ones, showed much interest in tenure decisions. In fact, by the end of 1976, these decisions were becoming a major issue in faculty affairs at many colleges and universities. Where a campuswide governance structure existed, as at most of the institutions in this study, students voiced an interest in the procedure and substance of these decisions. At one college, the principal subject of conflict between students and the institution as of 1976 was the question of student participation in tenure decisions. Academic administrators in the college agreed with faculty leaders; tenure decisions were matters to be resolved by a faculty committee without student participation. Student leaders argued that this procedure denied students an opportunity to effectively participate in or influence actions that were of great importance to them.

A part of this conflict arose from quite different faculty and student perceptions of desirable faculty behavior. Undergraduate students tended to value faculty members who were entertaining lecturers, who voiced antiauthoritarian points of view, who were critical of social behavior in the world beyond the campus, who spent a good deal of time in small group or individual discussion with students, and who identified themselves with student "causes." Academic department members tended to value a colleague who complemented (not competed with) their own subject-matter specialization, who devoted time to scholarly research and writing, who participated in professional meetings, who kept abreast of scholarly developments in their subject-matter field, and cooperated willingly with departmental and faculty committee meetings and other activities. The classroom performance of the faculty member was likely to count less than these other criteria when departments and faculty committees made tenure recommendations.

Campus governance, particularly at smaller institutions where separate faculty enclaves were less powerful, had to wrestle with the substance of the appropriate standards for decisions about faculty tenure. In this circumstance, "teaching effectiveness" then became a recognized standard in order to satisfy student expectation. But faculties continued to insist that the application of generally worded standards to specific individual cases was a process in which faculty judgment should prevail.

At some institutions, campus governance did succeed in establishing procedures for handling student grievances against a particular faculty member. At one university in this study, in 1974, the university council, the university senate, and the board of trustees approved a procedure of academic appeals for students. This procedure was coupled with a statement of "good teaching practices" and a statement of student responsibilities in classroom conduct and course performance.

Student representatives in campus governance pressed hard for a system of student evaluation of faculty performance in the classroom. Faculties tended generally to go along with this demand,

and formal or informal arrangements were made on most campuses
in this study to enable students, at the end of a course, to evaluate
the competence of the instructor. The real issue, however, was not
student evaluation of faculty performance, but faculty use of it. On
some campuses the evaluation information was made available only
to the instructor. On other campuses it was also made available to
the department chairman. Faculty members insisted that the use
to be made of student evaluation was a faculty matter rather than
a joint faculty-student matter.

### Evaluation of Program Accomplishment

The evaluation of program accomplishment differs from the
evaluation of faculty performance or of student performance in the
classroom. Program accomplishment has to do with the evaluation
of the achievements of a degree program. There was no indication
in any of the case studies that organizations of campus governance
had undertaken to raise issues about, let alone to evaluate, program
accomplishment.

One of the difficulties of higher education is that faculties
and academic administrators are not agreed on how to determine
or measure program accomplishment. The most commonly used
operating statistic is the relationship of the number of students who
enter a degree program to the number who obtain a degree at the
conclusion of the prescribed curriculum. If the proportion of students who obtain a degree is low, then the fault is usually identified
as low admission standards. If the proportion is high, then the credit
is usually attributed to appropriate standards of admission and good
instruction.

There are other criteria that may be employed to determine
something about program accomplishment. One measure is the
number of graduates who obtain job placement upon completion of
a degree program. But this measure may be more closely related to
labor market conditions than to effectiveness of the instructional
program. Another measure has been the number of undergraduate
students in the arts and sciences, or some other area of instruction,
who obtain admission to a graduate or graduate professional schools.

But here again the measure may say more about the economics and the capacities of graduate programs than about the effectiveness of undergraduate instruction.

It is possible to utilize standardized tests as a means of determining the learning accomplishments of students at the conclusion of a degree program. At the institutions studied, however, faculty members often disapproved of any such practice, and students tended to resent the erection of another barrier to completion of degree requirements. To some extent, faculties and academic administrators accumulated data about undergraduate performance on various graduate program admission tests, but this information was regarded as of general rather than evaluative usefulness.

Research accomplishment tends to be evaluated in terms of grants received, papers and books published, peer judgment expressed in reviews, and professional recognition and awards. Public service accomplishments are likely to be evaluated in terms of income produced and of general client satisfaction as evidenced by letters and other comments. In the area of public service, at least, there can be an economic evaluation: the willingness of persons to continue to pay money in order to obtain the service.

Student financial aid can be evaluated in terms of the number of students of low family income who are enabled to enroll in the college or university or in terms of the number of students of high academic potential who are recruited and enrolled. Either one of these measures permits a college or university to determine just what it was accomplishing by means of its financial assistance program.

To be sure, support programs as well as output programs need evaluation. But in our study the consumers of support programs were on the campus. Support programs underwent evaluation every day by faculty members, students, staff, and guests who made use of these services. Earlier we observed that one of the consequences of campus governance was the provision of a central forum for continuing comment and criticism about the adequacy of support programs.

The consumer of the output programs of higher education is society. The educated student might obtain an inherent satisfaction from his or her learning achievement, but society also has an investment and a stake in the graduate. Society is also a major beneficiary in the research and public service performed by higher education. In our study, however, the determination of social satisfaction with colleges and universities remained elusive.

Notable in this study was the absence of any evaluation by agencies of campus governance of the whole subject of output. On every campus there were pronouncements from time to time by presidents and others on such matters as program utility, cost effectiveness, public accountability, and public interest. These pronouncements might be made to campus senates and council as well as to other bodies. In turn, committees of the governance structure might occasionally echo these concerns in various reports and statements. But there was no evidence of any systematic discussion of or attention to program outputs on the part of campus governance. The "good" of higher education was a given for campus governance, apparently. There was no need then to consider just how much of a good the campus outputs actually were.

## Conclusion

Campuswide governance, like every other aspect of higher education, deserves careful and comprehensive evaluation. The evaluation undertaken here has been impressionistic rather than statistical. It was clear at an early stage in this inquiry that statistical data about the eight areas that I considered of major importance could not be obtained in any meaningful way. As a consequence, the case authors were asked to express their own judgments and those of persons with whom they discussed their experience. And I have relied upon these impressions as well as personal observation from visits to each campus in order to set forth my own impressions.

It seems apparent from the available evidence that the performance of campuswide governance in general from 1966 to 1976 was somewhat checkered. The assumption underlying campuswide governance was that if faculty members, students, professional staff, and academic administrators were brought together in a common deliberative body, "better" decisions would be produced than in any previous structural arrangements. There was no evidence that structures of campuswide governance played any role in relieving the particular campus tensions that helped to spark dissension and disruption during the 1960s. Campuswide governance arrangements undoubtedly did help to establish the proposition that there were socially acceptable means for bringing about change in the behavior of higher education, as well as in the behavior of other social institutions. The symbolic importance of campuswide governance should not be underestimated. Yet it cannot be said that campuswide governance actually brought about the uneasy truces or cessations of conflict on troubled campuses.

In other areas, campuswide governance did make positive contributions in providing a forum for clarifying institutional purposes, for subjecting institutional support programs to continuing and constructive assessment, for modifying standards of expected student behavior on campus, and for the expression of student interest in the degree requirements and faculty handling of instructional programs. These accomplishments of campuswide governance should not be underrated.

In contrast, campuswide governance had much less impact upon the clarification of the objectives of output programs, the evaluation of output-program accomplishments, the determination of budget priorities, the determination of program technology and management, and the development of institutional income. In these important areas, either faculty or administration domination of the decision-making process continued with little apparent change. There may have been greater sensitivity to the attitudes and concerns of various campus groups as a result of the existence of a structure of campuswide governance, but the essential dynamics of the process and the role of key actors in it were not altered.

Probably the most important single contribution of campuswide governance was its encouragement of more extensive communication within the academic community. Certainly academic administrators and the professional administrators of support programs had to give a great deal more time and care to the presentation of information about policies and program performance than ever before. Management information systems were developed not just in response to external pressures but also in response to internal needs of communication. Administrative officers were unanimous in declaring that they spent a great deal more time in 1975 and 1976 in extensive meetings with committees and with senates and councils than they had in 1966. Faculty members also testified that they were devoting more time to committee and other meetings than had been the case in the 1950s and early 1960s.

Student interest in campuswide governance appeared to be on the wane as of 1976. Student participation in campus elections and in governance structures was declining. The issues that continued to attract student interest were the remaining bits of restriction upon campus residence-hall life, faculty acceptance of a student role in evaluating instructional performance and in consequent faculty personnel decisions, and student fees. There was also continued concern with available student services, such as counseling, health care, and cultural and recreational opportunities. As one group of students declared to me, they did not want the college to control their lives but they did want the college to express an interest in their lives. And another group agreed that faculty members treated students as intellects, while student service personnel treated students as persons. Campuswide governance remained an opportunity for students to express their interest in the campus learning environment, if only students could decide what that interest was.

# CHAPTER SEVEN

◇◇◇◇◇◇◇◇◇◇◇◇◇

# A Workable Model of Campus Governance

◇◇◇◇◇◇◇◇◇◇◇◇◇◇◇◇◇◇◇◇◇◇◇◇◇◇◇◇◇◇◇◇◇◇◇◇

The literature on campus governance has presented essentially four models, or generalizations, about the decision-making process within colleges and universities. Corson (1960) presented a dual-organization model; Millett (1962) presented an academic community consensus model; Baldridge (1971b) presented a political or interest-group conflict model; and Cohen and March (1974) presented the organized anarchy model. One of the objectives of the thirty-campus study was to examine the experience in campuswide governance between 1966 and 1976, in order to determine the extent to which any of these models did in fact correlate with that experience. The case authors were asked to review the experience they reported and to state which model seemed best to describe or predict the performance of campuswide governance at their particular institutions.

As perhaps should have been expected, case authors differed widely in determining which, if any, of these models most accur-

ately described campus governance overall. If there was a consensus, it was that none of the models was quite adequate in presenting a generalized concept of prevailing decision-making behavior at
any given time. Moreover, the case authors interpreted their campus experiences according to the various models; that is, there were
case authors inclined to use all four of these models to describe the
campus experience that they had examined. No author was satisfied,
however, with the exact fit of the model he or she selected as the
basis for generalizing actual experience at his or her particular
campus.

## The Dual-Organization Model

Almost all the case authors agreed that the dual-organization model best described the structure and process of campus decision making that existed prior to 1965, and some were inclined to
suggest that the evolution of experience with campuswide governance was tending to return to this model. All case authors as of
1976 had sensed some diminution of faculty interest in campus governance, and most found evidence of a declining student interest.
Most of the case authors surmised that, if the dissatisfaction with
campus governance were to become pronounced enough to result
in the abolition of such governance, return to some kind of a dual-
organization structure and process would occur.

As pointed out in the preceding chapter, faculty members
were inclined to find four basic faults with the structure and process of campus governance: (1) it was time-consuming; (2) it
mixed student and sometimes other influence in decision making on
issues considered to be primarily matters for faculty decision; (3) it
involved faculty in conflicts that faculty members would prefer to
avoid, such as standards of student conduct and the determination
of budget priorities; and (4) it encouraged a centralized or campuswide decision-making process rather than a decentralized process.
From the faculty point of view, all of these deficiencies were of
fundamental importance, and all in combination justified some
modification or even termination of efforts at campus governance.
Each of these faults deserves further comment.

The argument about time is obvious. In the official review of the experience at Cornell University with a representative university senate, the task force on governance in 1976 presented data to demonstrate the substantial blocks of faculty time devoted to senate meetings. In addition, lengthy committee meetings preceded the senate meetings. All of these meetings took faculty away from the productive activities of instruction, research, and public service. Moreover, faculties were beginning to breed a particular type of individual who might be described as a campus politician, one who not only participated extensively in campus governance but also came to regard this activity as his or her professional role. Faculty members especially productive in research and public service endeavored to avoid service in campus governance and began to have serious doubts about the professional competence of faculty colleagues who did render such service.

The differing perceptions of faculty members and students about faculty competence were outlined in the preceding chapter. It bears repetition that these differing perceptions were quite deeply seated in the attitudes of both groups. Somewhat reluctantly, faculty members were inclined to consider student opinions about their performance, but they were less than willing to accept that such opinions were anything more than interesting information. The essence of faculty professionalism was the exclusive competence to decide the professional abilities of any other person in the same or similar academic specialization. Faculty members in the first part of this century won the privilege of determining who should and who should not be invited to join the membership of an academic department. Deans, academic vice-presidents, and presidents might in some situations exercise a veto over these determinations, but they were not expected to exercise any initiative. Now, suddenly, faculty members in the 1960s were being asked to share this determination with students. Having won one conflict about the authority to determine professional competence, faculty members were not about to surrender that authority to another constituent group of the academic community.

In the circumstances of the 1960s, faculty members were not very enthusiastic about their role in determining standards of student social conduct. The faculty role, it was argued, was to evaluate student academic conduct: the student's performance in the classroom, in the laboratory, in the study of assigned reading, and in the execution of specialized tasks. If the student fulfilled all course requirements in a satisfactory manner, the faculty member believed that this determination was the only one relevant to the faculty member's professional role in the college or university.

Student personnel staff and academic administrators had additional concerns beyond those of the faculty member. Student counselors noted that many students emerging from high school and the family environment were not prepared to assume full individual responsibility for their academic performance. Such students, even those with a high level of academic aptitude, might fail in their academic performance because of preoccupation with social freedom. Academic administrators shared this concern of student counselors and also worried about the external image of the institution occasioned by student behavior. Faculty response to these concerns was generally to let the student personnel staff, the academic administrators, and boards of trustees worry about student social conduct; the faculty basically wanted no part of the whole mess.

Faculty members were also disposed to withdraw from the budget process—for two important reasons. They had no desire to determine the income resources available to other departments any more than they wanted other departments to determine their own income resources. And faculty members perceived that if they participated in the budget process they might well be expected to endorse or assume responsibility for the budget results. Faculty members were inclined to prefer that presidents and governing boards should assume full and undivided responsibility for institutional budgets. In this way, the faculty privilege to be dissatisfied with the budget remained undiluted.

Faculty experience with campus governance began to reveal the fact that a centralized decision-making mechanism was beginning to emerge. Faculty members perceived that such a mechanism might well, with time, seek to bring more and more of faculty affairs under centralized rather than decentralized authority. Individual and departmental autonomy could be threatened by this arrangement. The former faculty senates had been acceptable because the rules of the game prescribed that what one department requested all other departments granted, lest the time come when a department would encounter the combined wrath of all those that it had opposed in the past. Faculties could not be sure that college or university campuswide senates and councils would be amenable to playing by these rules.

Faculty disillusionment with campus governance is relevant here because the alternative clearly seemed to be a dual-organizational structure. Another faculty choice, of course, might be faculty collective bargaining. But in the absence of a disposition to collective bargaining, faculty members were inclined to wish to return to organizational arrangements whereby faculty senates and faculty committees dominated the decision-making process as far as faculty affairs were concerned. In return, faculties were disposed to let academic administrators, the professional support staff, and governing boards worry about institutional affairs, including student affairs.

### The Academic Community Model

The new structures of campuswide governance developed in the mid 1960s were in effect an effort to construct a structure and process of community governance. When I wrote about the academic community in 1962, I did not envisage the kinds of structures and procedures that were to emerge in the next several years on so many campuses. I had identified four constituent groups within the academic community: the faculty, the student body, alumni, and administration (staff and governing board). The structures of campuswide governance that developed tended to recognize three of these constituent groups: faculty members, students, and administrative officers. Alumni were usually ignored, and the distinction I now believe appropriate between academic administrators, professional staff, and operating staff was recognized only in a few instances.

As discussed above, as of the end of 1976 the future of the practice of academic community governance was uncertain. We shall return to this theme in the next and concluding chapter.

### The Political Model

The political model of campus governance was essentially a modification, perhaps a refinement, of the academic community model. Whereas the academic community model assumed a common interest or consensus as emerging among the constituent groups of a campus, the political model assumed that the constituent groups had decidedly different interests and that campus governance was the process of finding and accepting appropriate compromises among these competing interests in the concern for survival of the enterprise.

There is little doubt that there were competing interests, and competing points of view, within the academic community. The difficulty in this study began when one endeavored to define exactly what those interests were, including what the objectives of various groups were. In the 1960s student activists had certain fairly clear objectives: to repeal college or university rules governing social conduct and especially the restrictions governing residence-hall life. In addition, some student activists wished to use the campus as a base for launching social protests. When student conduct regulations were substantially altered, student objectives became less clear; this situation continued as the decade of the 1970s progressed. Faculty interests as a group also appeared to be fairly limited: to guarantee academic freedom, to ensure employment security, to obtain increased compensation, and to protect faculty autonomy (individual and departmental). Beyond a few basic objectives such as these, the faculties in this study tended to have quite divergent concerns. So did students. And academic administrators were interested in preserving the institution as a viable enterprise and in obtaining increased public support for it.

The political model of campus governance further assumed a political product to be derived on a campuswide basis. Experience on various campuses called this assumption into serious question. For the most part it was evident that faculty and student actors on the campus scene were too individualistic, too little inclined to a common group viewpoint and to a common group action, too self-centered and inner-directed to be able to join together to advance more than a very simple common interest. In this kind of environment, the art of political compromise could not and did not flourish. Perhaps because the learning process is so highly individualistic, perhaps because the pursuit of learning is a personal rather than a group activity, both faculty members and students tended to value the person above the group. In any event, the role of campus governance turned out to be that of making such minimal central de-

cisions as were absolutely essential and to permit faculty members
and students to go their separate and individual ways, unhampered
by collective obligations. A political product was not the achievement of campuswide governance.

One of the major findings of this study, furthermore, was
the evidence of a very sharp difference in the voiced or perceived
interests of undergraduate and graduate students. Perhaps because
of the inherent nature of the maturation process, undergraduate
students were concerned about their identity and about their relationship to society in general, as suggested by Chickering (1969)
and others. On the other hand, graduate and professional students
were concerned about careers, about the quality of their professional preparation, and about the prospects for useful and rewarding
employment. At one research university, the tension between representatives of undergraduate and graduate students within the university senate became so pronounced that undergraduate leaders
tried to mount a student boycott of campus governance. Graduate
students tended to identify more closely with faculty interests and
concerns than did undergraduate students.

The political model, then, did not seem to fit the actual
experience of campus governance as indicated by these case studies.
If the political model was considered to have as a major characteristic the promotion or achievement of a compromise among competing interests, there was no evidence that the structure and process
of campus governance had indeed achieved any such compromise.
As already noted, many faculty members and many student representatives were more familiar with the budget and with the scope of
institutional activities in 1976 than they had been in 1966. Yet
familiarity with information had not necessarily promoted an acceptable political objective to be accomplished by the essentially
political process of campus governance.

## The Organized Anarchy Model

The very term *organized anarchy* turned out to be sufficiently unfamiliar and fearsome in the course of this study as to be
rejected as a descriptive generalization about campus governance.
None of the case authors and none of the administrative officers in-
terviewed were comfortable with this label. Perhaps a more apt

phrase would have been *organized autonomy*. Certainly the underlying assumption of all efforts at campus governance was one of
community, not of anarchy. The advocates of representation of campus constituent groups in a campuswide legislative assembly expected organized community behavior to result from the new
arrangements.

One might argue that the deficiencies or failures of campuswide governance came about because campuses really were organized anarchies. I personally would prefer to assert that the deficiencies and failure occurred because campuses were, after all,
organized autonomies. The organization of a college or university was
essentially autonomous in the extensive scope of authority over instruction, research, and public service vested in the individual faculty member and in the separate academic departments. The com-
posite organization of a college or university was essentially an
organized entity or enterprise only in the operation of support programs, in the structure and constraint of a budget, and in its external relationship to society at large.

Even more than organizational dualism, organized autonomy
appeared to be the descriptive generalization appropriately applicable to higher education structures and processes of governance.
The experiments of 1966 to 1976 in campus governance were in
effect an effort to substitute community governance for organized
autonomy. The complexities of campus governance arose largely
because community governance and the tradition of organized
autonomy proved irreconcilable.

Campus governance sought to achieve community governance, the alternative being organized autonomy. The presence of
that alternative constantly plagued the efforts at campuswide governance. For all the rhetoric and high expectations on behalf of community governance, faculty members and student representatives
remained aware of another way to go. The alternative, moreover,
was one of prior experience, an experience that in retrospect began
to acquire new virtues.

## A Different Model

One of the case authors, Bardwell L. Smith of Carleton
College, has proposed that I should pay more attention to the model

for "effective decision making" put forth by Robert E. Helsabeck
(1973) in *The Compound System*. In his foreword to the Helsabeck
thesis, Harold Hodgkinson argued that management theorists, production theorists, and political science theorists had applied their
specialized point of view to a field of experience, college and university operation, inappropriate to their concepts. Hodgkinson hailed
Helsabeck's study as a "courageous attempt" to develop a new perspective about the decision-making structure and process in higher
education. Helsabeck himself was more modest in his claim, asking
only for a wedding of theory and practice in the description and
prescription of decision-making structures appropriate to colleges.

Helsabeck propounded the proposition that decision-making
structures should be described in terms of democratic or oligarchic
participation. Furthermore, he called attention to the number of
decision-making units in an organization structure, making a distinction between a "corporate" structure and a "federated" structure. Helsabeck further set up a "decision typology" of four basic
types: authority allocation, resource allocation, resource acquisition
(personnel), and production.

The practice studied by Helsabeck was that of four colleges
identified only by titles descriptive of decision-making structure. All
four colleges were and had been church-related. Political College
had severed its church affiliation; the others retained a relationship
to the Society of Friends, the Mennonite Church, and the Free Will
Baptists. Helsabeck found authority allocation decisions to be highly
democratic and corporate in Political College, highly democratic
and corporate in Consensus College, oligarchic and corporate in
Brotherhood College, and oligarchic and corporate in Conservative
College. He found resource allocation decisions to be highly democratic and corporate in Political College, democratic and corporate
in Consensus College, and oligarchic and corporate in both Brotherhood College and Conservative College. He found resource acquisition decisions to be moderately democratic and moderately corporate
in Political College, highly democratic and corporate in Consensus
College, highly democratic and corporate in Brotherhood College,
and moderately democratic and corporate in Conservative College. Helsabeck found production decisions to be highly democratic
and moderately federated in Political College, highly democratic and

moderately federated in Consensus College, highly democratic and moderately federated in Brotherhood College, and moderately democratic and moderately corporate in Conservative College.

Helsabeck set forth the concept of a compound system, in which both a corporate role and a federated role existed within the same decision-making structure. He argued that participation alone was an inadequate criterion for explaining the nature of academic operation. The determination of the appropriate level of decision making was equally important to an academic structure. And, in effect, he found a compound system within the colleges combining elements of both corporate and federated action. Helsabeck also reflected upon various factors that might influence a decision-making structure: the existence of an external threat, the political structure, and the attitude and expectation of agencies external to the campus.

In essence, although the concept was by no means elaborated in the detail it deserved, Helsabeck found the four colleges he examined to represent a compound system in which there were elements of both a corporate and a federated structure. This concept or model of a compound system is not basically different from the concept I have in mind in using the phrase "organized autonomy." I would not be disposed to quarrel about labels. The compound system described by Helsabeck sought to justify both federated autonomy and centralized organization in the decision-making structure of a college or university. The degree of participation in the process of decision making might be democratic or oligarchic at the level of the federated unit and of the corporate whole. The critical question in the compound system is, What degree and kind of decision-making authority should be allocated to autonomous units in a federation and to the centralized corporate body. This question was not addressed nor answered in Helsabeck's treatise.

## Contrasts in Experience

Before we consider the future of campus governance, we need to look at one further aspect of the experience reported by the thirty case authors. As explained earlier, the thirty institutions selected for this study were intended to constitute a stratified sample of the kinds of campuses (other than two-year institutions) comprising the universe of higher education in the United States. Thus, fifteen of the colleges and universities operated under independent or voluntary sponsorship and fifteen operated under state government sponsorship. Six of the campuses were those of leading research universities, nine were comprehensive universities, and fifteen were general baccalaureate colleges. Moreover, there was a broad geographical distribution: three in the New England area, six in the Middle Atlantic states, six in Southern states, seven in Middle Western states, two in the Southwest, and six in the Far West. It is appropriate therefore to inquire what differences in experience were found among institutions based upon these classifications.

First, it is noteworthy that very few differences seemed to be based upon the distinction between independent sponsorship and public sponsorship. This distinction is important for other characteristics, but it proved to have almost no importance as far as experience with campuswide governance was concerned. Internally, with respect to the relationship between faculty, students, academic administrators, and professional staff, independent sponsorship versus state sponsorship made no observable difference.

It had been thought at the outset of this inquiry that colleges and universities having state government sponsorship might be less concerned with the attitudes and pressures from student groups and leaders than were the independent institutions. The reason for this expectation was the fact that independent institutions tend to obtain two thirds to four fifths or more of their instructional income from charges to students. But state colleges and universities tend to receive an allocation of state government appropriations upon the basis of enrollment. State colleges and universities, we found, were by no means indifferent to student attitudes. On the contrary, the study clearly indicated just as much student activism and student dissension at state institutions as in independent institutions and just as much extended negotiation with student groups and leaders.

Moreover, somewhat to my own surprise, I found no evidence that faculty attitudes toward students, academic administrators, and professional staff were any different in a state college or university than in an independent college or university. The customs and habits of academic communities vary somewhat by type of institution but not according to sponsorship. Indeed, the remarkable fact was that the customs and habits of the various constituent groups within an academic community were so similar.

Some differences were found among state colleges and universities on the basis of the structure of governing boards. Of the fifteen public institutions of higher education included in this study, eleven were campuses in a multicampus system, subject to the authority of a governing board with jurisdiction over several colleges or universities. Only four state colleges and universities had a separate board of trustees or board of regents with governing authority for a single campus. This distribution, which resulted from happenstance, was not too different from what I have found for public higher education in general in the United States. The prevailing pattern for public governing boards is authority over several campuses or institutions rather than a single campus.

The campus in a multicampus system found the authority of the governing board somewhat remote and distant from campus concerns. In some respects, the campus president in a multicampus system might be left largely on his own in dealing with issues of internal governance. At the same time, the multicampus governing board and its chief executive found it desirable to reinforce and strengthen the authority of the campus president in some circumstances. Certainly a campus in a multicampus system must be ever mindful of the point of view of the distant governing board and its executive officer. Among the multicampus systems, I found six in which the system looked to the campus president as its agent and in which the system expected the campus president to oversee all campus matters fairly closely. In five instances the authority of the governing board was less fully articulated and less evident on the individual campus.

Among the four state colleges and universities with separate or individual governing boards, the boards played an active role in campus governance, insisting that faculties and students be alert to their collective judgment about the public interest in the operation of the institution. Within limits largely self-imposed, these boards presented their position to presidents and, in turn, carefully arbitrated conflicts between college councils or university senates and the president.

Of the three leading research universities under state sponsorship, all three were parts of a multicampus system and decidedly restive under this governing arrangement. All three considered their flagship status and their equal commitment to research and public service along with instruction to be threatened by the pressures for equal treatment of different campuses within the system. This threat had a very real impact upon campus governance, where the overriding interest became one of preservation of special status.

Apart from some difference arising from operation within the context of a multicampus system, I found no evidence that sponsorship was a major factor in understanding differences in the experience with campus governance.

## Types of Institutions

The record is different when one looks at contrasts in experience based upon types of institutions. There were quite observable differences between leading research universities, comprehensive universities, and general baccalaureate colleges. In leading research universities, faculties tended to resist more strongly than elsewhere the intrusion of student interests in faculty affairs. Perhaps it could be argued that faculty members in leading research universities had more to protect in the way of a faculty interest. The more accurate statement would be that faculty members in leading research universities did not have the same preoccupation with undergraduate instruction as the other types of institutions, and especially the general baccalaureate colleges, tend to have.

In those institutions with a large proportion of undergraduate students in relation to graduate students and in those with relatively modest budgets for sponsored research and sponsored public service, faculty members had a closer affinity to students, evidenced more concern with student attitudes and interests, and were more inclined to enter into extended discussion with students about instructional and institutional affairs than in leading research universities. In three of the six leading research universities, the faculties refused to enter into a structure of governance involving student participation. In the other three research universities, a university senate was established with tripartite representation (faculty, students, administrators), but students (especially undergraduate students) experienced considerable frustration in the actual operation of this structure. Faculty members, moreover, were not disposed to have faculty matters decided by any such senate.

At the general baccalaureate college, faculty members tended to have a closer involvement with students than at other types of institutions. Some faculty members in these colleges were disposed to give a great deal of time and attention to students individually and in groups. Other faculty members were more remote from student contact outside of the classroom or laboratory but nonetheless inclined to enter into discussion about instructional practices through the formal and informal contacts of campus governance. Faculty attitudes toward campus governance were indeed influenced by the role of the institution in relation to undergraduate instruction.

At the comprehensive university, the experience was ambivalent. As the institution moved toward claiming the prestige and the financial support of a leading research university, faculty attitudes tended to coincide with faculty attitudes in the research university. Where the comprehensive university was more comparable to a general baccalaureate college, faculty attitudes were more likely to resemble those of the latter. Much of the experience in governance reflected the orientation of the institution toward multiproduct output, as contrasted with an undergraduate instructional ouput.

Another important influence upon campus governance was institutional size. The smaller the college or university, the more effective the effort at campuswide governance appeared to be. In an institution of 15,000 to 20,000 students, the relationships between faculty, students, and administrators were likely to become more highly formalized than on a campus of 1,000 to 2,000 students. Smallness seemed to encourage contact and concern; it was possible in the small institutions for various persons within the academic community to know each other by name and to become more intimately acquainted with both their aspirations and their anxieties.

I had expected that church-related institutions would be more inclined toward authoritarian relationships among the constituent groups of the academic community than nonsectarian institutions. Of the fifteen independent colleges and universities in this study, only six acknowledged any ties to a church denomination, and in two of these instances the ties were nominal. In fact, my observation on these various campuses suggested that church affiliation appeared to have very little impact upon faculty, student, and administration interaction. Faculties behaved in remarkably similar fashion, regardless of the sponsorship; much the same comment could be made about the behavior of students and administrative officials. In one instance, the church constituency beyond the campus was quite critical of campus "liberalism" and, in another, was expressed in the conservative life-styles of the student body and faculty. But these attitudes seemed to reflect geography as much as or even more than religious tradition.

Three of the thirty institutions in this study were of predominantly black racial composition in faculty, students, and administrative staff. One of these institutions operated under state government sponsorship and two operated under independent sponsorship. All three evidenced an observable contrast with other institutions in campuswide governance. A history of strong presidential leadership was a characteristic of these institutions, and even in the turmoil of the 1960s this historical background continued to influence the structure and process of campus governance. Some adjustments were made in structure to accommodate student participation and even a greater degree of faculty participation in the deliberative process preceding decision making. Both students and faculty members in these institutions appeared to be concerned that behavior patterns attracting widespread public notice would affect patterns of institutional support. A precarious status in society seemed to breed caution rather than exuberance, a low profile rather than a craving for notice.

## Geographical Contrast

Finally, there was the factor of geographical location to consider. Interestingly enough, geography did seem to make some difference but not as far as student disruption was concerned. Two West Coast universities experienced as much violence and destruction of property as two East Coast universities. A major state university in the Pacific Northwest had even more conflict and violence than a comprehensive state university in the Middle West. A major state university in the Southwest experienced more student hostility than a major independent university in the Southeast. A college in the Middle West had as much student disorder as a college in the Middle Atlantic area. There was no basis in this study for assigning any geographical distribution to the incidence of campus troubles in the 1960s.

What tended to be different in geographical terms was the response of various colleges and universities to their times of trouble. For some reason, the colleges and universities in New England, the Middle Atlantic states, and the Middle West responded more readily than colleges and universities in other areas to the impulse to establish new structures and processes of campus governance. Institutions in southern states and in the West seemed to respond the least in developing new structures and processes. The two universities in the Southwest underwent only partial change as a result of student difficulties.

The two notable exceptions to this geographical generalization were the two new and innovative state colleges created in the late 1960s, Bakersfield in California and Evergreen in Washington. Born during the years when national attention was being focused on campus disorders, both of these state colleges incorporated provisions for campuswide participation in their governance as an integral part of their academic planning. While the two approaches were quite different, both colleges established the principle of faculty and student contribution to the decision-making process. In this respect both colleges were ahead of other colleges and universities in the western half of the United States in terms of the scope entrusted to campuswide governance. Perhaps the innovative character of the two colleges in contrast with the more established tradition of the universities in the West explained the difference.

As mentioned earlier, only six of the thirty institutions included in this study enrolled predominantly commuting students. The others accommodated large numbers of students in residence-hall facilities and in private housing around the campus area. Residence-hall student life contributed to student activism during the 1960s in two ways: student living in common groups encouraged student interaction and student inclination to express dissatisfactions; and institutional restrictions upon student behavior in residence halls afforded students an immediate object for complaint. Commuting students were less likely than residential students to identify other aspects of daily life with their college or university experience. And commuting students tended to be less interested than residential students in campuswide governance. It was the residential institution where student concern with campuswide governance flourished.

## Contrast in Leadership

An effort was made to determine if the governance experience of colleges and universities could be analyzed in terms of institutional leadership. It quickly became apparent that this effort had to be carefully qualified. One obvious difficulty was that of determining the characteristics of leadership: authoritarian versus consultative, decisive versus vacillating, positive versus uncertain, open and friendly versus secretive and withdrawn, widely respected versus disliked or actively opposed, courageous versus timid. While faculty members and student representatives were fairly quick to size up presidential leadership and to describe its attributes, we encountered quite varied reactions. What one faculty member or student perceived as vigorous and effective leadership could be perceived as quite the opposite by another.

No one can assert that college and university leadership is of little importance in the affairs of higher education. But circumstances as well as personalities determine both the performance and the perception of leadership. Under one set of circumstances, an institutional leader might be seen as especially effective; under another set, the same individual might be regarded as inept.

Among the thirty institutions studied here, four presidents resigned in the aftermath of student disorders and a fifth died in a tragic automobile accident probably related to the stress of campus life. In all, there were fifteen presidential resignations or retirements at fourteen institutions during the decade 1966 to 1976; about half of these were related to some extent to issues of campus conflict, either with faculty groups or student groups. In the other instances, campus administrative officers resigned to accept comparable positions elsewhere.

In one state college, the development of a new structure of campuswide governance was almost entirely the creation of the president. In an independent university, the establishment of a new structure of campuswide governance was almost entirely the creation of a faculty group. In at least five instances, some adjustments were made in campus governance at the instigation of the president, but the changes were mostly a matter of accommodation rather than of substance. And in the two new and innovative state colleges, the two presidents were the primary movers in designing campuswide governance as an integral part of institutional planning.

Institutions tended to cluster around three kinds of presidential leadership: (1) presidential encouragement (avowedly or tacitly) of faculty and student participation in campuswide governance; (2) presidential accommodation (with varying degrees of reluctance) to new arrangements for campus governance; and (3) presidential failure to anticipate the storm of the 1960s, with subsequent abdication. In an effort to quantify these varying situations, I concluded that the experience of at least seven institutions fell in the category of presidential encouragement; that four institutions had the experience of presidential abdication; and that the remaining nineteen institutions experienced presidential accommodation to changing circumstances. Some of these presidents subsequently resigned because of various kinds of campus difficulty, including reluctance to offer a greater role in campuswide governance to faculty and student representatives.

The role of the college or university president is a difficult one to fulfill, especially considering both its internal and external dimensions and its ambiguities of both authority and responsibility. Nothing in the story of campus governance from 1966 to 1976, however, suggested that presidential leadership did not continue to remain the critical factor in institutional experience.

## Conclusion

There is no simple generalization to be made about campuswide governance during the decade of 1966–1976. There were some similarities in experience but great differences as well. Only two sure statements can be made upon the basis of the experience analyzed here—campus governance was a complicated endeavor, and campus governance reflected the unique characteristics of colleges and universities as organized enterprises.

Just as presidents of higher education institutions have an internal and an external dimension to their roles, so do colleges and universities have an internal and external dimension to their governance. Internally, there are distinct groups of individuals with certain specialized roles to fulfill: faculty members, students, professional support staff, operating support staff, and academic administrators. Externally, there are governments, alumni, associations of professional personnel, employers of college-educated talent, clients of services, private foundations and business corporations, interest groups, the media, friends, enemies, and the general public.

Internally, two constituent groups, the faculty and the students, aspire to self-governance. But, at the same time, they neither aspire nor endeavor to become economically self-supporting. Faculty members and students, for somewhat different reasons, aspire to behave as autonomous individuals committed to learning and to the benevolent uses of learning. These faculty members and students desire to retain an inner-directed or small-group-directed control over their thought and their deeds. Yet college and university faculties have only a relatively small number of common interests as a collectivity. And the same observation holds true for students— undergraduate, graduate, and graduate professional.

Professional support staff, operating support staff, and academic administrators are likely to manifest a greater degree of institutional interest or common concern than faculty members and students. It is being said that faculty members today have an increasingly common institutional concern: Will the institution continue to provide employment security and appropriate compensation while faculty members pursue their individual and departmental scholarly inclinations? If there should emerge a common institutional concern of students, it would be just this: Will society be ready to employ the student after completion of a degree program in the kind of job the student wants or to which the student feels entitled?

Externally, individuals and groups look to colleges and universities for a variety of services and a variety of persons prepared to lead socially beneficial lives. But few individuals or groups share a common concern with this variety; they are concerned only with a particular service and with a particular talent of immediate individual or group interest. If these external individuals and groups share a common interest, it is the desire or expectation that higher education shall be considered a serious business, that higher education should be a less costly business, and that higher education shall be a constructive rather than a disruptive force in American society.

Campuswide governance has made a limited but perhaps useful contribution to internal governance and almost no contribution to the external relationships of college and university to society. Perhaps a state of tension is the only possible relationship between higher education and society in a pluralistic and liberal democracy.

# CHAPTER EIGHT

◇◇◇◇◇◇◇◇◇◇◇◇◇

# Future of Academic Governance

◇◇◇◇◇◇◇◇◇◇◇◇◇◇◇◇◇◇◇◇◇◇◇◇◇◇◇◇◇◇◇◇◇◇◇◇

In this report on new forms of campuswide governance, several themes are readily evident. First, in the decade of the 1960s and especially after 1966, a great deal of discussion and a substantial amount of experimentation occurred about appropriate mechanisms for faculty and student participation in decision making on college and university campuses. Second, by 1976 it was apparent almost everywhere that the enthusiasm of the 1960s for new structures of governance was waning. Third, both the discussions and the experimentation left a great deal to be desired in providing a comprehensive, coherent theory of a college or university as an organizational enterprise.

Indeed, I believe that much of the dissatisfaction of the late 1970s with instruments of campuswide governance reflects not just a change in institutional circumstances, profound as this change has been, but also an implicit recognition of inadequacy in the point of

244

view of those who urged new structures in the 1960s. By 1976, and almost everywhere that new structures had been tried, advocates seemed to want to undo the mistakes of the past. Unfortunately, the revisionists of the 1970s tended to suffer from the same deficiency as the reformers of the 1960s: lack of a comprehensive and coherent view of the structure and process of the academic enterprise in terms of governance, management, and leadership.

In this concluding chapter I wish to move away from the details of this study as such in order to speculate about the future organization and governance of our colleges and universities. Obviously, these observations reflect my personal experience as a faculty member and as an academic administrator, personal studies such as that reported in this volume, and personal insight. I claim no special dispensation of prophecy. I hope to put forth a common-sense analysis that will interest and perhaps guide others in their future thinking and action.

### Essential Characteristics of the Academic Enterprise

Any concern with colleges and universities as organized academic enterprises must surely begin with an appreciation or understanding of their basic characteristics. I hold that these essential characteristics are: (1) a highly individualized productive enterprise concerned to conserve and advance learning; (2) a productive enterprise that does not charge the cost of its service to its direct clients (students) but obtains a substantial part of its financial resources from society; and (3) a productive enterprise whose outputs are produced by professionally educated and professionally experienced faculty members. These three characteristics are closely interrelated and, in combination, make the academic enterprise the unique endeavor, and the unique organization, that it is.

Regarding the first of these three basic characteristics, the learning process encompasses the method or methods by which individuals acquire, store, and use knowledge. In the higher learning process, this involves a formalized relationship between a faculty member and a student, individually or in groups. The learning process proceeds from an interaction of faculty member and student, reinforced by reading, laboratory exercise, the preparation of papers and reports, various kinds of instructional materials, and independent inquiry. In the higher learning, the emphasis is upon concepts and abstractions that generalize experience and upon other methods of thought and expression indicative of the human condition and of human capabilities.

Although the psychology of the learning process is anything but a precise science, there appear to be principal theories about learning that implicitly or explicitly guide the efforts of faculty members. One of these theories is that of stimulus and response; another is of cognitive development. Many, perhaps most, faculty members have an intuitive rather than a systematic understanding of learning theory and tend to employ both methods of learning in varying degrees. Faculty members are also aware that there are important variables in the learning process, involving stages of learning, the content of learning, the characteristics of the faculty member, the characteristics of the student, and the characteristics of the learning environment. In addition, the student's own behavioral and motivational orientation becomes critical to the learning process.

Organizationally, the circumstances of the learning process are of vital importance in two respects. First, the learning process is not a technology that can be planned and directed in some standardized fashion by "top management" of a college or university. Second, the learning process is so highly individualized that each faculty member can and does enjoy substantial personal authority and autonomy in devising the technology appropriate to his or her course and his or her group of students. To the extent that there is management of the learning process superior to the authority of the individual faculty member, that management is vested in an academic or instructional department and in the executive officer of the department. In schools and colleges where there are no departments as such, there may be instructional divisions or simply schoolwide or collegewide management. This management tends to be limited in scope and to involve personnel management more than instructional or learning management as such.

To be sure, separate colleges and sometimes universities become involved in fixing the instructional requirements for awarding degrees and may even become involved in the approval of individual courses and of what they cover. We shall say something more about this approval process in a moment. In addition, divisions, schools or colleges, and universities as organizational units may become involved in establishing policies for faculty personnel management, if not for instructional management. Regardless of these arrangements, the basic proposition remains as stated: the learning process is highly individualized and each faculty member personally exercises substantial authority in planning and managing this process.

The second essential characteristic of the academic enterprise, that it does not charge the full cost of its instructional service to students, results from one of the basic social purposes of American higher education: to promote social mobility by providing access to higher education to students regardless of their socioeconomic status. The independent college and university depends upon philanthropic support (endowment income and annual giving) in order to balance the gap between instructional charges to students and instructional costs. The public college and university depends upon government (mostly state government) subsidy to balance the gap between instructional charges to students and instructional costs. Moreover, public higher education has cultivated a tradition of low or modest student fees in order to encourage equality of educational opportunity; the consequence is a policy that places an ever-increasing subsidy demand upon state appropriations.

Other outputs of higher education—research, creative activity, public service, educational justice—depend upon an admixture of government subsidy, philanthropy, and charges to a clientele. Some 80 percent of all sponsored research is paid for by the federal government. Federal, state, and local governments today spend a great deal to promote educational justice. And colleges and universities spend general income in order to reduce their prices to students. Of income for all outputs, on all campuses, about 40 percent is derived from charges and about 60 percent from governments and from philanthropy. And it is likely that about one-fifth of the charges paid by students come from governmental sources and from philanthropy.

The social benefit to be derived from higher education justifies the pricing and the financial practices of higher education.

At the same time, each college or university acquires some of the characteristics of a government agency—the delivery of a service free of charge or at low charge to a particular clientele—and some of the characteristics of an eleemosynary enterprise dispensing "charity" to students and others. There is a high degree of competition among independent and public colleges and universities: for students, in pricing, for governmental subsidies, for philanthropic dollars. Colleges and universities depend upon a market, upon government, and upon philanthropy—a situation with few if any parallels in other social institutions.

The third essential characteristic is that the role of the faculty in a college or university is more than one of management of the learning process. Teaching requires highly specialized knowledge and creative ability, as well as professional competence in transmitting knowledge and in utilizing it for individual and social benefit. Faculty expect and deserve a major role in making decisions about the objectives, the process, and the resources (professional qualifications) of learning. Decisions on academic affairs and on faculty affairs cannot be made by deans, academic vice-presidents, presidents, and governing boards on their own initiative, simply because they lack the professional expertise to make such decisions in all disciplines. The faculty—individually, by departments, by divisions or schools, by colleges, and by university—must be involved in the decision-making process because of their professional role in the learning process.

These three essential peculiarities—the nature of the learning process, the economics of the learning enterprise, and the professional role of faculty members—confer upon every college and university unique organizational attributes. They underlie in every case the peculiar structure and process of governance, management, and leadership in the actual operation of any college or university.

## Organizational Characteristics

Three organizational characteristics of colleges and universities relevant to their governance, management, and leadership arise out of the three peculiarities sketched above. One is the high degree of autonomy, or decentralization, of the productive units. A second is the high degree of centralization in the performance of support services. And a third is the need for linkage of the enterprise with society.

The basic organizational unit of a college or university is the academic department, representing either an academic discipline or specialized field of professional practice. There are alternatives to the academic department, such as divisions of related disciplines or schools and colleges without formalized subdivisions, but the fact remains that the academic department constitutes the prevailing pattern of organization for the planning and management of the learning process and of research, creative activity, and public service.

It has become popular for some scholarly commentators and even for some colleges to decry the high degree of specialization among academic disciplines and within fields of education for professional practice. There have been various efforts at so-called interdisciplinary study and at problem-solving learning which supposedly ignore the disciplines as such. It is noteworthy that these efforts occur mainly within colleges rather than within universities, at undergraduate rather than at graduate or professional levels. And the escape from academic specialization, I would argue, is more apparent than real, since there is no real substitute for academic specialization as it is generally practiced in higher education.

I see no effective organizational arrangement for the learning process other than the academic department in a discipline or in a field of professional practice. Colleges may need to encourage at the undergraduate level a greater awareness of organic relationships among particular specializations. But, in doing so, colleges will continue to draw upon specialized competencies representing learning in depth rather than learning in general.

The academic department brings together specialists in a given discipline or professional field who share a common approach to a particular area of knowledge, a common methodology for advancing that knowledge, a common skill in utilizing knowledge, and a common ethical commitment in the cultivation of knowledge. As an organizational unit, the academic department seeks to recruit and retain individuals who know a subject or content of knowledge, who at the minimum can and will remain knowledgeable about advances in knowledge, and who can stimulate learning for individual students. The department expects the scholar to act on his or her own initiative in planning and managing learning for students. It undertakes to make such plans and to manage departmental affairs only in such fashion as will best advance the performance of the individual faculty member. If an individual faculty member is not as productive as the standards of the departmental group require, presumably the department will take action for the improvement or replacement of that individual. The "anarchy" of the organizational structure of a college or university observed by Cohen and March was both substantive and structural. Cohen and March spoke of the problematic goals, the unclear technology, and the fluid participation of the learning process. But this high degree of autonomy is the vital organizational characteristic of the academic enterprise.

The support programs of a college or university tend to be quite highly centralized, performing their essential tasks for the benefit of all the autonomous academic departments of the enterprise. Thus, there exists a set of units providing support services on a highly centralized basis alongside of highly decentralized operating or output units.

As for links with society, every college or university has an organizational device to connect the campus, as producer of learning, with society, the financial supporter of this process. If students paid entirely for instructional service and other clients paid entirely for all other services rendered, a college or university might concentrate the same energies in a marketing operation. Since a college or university desires governmental subsidy and philanthropic support in addition to sales, some organizational arrangement is needed to help obtain it. Moreover, since the justification for governmental and philanthropic assistance is the social benefit resulting from the learning process, some mechanism must be provided that does assure that, in the planning and management of the academic enterprise, appropriate attention has been paid to social expectation and social benefit.

In sum and as a consequence, the organizational arrangements of colleges and universities reflect the autonomy of academic departments, the centralization of support services, and the linkage of learning with society. It is within this organizational context that the structure and process of governance, management, and leadership function.

## A Decade's Experience of Governance

Prior to 1966, arrangements for governance within the thirty institutions of this study were varied. In general, the authority to make decisions about the operation of the academic enterprise was clearly vested in their governing boards. But these boards had in effect delegated substantial authority to faculty bodies to make decisions about academic affairs and faculty affairs under the general leadership of the president. The authority to make rules and regulations governing student conduct was also delegated to the general faculty or to a faculty senate. Student senates tended to have little if any delegated authority. Decision making about support services was also usually delegated to the president. Governing boards expected the president to advise the board on actions requiring board decision, but boards were satisfied with the existing governance arrangements as long as faculty and other decision making brought about minimal internal conflict and minimal external criticism.

Despite this similarity of authority, there was no common pattern of campus decision making in this thirty-campus study. Some of the institutions had a history of strong presidential leadership. This leadership was generally effective in reflecting faculty aspirations, in finding or providing new resources for college or university development, and in achieving student enrollment objectives with a minimum of student disorder or dissent. Other colleges and universities had had a considerable history of faculty-president collaboration. A few had experienced faculty domination of academic and faculty affairs and of student conduct, with a minimum amount of institutional concern for the management of support programs.

Governance by consensus—consensus of governing board, president, faculty, and students—broke down in the mid 1960s. The events that precipitated change were not the same at all institutions. Of fifteen universities, ten experienced serious or critical episodes of student disruption and violence. In two other universities, a concern about campus governance arose primarily because of external threats to survival. In the remaining three universities, the attention given to campus governance reflected a general interest encouraged by the temper of the times. None of the fifteen colleges had experienced any substantial student disorder, although there had been student demonstrations requiring special attention at seven of them. On all college campuses, the concern with structures and processes of governance reflected both faculty and student interest in a more definite and representative arrangement for participation in campus decision making.

The response to campus disruption and argument was to enlarge the opportunity for participation in the processes of power. The response was not unique to campus governance. Participation in power was thought to be a value in and of itself. The U.S. Congress, distrustful of presidential leadership in the 1960s and 1970s, expanded its participation by a proliferation of subcommittees and legislative staffs. The extension of the voting privilege to persons eighteen years through twenty years of age was another kind of participation. So was the expansion of presidential primary elections.

In our higher education sample, five universities established university senates with faculty, student, and administration participation. At three other universities, existing faculty councils were enlarged to include student representation. In another three, the faculty councils refused to admit students to their membership but added student membership to some of their standing committees. Four universities devised their own unique arrangements for faculty and student participation in a formalized structure of governance, the most unusual and perhaps least effective structure being the community forum instituted at the University of New Mexico.

At nine of the fifteen colleges, a college council bringing together faculty, students, and administrative officers was attempted after 1966. Variations on the idea of a college council came into being at the other six colleges. Because of their enrollment size and their commitment to undergraduate instruction, the older colleges tended to have a more extensive history of student participation than the universities, although this history was less evident in former teachers colleges.

All of the experiments in campuswide governance after 1966 had two characteristics in common. The new arrangements endeavored to formalize participation in a all-university senate or in an all-college council bringing together faculty members, students, and administrative officers, including the president, and involved elected, rather than appointed, student and faculty representatives. In addition, the senates and councils, while advisory to the president, expected a president to follow their advice in making recommendations to the governing board.

The new arrangements for decision making were primarily intended, although not generally so stated, to diminish the role of the president as professional and institutional adviser to the governing board. The assumption seemed to be that the senates and councils would readily arrive at important decisions on a timely and effective basis and that these decisions would greatly improve the quality of decision making by governing boards. This assumption was not borne out by experience.

A major weakness in the development of campuswide governance was the belief that faculty senates and student senates could be dispensed with when a collegewide council or a university senate was established. Thus, faculty members and students were brought together at the center of the enterprise on the assumption that all matters to be resolved at the center of the institution were equally important to both faculty and students. This assumption was another example of a mistake in organizational planning.

Students tended to be satisfied to make campuswide bodies the vehicle for revising and modifying student-conduct regulations. Faculty members tended to resent the amount of time devoted to this subject, while administrative officers and governing boards were necessarily concerned about the public reaction to coed dormitories, the removal of visitation limitations, and relaxation of controls over the consumption of alcoholic beverages. As in the past, the behavior of student editors and of some student organizations continued to result in some adverse public comment. And, of course, preparation of regulations to prevent or control campus disruption required considerable care.

Faculty members as a body were accustomed to develop

degree programs, determine degree requirements, and establish policies and standards affecting faculty personnel actions and to present their decisions for presidential and board approval. The participation of student representatives in a central body where such issues were now considered appeared to faculty members as a diminution of their own authority.

Administrators found it necessary to spend a great deal more time and effort than in the past in explaining and justifying various support services, including auxiliary enterprises. Management's role in the delivery of support programs became subject to a degree of faculty and student interest that generally had not existed in the 1950s. There was even some disposition on the part of presidents and their administrative colleagues to assert that faculty and student interference was causing increased costs and decreased efficiency in the rendering of support services.

Presidents and their colleagues sought to communicate to students and faculty the consequences of campus indifference to social expectations and social support. However, some faculty members and students seemed determined to bring about social hostility, without ever answering the question whether or not they were willing to accept diminished social support.

## Future of Governance

As campuswide governance continued to evolve, by early 1977 several needs had become clearly apparent. One was the need to distinguish campuswide governance from faculty and student governance. A second need was to define more precisely the scope of campuswide governance as an advisory process for the president. A third need was to distinguish campuswide governance from management. The fourth was to assert the leadership role of the president. We shall consider these last two needs in some detail in subsequent sections. Here we need to look more closely at the first two.

It is clearly not feasible to argue against a dominant role for faculty members in planning and managing the delivery of instructional and other products of the academic enterprise. Moreover, this faculty role in management further necessitates a major role in decision making about instructional programs, degree requirements, faculty personnel policies, and faculty ethics. The need of the future is not to reaffirm the faculty voice in academic and faculty affairs but to structure the process of expressing this voice.

Clearly the faculty governance structure and process should parallel the faculty management structure and process. Faculty initiatives will be exercised at the departmental level. The first issue is to decide what departmental initiatives shall require approval at the college level, and the second issue is to decide what college decisions shall require approval at the university level. These questions raise substantive matters about the decision-making process. There remains, then, the structuring of this decision-making process. There is probably need for a faculty council at the college level and for a faculty senate at the university level. The college council would be advisory to the dean of the college; the faculty senate would be advisory to the president of the university through the vice-president for academic affairs.

I believe strongly that the dean of a college should preside over the college council and that the vice-president for academic affairs should preside over the faculty senate. I shall say something about the veto authority of these academic officers in a later section. I do not see how academic officers can serve as academic officers and not have this authority of presiding over faculty advisory groups. While appointment of deans and the academic vice-president after faculty consultation may be the preferable method of selection, faculty election holds no terrors for me as such. The essential need is for the governance structure to have leadership.

Whether or not students should participate in faculty departmental meetings, in faculty council meetings, and faculty senate meetings is not a simple question to resolve. I am inclined to favor student participation in all committee meetings as a means of obtaining student viewpoints. I believe students should be excluded when a committee wishes to go into executive session, and I believe students might be observers at council and senate meetings, rather than participants in discussion and voting.

There is need for a student senate of elected representatives to serve as a central forum for consideration of standards expected of student organizations receiving permission to make use of any campus facility or campus resources, for recommendation about desirable student services and their financing, and for periodic review of student-conduct regulations. A student senate should not be considered representative of the student body unless at least 40 percent of all full-time students and at least 25 percent of all part-time students exercise the privilege of voting. I think there should be a separate college or university council on student affairs to be presided over by the vice-president for student affairs. This council might be composed one third of students selected by the student senate, one third of faculty members selected by the faculty senate, and one third of student service administrators appointed by the president. The actions of the council on student affairs would be advisory to the president.

Finally, in this structure and process of campus governance there is need for a campuswide council or senate; for reasons of convenience I shall refer to this body as a university senate. I believe such a campuswide senate should be comprised 40 percent of faculty members selected by the faculty senate, 40 percent of student members selected by the student senate, and 20 percent of administrative or support personnel selected by the president. The president should serve as presiding officer of this university senate. The jurisdiction or authority of the university senate might be three-fold: to discuss any actions of the faculty senate or the student affairs council that the president might refer for further consideration, to recommend to the president policies and procedures involving support programs of the enterprise, and to review institutional plans and budgets as submitted by the president for senate comment.

In any event, the structure and process of campuswide governance should operate as a delegation of authority from the governing board of the college or university. The actions of faculty senate, student affairs council, and university senate should be clearly understood as advisory to the president, just as the role of the president is advisory to the governing board.

One important objection to this structure is that presidents may decide to veto recommendations from faculty senates, student affairs councils, and the university senate. The advisory status of these bodies for campus governance suggests the possibility that the advice will be rejected. In general, I am inclined to believe that presidents are well advised to let the power of veto be exercised by governing boards rather than by themselves. But I recognize that there will be situations in which a presidential veto may well be justified, particularly where timely action or decision is needed in order to clarify expectations. Certainly presidential vetos ought to be reported to a governing board; I assume that the process of informal discussion with board members will ensure that such vetoes are not questioned.

It may be noted that, to an increasing degree because of federal government actions and because of the concern of courts about the equal protection of the laws and about due process of law, more and more policies, programs, procedures, and structures within an academic enterprise will require formal action by a governing board. The informal understandings and traditions of the past will not suffice. The considerable attention of the courts to matters academic means that the structures and processes of governance within colleges and universities will need to be considerably more legalistic in the future than in the past.

It should be emphasized that the final authority of decision making within a college or university is vested in the governing boards. Although boards of trustees have received considerable criticism over the years—on the grounds of unfamiliarity with academic matters and of representing only a particular segment of society—none of the experiments in campuswide governance particularly sought to abolish governing boards. There were hints on occasion that the elimination of governing boards might be desirable, but no sustained, frontal attack was evident to accomplish this overthrow. The issue seemed to be the means of communicating with and influencing decision making by governing boards. The final authority and responsibility of these boards remained intact throughout the experience of the 1960s and continued as such in the late 1970s.

The kind of governance structure I have outlined is intended to provide for participation of faculty and students, as well as of administrative officers, in the decision making of a college or university. Hopefully, such a structure is neither destructive of the requirements of leadership nor indifferent to the imperatives of management.

## Future of Management

The imperatives of management are so important that an earlier proposition bears repetition once again: A college or university is not a debating society, a legislative assembly, or a recreational center. It is first of all and primarily a productive enterprise, an enterprise to produce learning in all its various dimensions and forms. As a productive enterprise, a college or university cannot afford to be indifferent to the imperatives of production management.

The discussions and the actions about campuswide governance in the 1960s tended to overlook the fact that colleges and universities are enterprises with a productive output. Sandin (1969, p. 3) observed: "The simple reminder that a university is, among other things, a producing organization is occasionally in place in a time when the exuberance of would-be reformers distorts the vision of the earnest." Such a reminder was timely indeed, but it was generally ignored in the controversies of the 1960s. The productive nature of colleges and universities was seldom if ever articulated in the discussions of campuswide governance. The very antiintellectualism in society against which faculties had protested over the years suddenly found fertile soil within colleges and universities themselves.

I have a very simple definition of management which I am wont to use on every available occasion: Management is work planning and work performance. In other words, management is production. The traditional definition of management is the direction and control of work output, and, while I have no quarrel with this definition, I prefer to emphasize the act of production rather than the supervision of production. This preference is undoubtedly influenced by the nature of the learning process as a production process.

I have found it convenient, as in this present discussion, to think of the organization of the academic enterprise as a structure and process of governance, a structure and process of management, and a structure and process of leadership. All three elements of organization are essential, but in a producing organization surely the first consideration must always be that of management, of getting the job done, of turning out the intended product. Too many discussions about colleges and universities are inclined to emphasize governance and leadership and to steer away from management. For some reason *management* is a suspect word in the lexicon of academic discourse, a term appropriate to those who want to go into business but not a term for use by the academic intellectual.

The Carnegie Commission on Higher Education has identified the outputs of the academic enterprise as student instruction, research and creative activity, public service, educational justice, and the constructive criticism of society. There are many details and complications to be resolved in the program performance of these basic purposes, but the purposes indicate the kinds of outputs the academic enterprise is expected by society to produce—the kinds of outputs for which society provides support to higher education.

The details of management involve various processes: the determination of work purposes and strategies, the development of policies setting forth value judgments about work processes, the design of work outputs and of work programs, the definition of work technology, the acquisition and allocation of work resources (human, physical, and financial), the communication of a shared purpose and endeavor, the motivation of persons to accomplish intended work outputs, the encouragement of creative problem solving, and the evaluation of work effectiveness and work efficiency. All of these processes are present in an academic enterprise.

Management of the learning process is vested in academic departments, in academic divisions, or in academic colleges. There may be research centers, cultural centers, and public service centers to augment the performance of the academic departments. Departments and centers are engaged in production. Unfortunately, the art of teaching remains largely an art form rather than a carefully designed process founded upon scientific inquiry and a knowledge base about learning as a part of human behavior. The management of learning is embryonic because so much of learning is conducted under conditions of individual effort.

It is conventional wisdom to assert, as did Richman and

Farmer (1974, p. ix), that colleges and universities are "seriously mismanaged." The fault with such criticism is that it is too sweeping, too undiscriminating in scope. One must distinguish between the management of output programs (instruction, research, creative activity, public service, educational justice, constructive criticism) and the management of support programs (academic support, student services, institutional support, plant operation, and auxiliary enterprises). One must distinguish between instruction in agriculture, engineering, physics, medicine, and law on the one hand and instruction in administrative science, the behavioral sciences, the humanities, teacher education, and dramatic art on the other. Many or all of these instructional programs may be managed well in some colleges and universities, managed poorly in others.

As stated by Waltzer (1975), the academic department is where the action is. Or to state the proposition differently, we may observe with Anderson (1976) that to understand academic departments is to understand colleges and universities. Earlier studies by Dressel and his colleagues (1970, 1972) underlined the vital role of academic departments within universities. Yet somehow the managerial function of academic departments continues to escape general understanding and appreciation.

The academic department is the primary management unit of a college or university. It determines the work plan of a group of faculty members. It obtains and utilizes faculty and other resources to carry out desired work plans. The scope of departmental management includes departmental planning (policies and programs), academic affairs (degree requirements, courses, scheduling, guest lecturers), faculty affairs (faculty personnel actions), student affairs (academic advising, student evaluation, student grievances, prizes and awards, monitoring of student progress in fulfillment of degree requirements), budgetary affairs, office management, communication with college and university, and the evaluation of departmental performance. This array of management authority is impressive indeed.

Some departmental executive officers are more adept in departmental management and leadership than others. It is probably fair to say that too little attention is paid in academic education and in academic experience to the management role of the individual faculty member and of the academic department. A "successful" department almost certainly means the presence of a competent executive officer. The effective performance of instruction, research, and public service reflects the effective management of an academic department.

To some extent it is evident, as Spriestersbach (1975) has pointed out, that research management within a university may be subject to a somewhat greater degree of centralized supervision than instructional management. Although research projects originate with individual faculty members or groups of faculty members, and although research grant awards by federal government agencies involve careful review by academic peers, the grant awards are made to the university and the university has a responsibility to ensure that the terms of the grant are fulfilled. Moreover, universities may set up an office to ensure that research project proposals conform to the institution's mission and policies, competence, work load, and financial standards. These same concerns might well apply equally to the management of instructional programs and public service projects, but for some reason academic administrators are likely to be less rigorous in these areas than in research management in developing work plans and work performance standards.

Because the learning process is so highly individualized, management planning and management performance above the level of the individual faculty member, and especially above the level of the academic department, are likely to be limited in scope. College management might well give more attention to the interrelationship of departments, and university management might well give more attention to the interrelationship of colleges, but these levels of management authority in learning are not very well developed.

Just as vital as the management of output programs is the management of support programs. Here the record of higher education is more impressive than is generally realized. There has been a profession of library service for many years, and the librarians of colleges and universities have been well educated and usually well experienced in library management. Student services have been managed by a corps of professionally educated student personnel ad-

ministrators for some thirty years or more. Plant operation has found
professional management in the engineering profession. Fiscal affairs
have been entrusted to professionally educated accountants, business managers, and lawyers, and all business management personnel
have been well served by a professional association. Similar comments may be made about nonacademic personnel administrators,
lawyers, public affairs officers, doctors, nurses, computer center
directors, and others.

Two particular circumstances may give rise to the impression in some quarters that there are deficiencies in general academic management. One is the failure to understand the high degree
of autonomy characterizing the management of the learning process
by academic departments. The other circumstance is the common
inability of presidents and other spokesmen for the academic enterprise to be specific about the outputs and the benefits of the enterprise. These difficulties may be compounded by the fact of a collegial
rather than a hierarchical structure of governance within a college
or university when compared with a business enterprise.

It is popular for outsiders to ask about the academic enterprise: Who is in charge? Faculty members would be inclined to
answer that they are, and students give the impression that they are.
In fact, of course, faculty members manage the learning process and
thereby acquire considerable professional influence within the academic enterprise. And by their very numbers students cannot fail
to have their impact upon the academic community. Presidents and
their administrative colleagues must do what they reasonably can to
encourage faculty members and students at their productive efforts
in a shared community.

There is management within the academic enterprise, but it
is not clearly evident, it is not organized as a hierarchy of activity,
the production technology is not always clear, and the productive
output is not always apparent. Moreover, since so much of the learning process occurs within a student residential environment, many
outsiders fail to comprehend the difference between management of
learning and management of student residential life.

In addition, presidents and other spokesmen on occasion
have failed to describe in understandable ways what colleges and

universities do produce. It is fairly simple to describe the number of graduates in agriculture, or business, or nursing, or law, or engineering, or dentistry, or social work, or medicine. But what do you say about graduates in the humanities, the biological sciences, the physical sciences, mathematics, and the behavioral sciences? What do you say about all the time and effort devoted to research, part of which results in articles and books but part of which may never materialize in tangible form? What does one say about creative activity? What does one say about public service? What does one say about educational justice? What does one say about constructive criticism of society? I happen to think there is a great deal for a president to say, but it must be said in statistical and factual terms meaningful to persons outside the academic community.

There may be a third factor in conveying the impression of poor academic management, and that is the difficulty so many colleges and universities have in balancing their budgets. The constant appeal for more funds to legislators, alumni, and benefactors creates a sense that there must be something wrong with a management that is continually broke. Here again, we who have spoken out on behalf of higher education have failed to make real our needs, our accomplishments, and our dependence upon social support in return for social benefit.

Governance within the academic enterprise serves one and only one purpose: to advance work output. Leadership within the academic enterprise serves that purpose and none other. Academic enterprises need a new confidence in their work output, a new commitment to management, a new sensitivity to work planning and work performance. The social expectation is that colleges and universities shall be useful. American colleges and universities have long practiced utility but have been reluctant to acknowledge the fact or to proclaim their accomplishment.

The academic enterprise achieved affluence in our economy because of a public belief in its usefulness. It can survive only if the public continues to believe in its usefulness. That public perception depends upon the management of learning. Faculty members, students and academic leaders must stake their future upon management of the academic enterprise, upon its work planning and its work performance. I am willing to predict that the future of higher education rests with its management.

## Future of Leadership

Although the subject of leadership as such was not the principal focus of this study, this issue could not be avoided as one examined the experience with new arrangements for campuswide governance in the 1960s. Presidents tended to interpret the events of these years as an attack upon their role and authority, and without doubt there were overtones of just such intention in the efforts to reconstruct agencies of campus governance.

It is not easy to determine the reasons for this attack upon presidential leadership on college and university campuses. Social disillusionment with political leadership in the nation certainly had some impact on attitudes toward campus leadership. Some faculty members viewed presidential leadership in academic and faculty affairs as inconsistent with their own professional expertise and their authority arising from that expertise. Student leaders identified presidents with an external power structure perceived as hostile to student idealism and student determination to control their own individual and social behavior. John Gardner sadly observed in 1964 that the student generation of the day had been inoculated with an antileadership vaccine. The comment might well have been applied to more persons that just the students of the 1960s and 1970s.

The structures of campuswide governance developed in the 1960s were conspicuous in their studious avoidance of instruments or agents of leadership. In this sense the status and authority of presidents were secure. The reformers of the 1960s had no alternative to propose to presidential leadership; they seemed to want no leadership at all. As a consequence, campuswide governance arrangements ended up for the most part confirming presidential leadership but seeking to attach certain limitations to its exercise. By the late 1970s the indispensability of presidential leadership was again rather generally acknowledged, if not always appreciated.

One of the deficiencies of organization within academic enterprises has been an inability to define with any clarity the role and authority of the president. In the American college and university of the nineteenth century, all accounts clearly indicate that the president was a towering figure indeed. Except in some of the church-related colleges, the president usually had all the credentials of a faculty member, often taught a number of classes personally, and served as a faculty leader. Without an entourage of administrative associates, the president almost literally ran the college or university himself.

Two forces changed the presidential role in the twentieth century: the increase in enrollment and the academic revolution (the specialization of knowledge and the advent of research as a major purpose). Gradually the presidential role underwent change, without the subtleties of this change being clearly perceived. The campus conflicts of the 1960s reflected in part a catching up with the realities of role change that had been occurring for some time. Unfortunately, almost no one, presidents or otherwise, has been able to articulate the new role.

I believe that the presidential role today must be understood in two different dimensions: an internal or campus role and an external or social support role. The two roles are interrelated and equally vital. At some institutions there has been an effort to separate the two roles and to designate one person as "Mr. Inside" and another person as "Mr. Outside." In selecting presidents, selection committees and governing boards may settle for the person who can best perform whichever role will serve the institution's immediate needs. Finding the individual best qualified to perform both roles is the real challenge in presidential selection.

Internally, the president is presiding officer of the faculty and of the campus community, manager-in-chief of the support programs of the institution, and professional adviser to the governing board in the decisions the board must make about institutional purpose, values, programs, management, and financing.

Externally, the president is representative of the campus to the various publics interested in campus matters, representative of the campus in various associational activities seeking to assist campus effectiveness, and the linkage of campus with society and, more particularly, with social support of the campus.

I believe these are the principal roles of the campus president—roles that have not been clearly articulated in most discussions of campus organization and that have been overlooked or ignored in much of the experimentation with campuswide governance that occurred in the 1960s.

On the basis of my own personal experience, observation, and reflection, I am firmly convinced that a president should have faculty credentials and faculty experience, first of all. The president should be thought of as the chief academic officer of the institution. There are four major academic officers in a university: the department executive officer, the college dean, the university vice-president for academic affairs, and the president. I would argue that the relationship among these officers is not one of hierarchy, of subordination and superordination, but one of collegial collaboration. Moreover, each of these academic officers is both a manager and a participant in governance. The president, however, becomes the academic leader.

This faculty leadership role of the president needs careful delineation in terms of the faculty campuswide interest. In the academic organization of today, only a few kinds of academic and faculty decisions are made at the center, that is, for the organization as a whole. The organized autonomy of academic departments and even of constituent colleges within a university is such that many decisions and much of management are accomplished at less than the campuswide level. Institutionwide plans, policies, and budgets must be handled by the president, with such advice as agencies of governance are able to provide. Some faculty personnel actions may require approval before final decision by governing boards, but most of these actions will be recommended by faculty committees. The faculty leadership role of the president is to support the strengths of organized autonomy and to help establish only that degree of corporate or institutional coherence essential to maintain the academic enterprise.

The president is manager-in-chief of the support programs of the enterprise. Here a relationship of hierarchy exists. Here is the "bureaucracy" of the academic enterprise. Here the president must exercise the authority and responsibility of satisfactory service to the operating or output units of the organizational structure. As I have pointed out earlier, campuswide governance has brought presidential performance as manager-in-chief of support services under some degree of internal scrutiny, which I believe has some utility. Campuswide governance, like the governance of the U.S. Congress and of the state legislatures, still needs to understand the difference between policy formulation for support services and the management of these services.

Internally the president is the professional adviser to the governing board in making decisions about the institution. I think there can be only one professional adviser, and that adviser must be the president. The president will receive much advice from within the campus, but the president must also be mindful of the concerns of the governing board, which are externally oriented. The governing board will tend to reflect as best it can social expectation and social interest in the academic enterprise. Campus governance will reflect the interest of the campus, the desire to be self-governing. Governing boards will reflect the reality of campus dependence upon social support. The president is the leader in-between who must balance academic interest and values with social interest and values. It is not an enviable role, that of professional adviser to the governing board. But it is indispensable.

Externally, the president of necessity must appear as representative of the campus to all the groups and interests concerned with the campus: alumni, the local community where the campus is located, parents of students, donors and benefactors, community and other organizations, state and federal governments, the media. To these and other publics the president is the articulator and spokesman of a campus or institutional interest. The president must be a defender of the academic faith and a sympathetic adherent of the public interest in academic accomplishment. The president may have very sophisticated and helpful assistants in his external role of communicator, but it is always the president who must in the end serve as the representative of the academic community.

Colleges and universities participate in a variety of associational organizations: state associations of colleges and universities, regional and national associations. Such associations may serve as interest groups to formulate and advance a common social or political interest; they may be concerned with accreditation of academic quality; they may be concerned with intercollegiate athletics;

they may be concerned with the development of information and
knowledge about the academic enterprise. Whatever their purpose,
association relationships result in the exchange of experience among
institutions that can be very useful and reassuring. The problems of
leadership frequently turn out to be not unique but common to
many campuses. The association participation of the college and
university president is an important external function of the office.

Most importantly externally, the president is the formal,
full-time link between campus and society. If the academic enterprise were a self-supporting enterprise on the basis of charges to
clients, perhaps this linkage would be less important. But since in
the aggregate (for the United States as a whole and for all types of
institutions) currently only 40 percent of operating income is derived from charges and 60 percent from governments and philanthropy, linkage is vital indeed. Faculty members and students tend
to be self-absorbed, to be overwhelmed by the challenges and the
uncertainties of knowledge and of learning. They are likely to permit the walls of the campus actually to isolate them from the
struggles and conflicts of society at large. When they do go forth
from the campus, they are apt to believe that their faculty or student
status confers some special privilege of social authority. No president
can entertain any such illusion. Presidents confront the reality of
social interest, and of social disinterest, in the academic enterprise.

No presidential role is more exacting, more freighted with
the burden of conflict, more certain of generating criticism than
this one of linkage between campus and society. Faculty members
and students want increased social support without cultivating that
support or evidencing any responsibility toward it. Presidents are
supposed to assure social support without any infringement upon
faculty or student rights and behavior.

The only satisfaction a president can have is to know that
the history of higher education in Western culture for nearly eight
centuries has been a history of tension between campus and society.
In eight hundred years, no one has found any formula for diminish-
ing that tension. Colleges and universities have not recently found
any way to prevent it or play it down. Our increased knowledge
about academic behavior and social behavior has given us no certain procedure for reconciling one with the other.

Presidents have been suspect on campuses because of their perceived preoccupation with society external to the campus. Perhaps on our college and university campuses, as in the Persia of old, faculty members and students have been disposed to kill the messenger who brought bad news. In the 1960s presidents brought the news that society was not yet ready for many of the changes so eagerly wanted, apparently, by some faculty members and students. In the 1970s presidents have had to bring the news of changing social expectations in relation to higher education. Neither theme has been received with enthusiasm within campus communities.

Many explanations have been offered to account for an evident diminution in the capacity of presidents to lead academic communities: the loss of a clear sense of academic mission, financial stringency, the politicization of constituencies, the demands of crisis management. Many suggestions have been put forth about how presidents might recapture the ability to lead: increased attention to tasks rather than to unclear goals, greater concern with organizational relationships than with philosophical pronouncements, more effort for external accomplishment than for internal acceptance, mobilization of commitment to a rediscovery of values and to the potential of will over the tyranny of experience. The implication of these apologies and exhortations is that presidential leadership can be and must be reaffirmed as vital to the welfare and survival of academic communities.

Presidential leadership seems to have survived the crisis of the 1960s even as it survived earlier periods of important change. One hopes that the role and the limitations of presidential leadership will be more clearly understood in the future than in the recent past. And presidential performance may offer reassurance that presidential leadership can and does make a difference.

The presidential leadership of the 1980s will not be the same as the presidential leadership prior to 1965. Experiments in campuswide governance will have helped to accomplish the change, for in these experiences college and university presidents found a broadly representative forum for the exercise of leadership. Presidents have learned to share authority, to consult more widely and systematically, to communicate information more fully and extensively, to explain the realities of social expectation and support more convincingly.

Presidents obviously cannot fulfill their roles by themselves. Presidents must have associates in academic administration and in the professional management of support programs. They must have staff associates for public and campus affairs. The leadership and management of colleges and universities has become a team endeavor. Yet it is the personality and the competence of the president as an individual which in the long run determines the effective leadership of a college or university.

There are two indispensable tools of leadership for the president of a college or university: planning and budgeting. Both tools share a common characteristic, the linkage of campus with society. Both tools are intimately connected one to the other. Plans without budgets become unfulfilled dreams. Budgets without plans become wasted activity. Planning and budgeting are management obligations of every cost center within a college or university, as well as of every program grouping. But plans and budgets must eventually become an institutional whole. The leadership of a college or university relies above all other procedures upon planning and budgeting to fulfill the various roles the president must perform.

Campuswide governance need not result in the destruction of presidential leadership. On the contrary, it can assist and strengthen it. Participation of faculty members, students, professional staff, and operating staff in a college council or a university senate can offer advice to a president about the objectives of the learning process and the needs of the learning environment. But a college council or a university senate cannot substitute itself for institutional leadership, nor can it seek escape from institutional responsibilities to the public interest.

Sometimes the question has been asked: Can a college or university be led? How does a president lead the learning process? How does a president lead students toward intellectual and emotional maturity? The answer, if there is an answer, lies not in a leadership of command but in a leadership of understanding, empathy, and faith that individuals can do and be better than they are. The president leads by trying to bring together the resources that will accomplish purposes.

Leadership of a college or university in a structure and process of campuswide governance requires a great deal more time and energy devoted to the internal affairs of the institution. Campuswide governance is not just demanding upon the time of faculty members and students; it is demanding also upon the time of presidents and of their closest associates, who must devote more time and effort to internal communication, to committee meetings and council or senate meetings, and to the collection and analysis of information about the institutional enterprise. Leadership activity within the academic community has been changed by the development of campuswide governance.

I would like to believe that there is a *quid pro quo* in the changed circumstance of college and university leadership—that college and university leadership will become more involved in matters concerning the learning process, just as faculty members and students through campuswide governance have become more involved with matters affecting the learning environment.

But whatever the campus governance and process of tomorrow, one prediction is surely safe. The decision-making effort within colleges and universities will continue to require a structure and process of leadership. There is no viable choice except to vest this authority and responsibility of leadership in the president. Experiments in campuswide governance did not demonstrate a lack of need for presidential leadership. They did place new demands upon such leadership. At the same time they confirmed the indispensability of a structured leadership in campus, as in all human, affairs.

## Collective Bargaining

At the time of this study, none of the thirty colleges or universities had been through the experience of faculty collective bargaining, although several were facing the prospect of such a process. There are two major issues to be confronted in faculty collective bargaining. The first issue is economic: how faculty collective bargaining can bring about improved compensation for faculty members through increased income from students, governments, and philanthropy. The second issue is organizational: how faculty collective bargaining will affect the structure and process of governance, of management, and of leadership.

This is not the place to begin a discussion of either complex issue. In some instances, as in New York, faculty members in public institutions may see collective bargaining as a defense against other groups of public employees, including public school teachers. In other instances, faculty collective bargaining may be deemed essential as a counterweight to collective bargaining by the nonacademic personnel of a university. But it must be stated emphatically that faculty collective bargaining surely has the potential effect of altering substantially the organizational structure and process of the academic community. All that has been said here about the future of governance, of leadership, and of management can be profoundly altered by the advent of faculty collective bargaining.

In its report, *Governance of Higher Education* (1973), the Carnegie Commission argued that economic issues should be the sole objective of faculty collective bargaining and that matters of governance should remain undisturbed and unmentioned in negotiation agreements. The same point of view was expressed even more strongly in the 1977 report of the Carnegie Council on Policy Studies in Higher Education, *Faculty Bargaining in Public Higher Education*. It is possible that faculty bargaining agencies will observe this admonition, but I am doubtful.

I believe that faculty collective bargaining will profoundly alter faculty-student-administration relationships in colleges and universities, will generally relegate governance decisions to the bargaining table for resolution, and will undermine or eliminate the faculty role in academic management. I believe faculty collective bargaining will reduce faculty members to the status of professional employees of management and make academic management the province of departmental executive officers, academic deans, academic vice-presidents, and presidents. Time will tell.

The future of governance, management, and leadership is difficult to predict as to structure and process, given a continuation of current trends. The future seems to me more certain with the advent of faculty collective bargaining. Faculty status in the academic enterprise will be very different indeed, I think, when collective bargaining becomes the order of the day. Then it will be easier to answer the question: Who is in charge? But will the learning process then be equally effective?

## Conclusion

In recounting the story of the emergence of the American university at the end of the nineteenth century, Veysey (1965) identified four educational positions competing for control of the new institution: religious tradition and piety, utility, research, and liberal culture. As one examines the experience of American colleges and universities with new structures of power in the 1960s, certainly there was no recurrence of former struggles for control. There is no evidence of any clear and fervent educational point of view struggling for domination of higher education in the conflicts of the 1960s. There was a student hostility to society and a vaguely formed attitude on the part of some students that higher education should be an agent for bringing about change in social structures and processes. But there was limited advocacy of this point of view by faculty members, who were motivated to change primarily because they wanted to institutionalize the academic revolution.

The failures in the 1960s arose, I believe, from three principal circumstances. First, the new forms of faculty and student participation in decision making offered no response to the question of how to achieve campus democracy on the one hand and increased social support of each campus on the other. They offered no answer to the dilemma of aspiration for self-government without an aspiration for self-support. Second, the new forms of faculty and student participation in decision making offered no arrangement for leadership. And, third, they in effect imposed a centralizing tendency upon a highly decentralized management structure. In the excitement about maintaining law and order on campus, no one bothered to examine the college or university as a productive enterprise.

The future of governance, management, and leadership on college and university campuses will depend upon structures and processes that achieve certain required organizational ends: (1) appropriate recognition of colleges and universities as productive enterprises; (2) a necessary integration of governance, management, and leadership structures and processes appropriate to the unique nature of the academic enterprise; and (3) a necessary integration of campus and society. I would argue that the whole organizational history of higher education in America has been a history of efforts and struggles to achieve these ends. The experience of the decade 1966 to 1976 was an especially dramatic episode in that long history.

Organizational planning in any enterprise tends to employ three criteria of accomplishment: effectiveness, acceptability, and clarity. These criteria are useful both for planning organizational structures and for evaluating their performance. It is appropriate that the first consideration should be effectiveness: Does the arrangement for the exercise of power and for the performance of work accomplish the program objectives of the enterprise? Acceptability is important in terms of the human relations of organizations, in terms of the willingness of people to join together to accomplish a common purpose with a sense of fairness, justice, and benefit. The criterion of clarity asks whether or not working roles and relationships are widely understood by all participants.

I believe it may be said that campus organization for decision making became dysfunctional in the early 1960s because it had failed to clarify faculty power and had lost acceptability on the part of some articulate and determined students. The new arrangements of the 1960s responded to these failures but at the sacrifice of effectiveness, the most important criterion of all.

It is not easy to foretell the future. The real test of campus governance, management, and leadership will lie in the capacity of colleges and universities to respond to changing social circumstances. Glenny and his associates (1976) have set forth the dimensions of change as perceived by presidents. But it is not enough for presidents alone to "confront reality." Faculties, students, and all interested in higher education as a social institution must do the same—must perceive and adjust to change in the 1980s. The conflicts of the 1960s have already given way to the complexities of the 1970s. The 1980s promise to hold a fair share of uncertainties and anxieties.

Organizational structures of power, work performance, and leadership are human adaptations to human needs. The organizational structures for decision making, management, and leadership of campus communities will somehow adapt to the needs that lie ahead. Hopefully, the adaptation will be more peaceful for colleges and universities in the 1980s than in the 1960s, but there obviously can be no guarantee that such will be the case. Organizational structures and processes in higher education are still in a state of evolution. Upon the success of the organizational adaptation to a changing environment will depend the capacity of higher education to survive in the forms we have known in the past.

Society cannot survive without higher education. But a society will expect higher education structures and processes to serve it well. Society and campus drew apart in the 1960s, and the fault was not all on campus. Society and campus may draw closer together in the 1980s. If such a development does in fact occur, that event will determine the future of campus governance, management, and leadership.

◇◇◇◇◇◇◇◇◇◇◇◇

# Bibliography

◇◇◇◇◇◇◇◇◇◇◇◇◇◇◇◇◇◇◇◇◇◇◇◇◇◇◇◇◇◇

ANDERSON, G. L. "Organizational Diversity." In J. C. Swart and J. R. Montgomery (Eds.), *New Directions for Institutional Research: Examining Departmental Management*, no. 10. San Francisco: Jossey-Bass, 1976.

ANDES, J. *A Systems Approach to University Organization.* Gainesville, Fla.: Institute of Higher Education, University of Florida, 1970.

Assembly on University Goals and Governance. *A First Report.* Sponsored by the American Academy of Arts and Sciences, January 1971.

ASTIN, A. W., ASTIN, H. S., BAYER, A. E., and BISCONTI, A. S. *The Power of Protest: A National Study of Student and Faculty Disruptions with Implications for the Future.* San Francisco: Jossey-Bass, 1975.

BALDERSTON, F. E. *Managing Today's University.* San Francisco: Jossey-Bass, 1974.

BALDRIDGE, J. V. *Power and Conflict in the University.* New York: Wiley, 1971a.

277

BALDRIDGE, J. V. (Ed.). *Academic Governance*. Berkeley: Mc-Cutchan, 1971b.

BALDRIDGE, J. V., and KEMERER, F. R. "Academic Senates and Faculty Collective Bargaining." *The Journal of Higher Education*, 1976, *47* (4), 391.

BECKER, H. S. (Ed.). *Campus Power Struggle*. New York: Aldine, 1970.

BLAU, P. M. *The Organization of Academic Work*. New York: Wiley, 1973.

BROWN, J. D. *The Human Nature of Organizations*. New York: American Management Association, 1973.

BUCHANAN, J. M., and DEVLETOGLOU, N. E. *Academia in Anarchy*. New York: Basic Books, 1970.

BURNS, G. P. *Trustees in Higher Education: Their Functions and Coordination*. New York: Independent College Funds of America, 1966.

Carnegie Commission on Higher Education. *A Classification of Institutions of Higher Education*. A technical report. New York: McGraw-Hill, 1973.

Carnegie Commission on Higher Education. *Governance of Higher Education: Six Priority Problems*. A report and recommendations. New York: McGraw-Hill, 1973.

CHICKERING, A. W. *Education and Identity*. San Francisco: Jossey-Bass, 1969.

CLARK, B., and YOUN, R. I. K. *Academic Power in the United States*. An ERIC Clearinghouse on Higher Education publication. Washington, D.C.: American Association for Higher Education, 1976.

CLARK, K. B. "The Governance of Universities in the Cities of Man." *The American Scholar*, 1970, *39*, 566.

CLEVELAND, H. "How Do You Get Everybody in on the Act and Still Get Some Action?" *Educational Record*, 1974, *55* (3), 177.

COHEN, M. D., and MARCH, J. G. *Leadership and Ambiguity: The American College President*. A general report prepared for the Carnegie Commission on Higher Education. New York: McGraw-Hill, 1974.

CORSON, J. J. *Governance of Colleges and Universities*. A volume in the Carnegie Series in American Education. New York: McGraw-Hill, 1960.

CORSON, J. J. *The Governance of Colleges and Universities.* (Rev. ed.) New York: McGraw-Hill, 1975.

*Daedalus,* Journal of the American Academy of Arts and Sciences. "American Higher Education: Toward an Uncertain Future." Fall 1974 and Winter 1975, *1* and *2.*

*Daedalus,* Journal of the American Academy of Arts and Sciences. "The Embattled University." Winter 1970.

DEMARATH, N. J., STEPHENS, R. W., and TAYLOR, R. R. *Power, Presidents, and Professors.* New York: Basic Books, 1967.

DILL, D. D. *Case Studies in University Governance.* Washington, D.C.: National Association of State Universities and Land-Grant Colleges, 1971.

DODDS, H. W. *The Academic President—Educator or Caretaker?* New York: McGraw-Hill, 1962.

DRESSEL, P. L., JOHNSON, F. C., and MARCUS, P. M. *The Confidence Crisis: An Analysis of University Departments.* San Francisco: Jossey-Bass, 1970.

DRESSEL, P. L., and FARICY, W. H. *Return to Responsibility: Constraints on Autonomy in Higher Education.* San Francisco: Jossey-Bass, 1972.

DYKES, A. R. *Faculty Participation in Academic Decision Making.* Washington: American Council on Education, 1968.

EPSTEIN, L. D. *Governing the University: The Campus and the Public Interest.* San Francisco: Jossey-Bass, 1974.

*Faculty Bargaining in Public Higher Education.* A report of the Carnegie Council on Policy Studies in Higher Education, with two essays by Joseph W. Garbarino and by David E. Feller and Mathew W. Finkin. San Francisco: Jossey-Bass, 1977.

*Faculty Participation in Academic Governance.* Report of the AAHE Task Force on Faculty Representation and Academic Negotiations, Campus Governance Program. Washington, D.C.: American Association for Higher Education, 1967.

GLENNY, L. A., SHEA, J. R., RUYLE, J. H., and FRESCHI, K. H. *Presidents Confront Reality: From Edifice Complex to University Without Walls.* A report for the Carnegie Council on

Policy Studies in Higher Education. San Francisco: Jossey-Bass, 1976.

GOHEEN, R. F. The Human Nature of a University. Princeton: Princeton University Press, 1969.

GROSS, E., and GRAMBSCH, P. V. University Goals and Academic Power. Washington, D.C.: American Council on Education, 1968.

HARCLEROAD, F. F. (Ed.). Issues of the Seventies: The Future of Higher Education. San Francisco: Jossey-Bass, 1970.

HEILBRON, L. H. The College and University Trustee: A View from the Board Room. San Francisco: Jossey-Bass, 1973.

HELSABECK, R. E. The Compound System: A Conceptual Framework for Effective Decision Making in Colleges and Universities. Berkeley: Center for Research and Development in Higher Education, University of California, 1973.

HENDERSON, A. D., and HENDERSON, J. G. Higher Education in America: Problems, Priorities, and Prospects. San Francisco: Jossey-Bass, 1974.

HENDERSON, A. D. The Role of the Governing Board. An AGB report. Washington, D.C.: Association of Governing Boards of Universities and Colleges, October 1967.

HODGKINSON, H. L. The Campus Senate: Experiment in Democracy. Berkeley: Center for Research and Development in Higher Education, University of California, 1974.

HODGKINSON, H. L. College Governance: The Amazing Thing Is that It Works at All. Washington, D.C.: ERIC Clearinghouse on Higher Education, The George Washington University, 1971.

HODGKINSON, H. L., and MEETH, L. R. (Eds.). Power and Authority: Transformation of Campus Governance. San Francisco: Jossey-Bass, 1971.

HOWARD, J. A., and FRANKLIN, H. B. Who Should Run the Universities? Washington, D.C.: American Enterprise Institute, 1969.

JELLEMA, W. W. Efficient College Management. San Francisco: Jossey-Bass, 1972.

JENCKS, C., and RIESMAN, D. The Academic Revolution. Garden City, N.Y.: Doubleday, 1968.

JENKS, R. S. "Faculty-Student Participation in University Government: A Case History." *Educational Record, 54,* 236–242.

JENKS, R. S. "An Internal Change Agent's Role in Restructuring University Governance." *The Journal of Higher Education,* 1973, *44,* 370–379.

JOHNSON, E. L. *From Riot to Reason.* Urbana: University of Illinois Press, 1971.

KELLEMS, S. E. *Emerging Sources of Student Influence.* An ERIC higher education research report. Washington, D.C.: American Association for Higher Education, 1975.

KEMERER, F. R., and BALDRIDGE, J. V. *Unions on Campus: A National Study of the Consequences of Faculty Bargaining.* San Francisco: Jossey-Bass, 1975.

LEWIS, L. S. *Scaling the Ivory Tower: Merit and Its Limits in Academic Careers.* Baltimore: Johns Hopkins University Press, 1975.

MCCONNELL, T. R. *The Redistribution of Power in Higher Education.* Berkeley: Center for Research and Development in Higher Education, University of California, 1971.

MCGRATH, E. J. *Should Students Share the Power?* Philadelphia: Temple University Press, 1970.

MAGRATH, C. P., and SINDLER, A. P. (Eds.). *The Future Academic Community.* Washington, D.C.: American Council on Education, 1968.

METZLER, K. *Confrontation: The Destruction of a College President.* Los Angeles: Nash, 1973.

MILLETT, J. D. *The Academic Community.* New York: McGraw-Hill, 1962.

MILLETT, J. D. *The Multiple Roles of College and University Presidents.* An Occasional Paper of the Office of Leadership Development in Higher Education. Washington, D.C.: American Council on Education, 1976.

MILLETT, J. D. "Higher Education Management Versus Business Management." *Educational Record,* 1975, *56,* 221.

MILLETT, J. D. *Strengthening Community in Higher Education.* Washington, D.C.: Management Division, Academy for Educational Development, 1974.

MILTON, O., and SHOBEN, E. J., JR. (Eds.). *Learning and the Professors*. Athens: Ohio University Press, 1968.

MORRISON, R. S. *Students and Decision Making*. Washington: Public Affairs Press, 1970.

NASON, J. W. *The Future of Trusteeship: The Role and Responsibilities of College and University Boards*. Washington, D.C.: Association of Governing Boards of Universities and Colleges, 1974.

National Commission on the Causes and Prevention of Violence. *To Establish Justice, To Insure Domestic Tranquility*. Final Report, Chap. 9. Washington, D.C.: U.S. Government Printing Office, 1969.

NICHOLS, D. C. *Perspectives on Campus Tensions*. Washington, D.C.: American Council on Education, 1970.

PERKINS, J. A. (Ed.). *The University as an Organization*. New York: McGraw-Hill, 1973.

PERKINS, J. A. *The University in Transition*. Princeton, N.J.: Princeton University Press, 1966.

PERRY, R. R., and HULL, W. F., IV. (Eds.). *The Organized University*. Toledo: University of Toledo, 1971.

*President as Educational Leader, The*. Washington, D.C.: Association of American Colleges, 1976.

President's Commission on Campus Unrest. *Campus Unrest*. Washington, D.C.: U.S. Government Printing Office, 1970.

RAUH, M. A. *The Trusteeship of Colleges and Universities*. New York: McGraw-Hill, 1969.

RICHMAN, B. M., and FARMER, R. N. *Leadership, Goals, and Power in Higher Education*. San Francisco: Jossey-Bass, 1974.

RIESMAN, D. *Constraint and Variety in American Education*. Garden City, N.Y.: Doubleday, 1958.

ROSSMAN, M. *The Wedding Within the War*. Garden City, N.Y.: Doubleday, 1971.

SANDIN, R. T. *Power and Purpose in Collegiate Government: Role of the Faculty in Academic Planning*. Ohio: Center for the Study of Higher Education, University of Toledo, 1969.

SMART, J. C., and MONTGOMERY, J. R. (Eds.). *New Directions for Institutional Research: Examining Departmental Management*, no. 10. San Francisco: Jossey-Bass, 1976.

SPRIESTERSBACH, D. C. *Research Administration in Academic Institution.* An Occasional Paper of the Office of Leadership Development in Higher Education. Washington, D.C.: American Council on Education, 1975.

*Statement on Government of Colleges and Universities.* Jointly published as a pamphlet by the American Association of University Professors, American Council on Education, and the Association of Governing Boards of Universities and Colleges, 1966. Also published in the *AAUP Bulletin,* Winter 1966.

STOKE, H. W. *The American College President.* New York: Harper & Row, 1959.

VEYSEY, L. R. *The Emergence of the American University.* Chicago: University of Chicago Press, 1965.

WALTZER, H. *The Job of Academic Department Chairman.* An Occasional Paper of the Office of Leadership Development in Higher Education. Washington, D.C.: American Council on Education, 1975.

WILLIAMSON, E. G., and COWAN, J. L. *The American Student's Freedom of Expression: A Research Appraisal.* Minneapolis: University of Minnesota Press, 1966.

WILSON, L. *Shaping American Higher Education.* Washington, D.C.: American Council on Education, 1972.

WREN, S. C. *The College Student and Higher Education Policy: What Stake and What Purpose?* Berkeley, Calif.: Carnegie Council on Policy Studies in Higher Education, 1975.

WRISTON, H. M. *Academic Procession.* New York: Columbia University Press, 1959.

ZWINGLE, J. L. *The Lay Governing Board.* Washington, D.C.: American Council on Education, 1970.

ZYSKIND, H., and STERNFELD, R. *The Voiceless University: An Argument for Intellectual Autonomy.* San Francisco: Jossey-Bass, 1971.

◇◇◇◇◇◇◇◇◇◇◇◇◇

# Index

◇◇◇◇◇◇◇◇◇◇◇◇◇◇◇◇◇◇◇◇◇◇◇◇◇◇◇◇◇◇◇◇◇◇◇

## A

Academic community, 3; adversary/ partnership relation in, 19–22; constituent groups, 39, 228; literature on, 22–23; unique character, 38–39

Academic community model, 14–15, 224, 228

Academic council, at Eastern Montana, 178–180

Academic departments: autonomy, 266; management scope, 260–261; specialization in, 249–250

Academic enterprise, characteristics of, 245–248; organizational characteristics, 248–251; purpose, 263–264

Academic freedom, 32, 202

Academic governance, 1–23; future of, 244–275; history of, 251–254; studying, 24–39

Accomplishment, criteria of, 274

Accreditation, institutional purpose and, 198–199

Administration: at Berkeley, 64, 69; in dual-organization model, 12–13, 225–228; faculty in, 69; governance distinguished from, 6; hierarchy in, 12; at Howard, 124–126; at New Mexico, 106; personnel included in, 36

Administrative council: at New Mexico, 106; at Northern Kentucky, 188–190

Administrators: case authors, 26–28; in dual-organization model, 227–228; in political model, 229; student concerns, 227

Adversary/partner relationship, 19–22

Advisory participation / executive model, 134–135

Albertus Magnus College, 25, 27; case history, 169–172

**285**

and, 34, 36, 266–267
Support staff: in dual-organization
    model, 288; governance atti-
    tude, 242
Syracuse University, 25, 27, 90, 142–
    143; case history, 127–135; in-
    stitutional purpose, 200
Syracuse University Research Corpo-
    ration, 132, 135

**T**

Task Force on Faculty Representa-
    tion and Academic Negotia-
    tion of the American Associa-
    tion for Higher Education
    (AAHE), 4
TAYLOR, R. R., 3, 279
Teachers College, 42
"Teaching effectiveness," 218
Tennessee, State University and Col-
    lege System of, 112
Tennessee State University, 25, 26,
    27, 89–90; case history, 112–
    116
Tenure, 6, 7, 153–154, 189–190; stu-
    dent interest in, 217–218
TOLLEY, W. P., 128, 129, 130
Town-meeting tradition: at Central
    Connecticut, 175; at Oregon,
    102–105
Transitional (public) colleges, 194;
    case histories, 172–183; de-
    fined, 145
Tuskegee Institute, 25, 27; case his-
    tory, 155–158

**U**

Union Theological Seminary, 42
University Assembly, at Oregon, 103
University community forum, at New
    Mexico, 108–110
University council: at Austin, 76–78;
    at Columbia, 42; at Miami,
    93–95

University senates: at Berkeley, 65–
    67; at Columbia, 41, 43–48; at
    Cornell, 58–63, 226; at Emory,
    115–119; future, 256–257; at
    Miami, 92–95; at New Hamp-
    shire, 97–101; participation in,
    252–253; at Roosevelt, 137–
    141; at Syracuse 129–132

**V**

Vassar College, 22, 27; case history,
    145–150
VEYSEY, L. R., 273, 283
Vietnam War, 32, 48, 62, 99, 122

**W**

WALTZER, H., xxii, 260, 283
WASHINGTON, B. T., 155
WEBER, MAX, 17
West, institutions studied, 27
West Virginia Wesleyan College, 25,
    27; case history, 162–164
WHITNEY, C. B., xxii
WILDER, P. S., JR., xxii
WILLIAMSON, E. G., 21, 283
WILSON, L., 20, 283
Wisconsin Student Association, 52
Wisconsin University System, 50
Women/men equality issues, at Cor-
    nell, 61–62
WREN, S. C., 21, 283
WRISTON, H. M., 13, 283

**Y**

Yale University, Vassar and, 148
YOUN, R. I. K., 278

**Z**

ZWINGLE, J. L., 21, 283
ZYSKIND, H., 20, 283

DATE